Nigel Green is Headteacher of Sutton Manor High School. An ex-international athlete, he previously taught at Denstone College, Oundle, Collyers Sixth Form College and Hitchin Boys' School, and is an examiner for the Cambridge board.

Jean Potter is Vice-Principal of Strode's Sixth Form College, Egham. She has taught in three grammar schools, and was previously Head of Biology at Gloucester College of Technology.

Wilf Stout, who has been the co-ordinating author of this book, is Schools Liaison Officer, University of Cambridge Local Examinations Syndicate. He is an experienced teacher, examiner and author and has been fully involved in the development of GCSE syllabuses. He is currently Chairman of the Education Division of the Institute of Biology.

Pan Study Aids for GCSE include:

Accounting

Biology

Chemistry

Commerce

Computer Studies

Economics

English Language

French

Geography 1

Geography 2

German

History 1: World History since 1914

History 2: Britain and Europe since 1700

Human Biology

Mathematics

Physics

Sociology

Study Skills

PAN STUDY AIDS

BIOLOGY

N. P. O. Green, J. M. Potter and G. W. Stout

A Pan Original
Pan Books   London and Sydney

First published 1987 by Pan Books Ltd,
Cavaye Place, London SW10 9PG

9 8 7 6 5 4 3

© N. P. O. Green, J. M. Potter, G. W. Stout 1987

ISBN 0 330 29937 9

Text design by Peter Ward
Text illustration by M L Design
Photoset by Parker Typesetting Service, Leicester
Printed and bound in Spain by
Mateu Cromo SA, Madrid

CONTENTS

INTRODUCTION TO GCSE

From 1988, there will be a single system of examining at 16 plus in England and Wales and Northern Ireland. The General Certificate of Secondary Education (GCSE) will replace the General Certificate of Education (GCE) and the Certificate of Secondary Education (CSE) In Scotland candidates will be entering for the O grade and Standard Grade examinations leading to the award of the Scottish Certificate of Education (SCE).

The Pan Study Aids GCSE series has been specially written by practising teachers and examiners to enable you to prepare successfully for this new examination.

GCSE introduces several important changes in the way in which you are tested. First, the examinations will be structured so that you can show *what* you know rather than what you do *not* know. Of critical importance here is the work you produce during the course of the examination year, which will be given much greater emphasis than before. Second, courses are set and marked by six examining groups instead of the previous twenty GCE/CSE boards. The groups are:

Northern Examining Association (NEA)
Midland Examining Group(MEG)
London and East Anglian Group (LEAG)
Southern Examining Group (SEG)
Welsh Joint Examinations Council (WJEC)
Northern Ireland Schools Examination Council (NISEC)

One of the most useful changes introduced by GCSE is the single award system of grades A–G. This should permit you and future employers more accurately to assess your qualifications.

GCSE	GCE O Level	CSE
A	A	–
B	B	–
C	C	1
D	D	2
E	E	3
F	F	4
G		5

Remember that, whatever examinations you take, the grades you are awarded will be based on how well you have done.

Pan Study Aids are geared for use throughout the duration of your courses. The text layout has been carefully designed to provide all the information and skills you need for GCSE and SCE examinations – please feel free to use the margins for additional notes.

N.B. Where questions are drawn from former O level examination papers, the following abbreviations are used to identify the boards:

UCLES (University of Cambridge Local Examinations Syndicate)
AEB (Associated Examining Board)
ULSEB (University of London Schools Examination Board)
SUJB (Southern Universities Joint Board)
O&C (Oxford & Cambridge)
SCE (Scottish Certificate of Education Examination Board)
JMB (Joint Matriculation Board)
SEB (Scottish Examining Board)
ODLE (Oxford Delegacy of Local Examinations)
WJEC (Welsh Joint Examinations Council)

GUIDE TO REVISION

CONTENTS

To do well in examinations requires more than good luck. In fact, good candidates eliminate luck from the examination by adequate revision.

Your revision should be so complete that you are able to walk into the examination and know that, whatever topics come up and however the questions are worded, you will be able to answer them satisfactorily. It is important not to be overconfident but your revision should remove all panic and fright from examinations. There is only one way to guarantee success and that is by your own determination and hard work.

Ideally, revision should be a continuing process that begins when you start an examination course. Each topic should be revised as it is covered and questions answered and corrected at all stages. Term and end-of-year examinations should continue to provide familiarity with the subject and examination technique.

However, revision for the vast majority of students is a once-only event prior to examinations. With this in mind the following is a suggested approach to your revision. Remember that revision, like living organisms, requires a continual input of energy in order to be successful. The fuel in this case is hard work.

TIMING

Give yourself plenty of time to avoid last-minute panic and late nights. Aim at having completed all your revision by the date of your first examination. After this date your time will be required for keeping the facts fresh in your mind.

ORGANIZATION

1. Find out the dates of your exams and the form of each paper in terms of topic areas and style of questions.
2. Obtain a syllabus and recent examination papers. This is not essential but some students gain confidence from a familiarity with both.
3. Work out a programme of revision in terms of subjects and topics within them and keep to it. This is the sort of discipline needed for revision.
4. Ensure that your school or college notes are complete. All the information required for your revision should be in your notebooks and not in the textbook. Try to avoid having to use this for revision. From now on use it only as a reference book – it has done its job.
5. Tidy up your files or notebooks so that they are a pleasure to revise from.

In carrying out the above you have successfully begun your revision.

The use of multiple-choice questions and compulsory short answers means that questions can be set covering the whole of the syllabus. Therefore you must have a thorough knowledge of all of the syllabus.

Your method of revision is something which is personal but you may find this method helpful.

1   Revise the course, topic by topic, using the headings given in the contents of this book.

2   Read through your notes on a topic and make a list of sub-topics, e.g.:

Topic	Transport in animals
Sub-topics	Structure and function of the heart
	Heart disease
	Structure and function of:
	arteries
	veins
	capillaries
	blood
	The immune system
	The ABO blood group

(Use the relevant chapter in the revision guide to help you with this.) Take each one in turn and read through it several times. Make a list of the key facts involved in the structure or function being studied and check your understanding of all biological terms and definitions. Try to identify the principles which appear.

3   Any tables which appear should be thoroughly studied and the details learned. A useful way of memorizing tabulated information is by the use of a **mnemonic** (nem-on-ic). This involves arranging the facts so that their first letters spell out a word.

For example, the characteristics of all living organisms are:

Movement, Assimilation, Respiration, Reproduction, Irritability, Growth, Excretion, which spells out (phonetically) **marri(a)ge**.

4   The only satisfactory way to learn a diagram is to draw it several times. Simplify diagrams as much as possible so you can draw and label them in 3–4 minutes. For complex diagrams such as organs or organ systems you should be able to draw two diagrams.

(*a*)   A labelled sketch diagram showing structures and functions. This may be used to illustrate a point in an essay answer (*see* Fig 5.1).

(*b*)   A fully labelled and accurately proportioned diagram. This may be demanded by the question and time is allowed to draw this, e.g. 'Draw a labelled diagram of the mammalian heart showing the direction of blood flow' (*see* Fig 5.2).

All diagrams should be large, labelled and drawn in pencil. Shading should not be used and the use of coloured pencils should be restricted to blood vessels. Each diagram or drawing should have a reference (which may be used elsewhere in the answer) and a title, e.g. Fig 5.3 Structure of the human heart.

5 Read through the appropriate chapter in the revision guide and check your list to be sure that all points have been covered and are understood. Remember that the guide contains the minimum information considered necessary to obtain a good pass. The key words for each chapter list all the biological terms which are likely to appear on the examiner's mark sheet. Use them as a checklist during revision and be sure that you understand them and can use them correctly in your answers.

6 As an aid to learning, construct your own revision flow diagrams. This is a useful technique in revision and examinations since it is a good way to plan answers to essay questions and it shows the interrelationships which exist between topics. (Examiners use this technique in setting questions and preparing mark schemes.)

To construct a flow diagram you take a sheet of paper and lay out the main points, allowing plenty of space around each. Using these points to suggest other words to you (stimuli) build up the diagram, linking the words with lines and arrows to show functional relationships. In the example given below (*see* Fig 1.1) the three main points involved in a gaseous exchange in a mammal were listed as:

▶ **atmosphere** – the source of oxygen
▶ **lungs** – the gaseous exchange organ
▶ **tissues** – the source of carbon dioxide

Other terms were added, where appropriate, using the main points

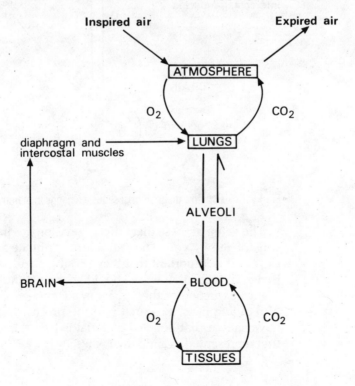

Fig 1.1 Flow diagram of gaseous exchange in mammals

as stimuli. You can add further information to Fig 1.1 to convert it into a more complete revision aid, as shown in Fig 1.2.

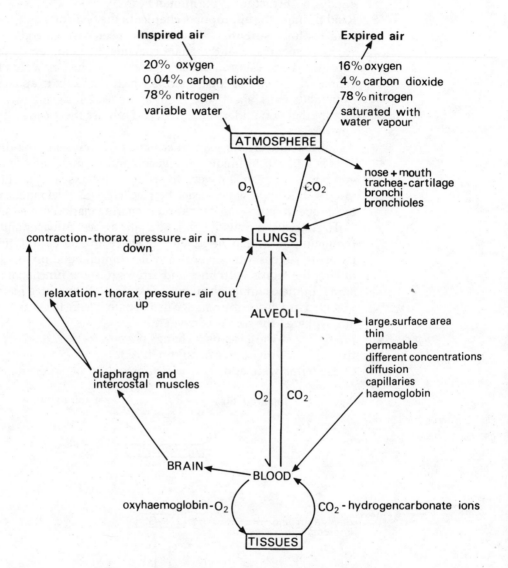

Fig 1.2 Revision flow diagram of gaseous exchange in mammals

The value of these diagrams in revision lies in the fact that they are constructed by you. Their structure is unique and means something to you. It is important that they should include all the key points and that each word you write should act as a stimulus for another word. The construction of these diagrams is one of the most efficient ways of recalling facts. Research into the processes of memory and recall have shown that detailed material is best retained in the memory if first represented in simplified ways.

Try this out for yourself and construct a flow diagram for the structure of the mammalian alimentary canal starting with the key words mouth, stomach, intestine, anus. You may be surprised by how much detail you can add. Remember to keep your diagrams simple.

7 Read Chapter 12 (p.309) and take note of all the advice given on how to understand the variety of questions and how to prepare answers to them.

8 Having revised a topic as suggested, the next step is to look at the past questions given in the guide. Now try answering some of the specimen questions which have been given at the end of each chapter. The questions given in the guide cover those topics which tend to crop up most frequently in examinations.

At first take your time and use references, but later you must practise answering questions without references and in the time allowed in the examination. Always have your answers marked.

THE CELL AND ORGANIZATION OF LIFE

CONTENTS

Cell The smallest unit of living material. It is made up of a single nucleus and cytoplasm surrounded by a cell membrane.

Nucleus A denser area within a cell, surrounded by a nuclear membrane and containing the hereditary material.

Cytoplasm The region of the cell where almost all the living processes take place.

Cell membrane The outer covering of all cells.

Tissue A group of similar cells performing the same function more efficiently than they would alone, e.g. muscle.

Organ A structure formed by two or more tissues working together to perform particular functions, e.g. stomach.

Organism A single individual of a species.

Diffusion The movement of molecules from a region of their high concentration to a region of their low concentration.

Osmosis The movement of water molecules from a region of their high concentration to a region of their low concentration through a selectively permeable (semi-permeable) membrane.

Active transport The movement of substances from a region of their low concentration to a region of their high concentration. This movement requires energy.

Enzyme A protein molecule produced by living cells to catalyse a chemical reaction.

Classification The means by which organisms are grouped together on the basis of characteristics which are unique to that group of organisms.

Key A means of identifying organisms on the basis of observing common external features.

CHARACTERISTICS OF LIVING ORGANISMS

All living organisms are made of one or more cells which show characteristics not displayed by similar non-living organic material. All living organisms show some or all of the following characteristics.

1 **Movement**. A change in position of the whole body, part of the body, or within a cell, using energy released by the organism (see Chapters 5, 7, 8).

2 **Assimilation and nutrition**. All living organisms need a supply of nourishment to maintain the structure of the body and to provide energy (see Chapter 3).

3 **Respiration**. The process by which energy is released in cells by the breakdown of food materials (see Chapter 4).

4 **Reproduction**. The production of other individuals of the same species (see Chapter 9).

5   **Irritability**. The ability to respond to a stimulus (see Chapter 7).
6   **Growth**. An increase in the amount of living material in an organism produced from substances unlike itself (see Chapter 9).
7   **Excretion**. The removal from the body of the waste products produced by chemical processes in the cells (see Chapter 6).

CYTOPLASM

Cytoplasm shows certain similarities wherever it is found. It is composed of the following.
1   **Water**, which is a vital constituent making up 80–90% of its mass. It contains dissolved mineral salts, e.g. chlorides, phosphates, hydrogencarbonates, sulphates and nitrates, of sodium, potassium, magnesium and calcium, and food materials, e.g. sugars, fats and amino acids.
2   A **protein framework** which has certain properties, including the ability to change between liquid (sol) and semi-solid (gel) states. The framework supports and separates the enzyme systems responsible for all the chemical processes which take place in the cytoplasm.

LEVELS OF ORGANIZATION

Living systems function at several levels, showing increasing complexity and organization with each level. Each level is built up from the preceding levels:

atomic → molecular → cell → tissue → organ

community ← population ← organism ← organ system
↓
ecosystem

The structures and functions which constitute life rely on about twenty different elements, e.g. hydrogen, carbon, oxygen, nitrogen. Atoms of these elements are arranged to make molecules, e.g. carbohydrates, amino acids, fats, and these form the basis of all other levels.

CELL STRUCTURE

Animal and plant cells have the basic structures shown in Fig 2.1.

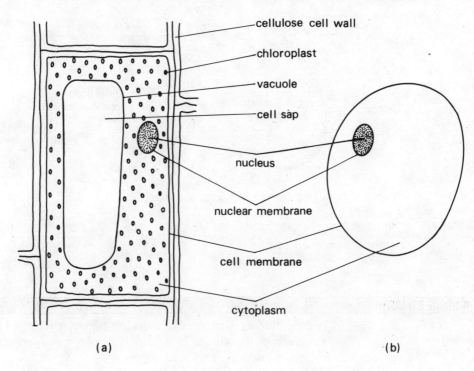

(a)   (b)

Fig 2.1   (a) Typical plant cell. (b) Typical animal cell – a cheek (epithelial) cell

DIFFERENCES BETWEEN PLANT AND ANIMAL CELLS

Plant cells are usually bigger than animal cells because they contain one or more large vacuoles. Many of the structures found in plant and animal cells are common to both, e.g. nucleus, cytoplasm and cell membrane. The main differences are shown in Table 2.1.

Table 2.1 Differences between plant and animal cells

Plant cell	Animal cell
Cell wall	No cell wall
Large permanent vacuoles	Small temporary vacuoles
Chloroplasts generally present	No chloroplasts present

Plant cells possess an outer rigid cell wall made of cellulose which supports the cell. Chloroplasts are distributed throughout the cytoplasm of most plant cells. They are relatively large structures containing the green pigment chlorophyll. Photosynthesis (see Chapter 3) occurs in the chloroplasts and starch grains are stored here. Under the electron microscope (EM) a chloroplast has the structure shown in Fig 2.2.

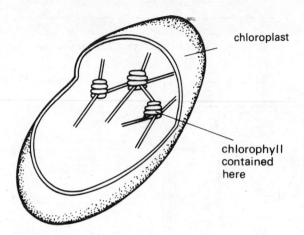

Fig 2.2 Electron micrograph of a chloroplast

TISSUE STRUCTURE

A collection of similar cells working together is called a **tissue**. The structure of these cells is modified to perform specialized functions such as shown in Table 2.2.

Table 2.2 Examples of plant and animal tissues and their functions

	Structure	Function
Plants	Palisade cells	Nutrition
	Epidermal cells	Protection
	Root hair cells	Absorption
	Xylem cells	Support, water and salt transport
	Phloem cells	Transport of sugars and amino acids
Animals	Epithelial (cheek) cells	Protection
	Bone cells	Support
	Muscle cells	Movement
	Blood cells	Transport
	Nerve cells	Communication

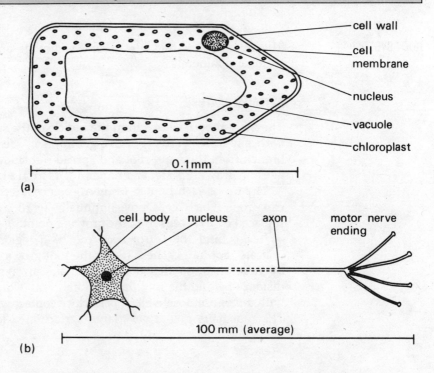

Fig 2.3 (a) Palisade cell, showing size. (b) Nerve (motor) cell, showing size

ORGANS AND ORGAN SYSTEMS

A collection of different tissues working together to perform a variety of functions is called an **organ**. For example the leaf is concerned with food production, the stem with support and transport and the root with anchorage and absorption. The heart is an animal organ which contains muscle and nerve cells; its function is to pump varying amounts of blood around the body under different conditions.

In both plants and animals, organs and tissues may be grouped together to carry out major functions, e.g. transport of food, waste products and hormones in animals. Such an arrangement is called an **organ system**. In this example the heart, blood vessels and blood form the circulatory system. Plants too have organ systems, e.g. the root system (below ground) and the shoot system (above ground).

STRUCTURE AND FUNCTION OF THE FLOWERING PLANT

Tissues, organs and organ systems have structures which enable them to carry out functions much more efficiently than they would do if they consisted of isolated cells. These interrelationships between the structure and function of tissues, organs and organ systems are clearly seen in flowering plants.

ROOT SYSTEM

The functions of this system are anchorage and the absorption of water and minerals.

EXTERNAL FEATURES

The main root develops from the radicle of the seed. It usually grows vertically downwards (positive geotropism, see p.175). Lateral roots branch from the main root and spread out sideways, giving anchorage and drawing water and mineral salts from a large volume of soil.

The tip of each branch of the root is covered by a protective **root cap** from which cells are continually worn away by friction and replaced by new cells from the growing point.

Just behind the tip of each root is a region bearing numerous delicate **root hairs**. These die as the root grows on, and are replaced by new ones, so that a band of hairs always exists at the same distance behind the root tip. Each hair is an elongated epidermal cell with a *thin* cellulose wall. It is in close contact with the soil particles. The root hairs give a very large surface area for the absorption of water and salts.

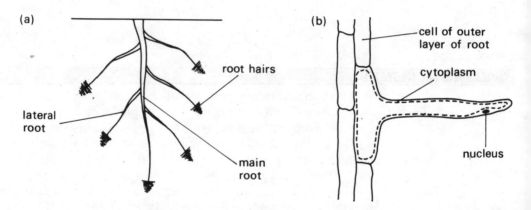

Fig 2.4 (a) Main tap root. (b) Root hair cell

INTERNAL STRUCTURE

Growth occurs as a result of the activity of the **growing point** at each root tip. Cells produced here elongate by absorption of water, and then became differentiated into tissues with different functions (see Fig 2.5).

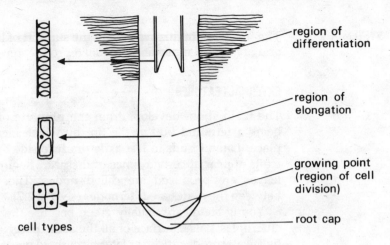

cell types

Fig 2.5 VS root tip

The **vascular** or **conducting tissue** of the root forms a central core (Fig 2.6). The **xylem**, which conducts water and mineral salts, also provides mechanical strength. This arrangement gives the root strength to resist the pulling strains which result from movement of the aerial parts of the plant.

The xylem is arranged in the shape of a star alternating with the phloem. A well-defined **endodermis** surrounds the vascular tissue. A wide **cortex**, which often contains storage tissue, separates the vascular tissue from the outer **exodermis**, which in a young root will bear root hairs. Roots are sometimes specialized for storage, e.g. **tap root** (carrot), **root tuber** (dahlia).

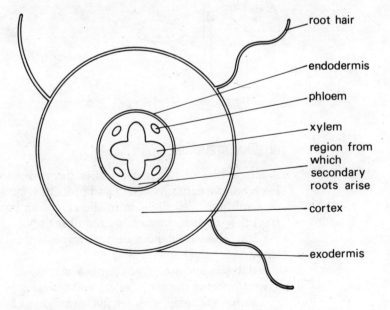

Fig 2.6 TS main root of bean

SHOOT SYSTEM

The functions of this system are the support of leaves in light and air, and of flowers and fruit for sexual reproduction.

EXTERNAL FEATURES

The main shoot develops from the **plumule** of the seed. It usually bears a **terminal bud** at the tip, by which increase in length takes place. **Lateral buds** in leaf **axils** produce side branches. Flowers and fruits appear at certain times of the year. Regions of the stem where leaves are produced are called **nodes**. Those parts of the stem between the nodes are **internodes** (see Fig 2.7).

Young stems are usually green because the outer tissues contain chloroplasts. The surface of all the aerial parts of the plant is covered by a waterproof cuticle, or later by cork, to prevent loss of water.

The general shape of the aerial part of the plant is formed by the reactions of the stem to gravity and light. The main stem grows vertically upwards away from gravity, and all stems grow towards light.

Fig 2.7 Shoot system

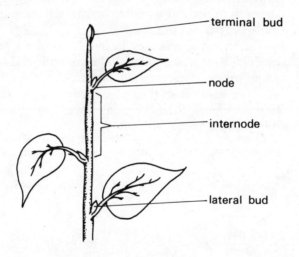

terminal bud

node

internode

lateral bud

INTERNAL STRUCTURE

A single ring of **vascular bundles** lies near the outside of the stem. Each bundle contains xylem and phloem separated by a narrow band of **cambium**. Cell division in the cambium increases the amount of the other tissues. In most plants **fibres** give additional strength (see Fig 2.8). The vascular bundles are important because they:

1 carry water and salts (xylem);
2 carry sugars and amino acids (phloem);
3 give support to the stem (xylem and fibres).

Central to the bundles are the turgid cells of the **pith** which provide support for the stem.

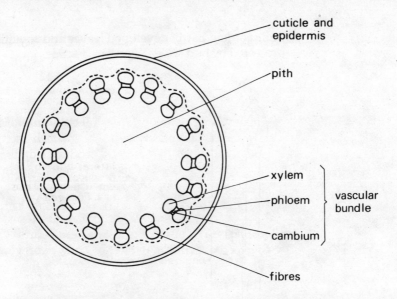

Fig 2.8 TS young stem of sunflower

Outside the bundles lies a narrow **cortex**. The inner part of this is made up of cells which may contain storage starch grains. The outer part may give strength to the outer layers of the stem (with its thickened cellulose walls). These outer cells which receive light may contain chloroplasts, enabling photosynthesis to take place.

On the outside of the stem is a single layer of cells called the **epidermis**. These cells have thickened walls and secrete a waterproof **cuticle**.

Questions are often set which require an understanding of the structure and functions of roots and stems. You should use the diagrams given and Table 2.3 in answering the following such question.

Specimen question Draw clearly labelled diagrams of transverse sections of (a) a stem and (b) a root of a herbaceous dicotyledon. Explain how the structures of stems and roots are suited to their respective functions. (25 marks)

Table 2.3 Structural differences between roots and stems

Roots	Stems
Do not bear buds, leaves or flowers	Bear buds, leaves and flowers
Bear root hairs	Do not bear root hairs
Tip protected by root cap	Tip protected by overlapping leaves
Cambium is not present in young root	Cambium present between xylem and phloem
White or brown	Usually green due to chlorophyll
No cuticle	Outer surface covered with a cuticle
No stomata	Bears stomata in epidermis

BUDS

Buds contain partly developed leaves and sometimes flowers, usually protected by bud scales.

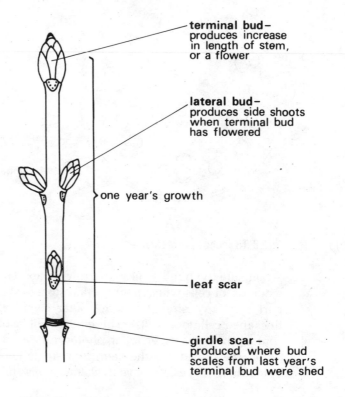

terminal bud –
produces increase
in length of stem,
or a flower

lateral bud –
produces side shoots
when terminal bud
has flowered

one year's growth

leaf scar

girdle scar –
produced where bud
scales from last year's
terminal bud were shed

Fig 2.9 Horse chestnut twig in winter condition

Buds are generally dormant in winter and are stimulated to grow in spring. Growth is controlled by chemicals in the plant called hormones which regulate which buds develop when.

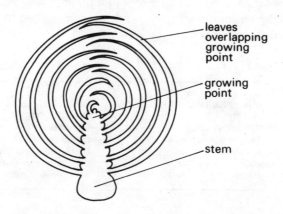

leaves
overlapping
growing
point

growing
point

stem

Fig 2.10 VS through large winter bud of Brussels sprout

LEAF

The functions of the leaf are:

1 photosynthesis (see p.53);
2 transpiration (see p.120);
3 gaseous exchange (see p.92);
4 protein synthesis (see p.36);
5 temporary starch storage (see p.55).

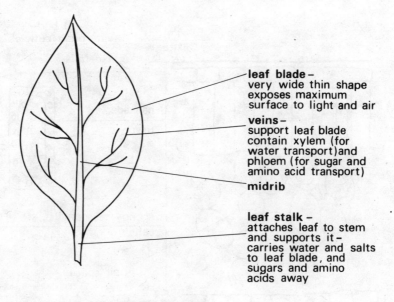

leaf blade –
very wide thin shape exposes maximum surface to light and air

veins –
support leaf blade contain xylem (for water transport) and phloem (for sugar and amino acid transport)

midrib

leaf stalk –
attaches leaf to stem and supports it – carries water and salts to leaf blade, and sugars and amino acids away

Fig 2.11 External features of a privet leaf

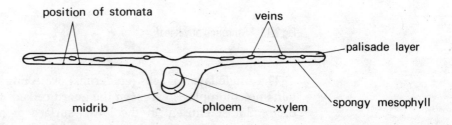

position of stomata   veins

palisade layer

midrib   phloem   xylem   spongy mesophyll

Fig 2.12 TS through leaf blade

The **leaf blade** contains an upper **palisade** tissue of closely packed cells. These cells are rich in **chloroplasts** containing the photosynthetic pigment chlorophyll. The leaf is extended, with the upper surface exposed to the light, so that it falls on the palisade layer. Photosynthesis occurs in the chloroplasts. The lower layer of the leaf blade is the **spongy mesophyll** containing fewer chloroplasts, but many air spaces between the cells. These allow diffusion of gases through the leaf.

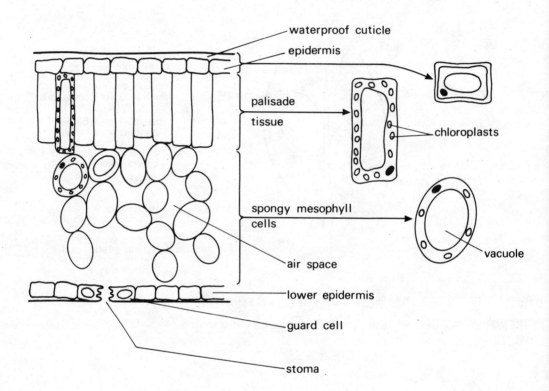

Fig 2.13 TS through privet leaf

The single layer of cells (epidermis) protecting the leaf blade contains no chloroplasts except in the **guard cells** of the **stomata**. These occur almost entirely in the lower surface of most leaves. Since evaporation of water vapour occurs mainly through the stomata, this position away from direct sun's rays protects the plant from excessive water loss. Oxygen and carbon dioxide diffuse in and out of the leaf through the stomata.

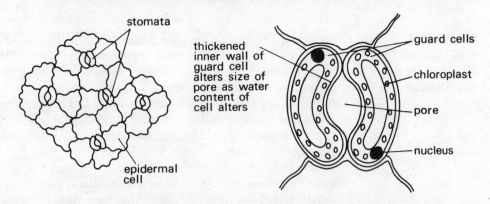

Fig 2.14 (*a*) Surface view of lower leaf epidermis. (*b*) Surface view of one stoma, enlarged

Re-read these notes and study the diagrams to find the information to answer the following question. Always qualify each structure with its function.

Specimen question In what ways are the leaves of plants adapted for photosynthesis? (6 marks)

PHYSICAL AND CHEMICAL FEATURES OF CELLS

THE IMPORTANCE OF WATER

Life is believed to have originated in the sea. The aquatic environments (marine and freshwater) present fewer problems to living organisms than life on land. All living cells are surrounded by water – it forms their immediate environment.

Water is a vital constituent of all cells and body fluids because of the following:

1 All chemical reactions, secretion, absorption and excretion of substances occur in solution. Water is the solvent in which substances are dissolved.

2 Transport systems in animals and plants all depend on water as the transport medium, e.g. blood plasma.

3 Water is a raw material of photosynthesis – the main energy-fixing process of living organisms.

4 Loss of water from terrestrial organisms, by evaporation and excretion, has led to the evolution of many structures and processes to protect them from desiccation, e.g. cuticle in plants, epidermis in mammals.

EXCHANGE OF SUBSTANCES BETWEEN CELLS AND THEIR ENVIRONMENT

All living organisms are composed of particles, called **molecules**, which are in a state of constant random movement. If the chemical composition of the cells is different from that of their environment, movement of substances in and out of cells will occur. The three processes involved are **diffusion**, **osmosis** and **active transport**.

A clear understanding of these processes is necessary – it is a popular topic with examiners. Consider the following question when reading these notes.

Specimen question (a) What do you understand by the term osmosis? (5 marks) (b) How does diffusion differ from this? (3 marks)

DIFFUSION

If the molecules of a liquid, gas or dissolved substance are unevenly distributed in a space, they will by their random movement become evenly distributed. This movement of molecules from a region of their high concentration to a region of their low concentration, down a concentration gradient, is called diffusion.

Any substance which can pass through a cell membrane will diffuse into or out of a cell, in the direction determined by the concentration gradient. For example, all cells respire and produce carbon dioxide; the concentration of carbon dioxide within the cell rises above that of the environment, and the carbon dioxide diffuses out of the cell, down the concentration gradient.

OSMOSIS

This is a special type of diffusion. It is the movement of water molecules from a region of their high concentration to a region of

Fig 2.15 Demonstration of osmosis

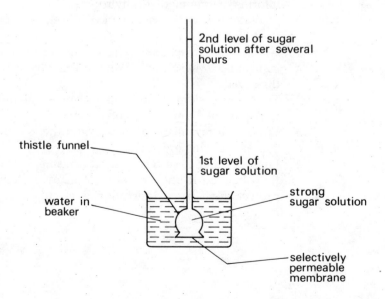

2nd level of sugar solution after several hours

thistle funnel

1st level of sugar solution

water in beaker

strong sugar solution

selectively permeable membrane

their low concentration across a **selectively permeable membrane**. It may also be thought of as the passage of water molecules from a weak solution to a strong one, across a selectively permeable membrane.

A membrane which allows the passage of all substances across it is said to be freely permeable. One which prevents the passage of all substances is said to be impermeable. One which allows water to pass through but not dissolved substances is selectively permeable, e.g. the cell membrane surrounding all cells.

Water can pass through the selectively permeable membrane but not the sugar molecules (see Fig 2.15). Because of the higher concentration of water molecules in the beaker, more water passes into the thistle funnel than out of it and the level in the tube rises.

The sugar solution is said to have a low **water potential**. The water could be replaced by a weak sugar solution, and water would still enter the thistle funnel by osmosis, as long as the sugar solution it contained was stronger (had a lower water potential).

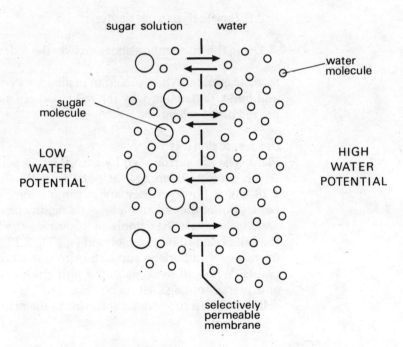

Fig 2.16 Explanation of osmosis

The water potential of the fluids in cells is related to their concentration of dissolved sugars and salts. The cell is surrounded by a selectively permeable membrane, so if the fluid outside the cell has a different water potential from that inside, water will either leave or enter the cell, perhaps with damaging results. Animal cells therefore are either surrounded by body fluids of the same water potential as themselves, or they have a means of adjusting their water content if it changes (see p.163).

Osmosis and red blood cells

Red blood cells are normally surrounded by a fluid of almost constant water potential, the plasma. If we experimentally surround red blood cells with water or a very strong salt solution, the effect on the cells can be compared with normal cells. The arrows in Fig 2.17 show the water movement.

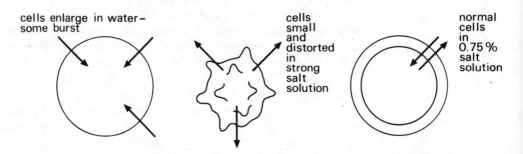

cells enlarge in water – some burst

cells small and distorted in strong salt solution

normal cells in 0.75% salt solution

Fig 2.17   Osmotic effects on red blood cells

Using the information above answer the following question.

Specimen question   When placed in distilled water, red blood cells swell and burst. (*a*) Explain why the red blood cell swells. (*b*) Explain why the red blood cell bursts.

Osmosis and plant cells

Plant cells are surrounded by a firm, freely permeable cellulose wall which protects them against bursting if they absorb water (see Fig 2.18 (*a*)). If however they are put into strong sugar solution, water passes out of the cell and it loses its rigidity (see Fig 2.18 (*b*)). Further water loss causes the cytoplasm to shrink away from the cell wall and the cell is said to be **plasmolysed** (see Fig 2.18 (*c*)). **Turgid** cells as in (*a*) have an important supporting role in herbaceous (non-woody) plants. When all the cells in the pith absorb water, each cell swells and presses out against its neighbours. The result is a rigid mass of cells which can support the soft parts of the plant (see p.202).

Fig 2.18   Osmotic effects on plant cells

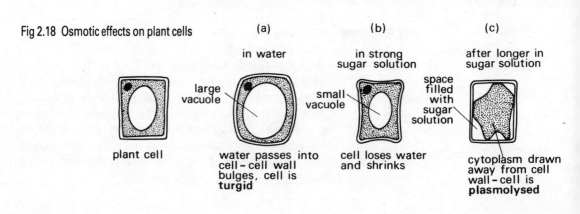

(a) in water

(b) in strong sugar solution

(c) after longer in sugar solution

large vacuole

small vacuole

space filled with sugar solution

plant cell

water passes into cell – cell wall bulges, cell is **turgid**

cell loses water and shrinks

cytoplasm drawn away from cell wall – cell is **plasmolysed**

ACTIVE TRANSPORT

This is the movement of substances from point **A** to point **B** against a concentration gradient and requires energy produced during respiration. It occurs in the movement of substances across the cell membrane either to maintain the constant composition of the cell or to take in raw materials for growth or maintenance of normal functions. **Carrier molecules** situated in the cell membrane are thought to be responsible for moving these substances.

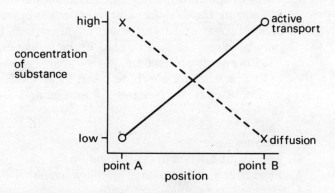

Fig 2.19 Graph illustrating active transport

Examples

1 The active absorption of mineral salts by the root hair cells of a plant (see p.60).
2 The completion of the absorption of digested food in the intestine of a mammal (see p.70).
3 The selective reabsorption of substances back into the blood capillaries in the first convoluted tubule in the kidney (see p.160).

FOOD MATERIALS IN PLANTS AND ANIMALS

Photosynthesis is the basic process in the production of all food materials in plants. It is the process whereby simple inorganic substances such as carbon dioxide and water are combined to produce complex organic compounds (carbohydrates) (see Chapter 3). From these carbohydrates the leaf forms fats, and by combination with mineral salts it forms proteins and vitamins.

Similar materials found in animals originate in plants. Animals cannot build up organic materials, and must obtain them from plants or other animals which themselves are dependent on plants.

CARBOHYDRATES

These contain the elements carbon, hydrogen, oxygen.

Table 2.4 Different categories of carbohydrate

Type of carbohydrate	Solubility in water	Examples
Simple sugars (monosaccharides)	Soluble	Glucose Fructose
More complex sugars (disaccharides)	Soluble	Maltose Sucrose
Large molecule carbohydrates (polysaccharides)	Insoluble	Starch Glycogen Cellulose

Carbohydrates formed by photosynthesis are stored as starch in the leaf during the day. At night the starch is broken down (see p.54) to soluble sugar and translocated to other parts of the plant where it may be stored (as starch), used in the formation of cellulose walls or used in energy production.

In animals, carbohydrate taken in as food is digested to simple sugars by enzymes (see p.68), absorbed and used for energy release or stored as glycogen.

Functions

1 Energy production in cell respiration.
2 Storage as starch in plants, glycogen in animals.
3 Formation of cellulose cell walls.

FATS

These contain carbon, hydrogen and oxygen, and are formed by plants from sugars, stored as oil droplets in plant cells and as adipose tissue in animals.

Functions

1 Release large amounts of energy when broken down during respiration.
2 Protect internal organs of mammal from damage.
3 Act as a heat insulator in mammal skin.

PROTEINS

These contain carbon, hydrogen, oxygen, nitrogen and sometimes sulphur. They are very large molecules formed of a chain of **amino acids** joined end to end. There are twenty different amino acids which can be joined in any order and any length to make a great variety of different proteins.

Amino acids are formed in the leaf of the green plant by combining sugars with mineral salts (particularly nitrates) absorbed by the root. These amino acids are then combined to form proteins.

Functions

1 As an important structural part of all cells, and therefore necessary in growth and tissue repair.
2 Formation of enzymes and other functional substances, e.g. haemoglobin, insulin.

VITAMINS

These are substances vital to life, but only needed in small quantities. They are made by plants. Animals must obtain most of their vitamins from plants because they cannot manufacture their own.

Functions

Many vitamins combine with proteins in the formation of enzymes (for special functions see p.70).

Specimen questions Several simple questions are usually set on the structure and functions of biological molecules. It is a pity to lose easy marks so learn them, e.g.:

1 Of what organic units are proteins composed? (1 mark)
   Give two functions of proteins in the cells of an organism. (2 marks)
2 What are carbohydrates? (6 marks)

ENZYMES

Enzymes are chemical substances which increase the rate of chemical reactions in living organisms or allow them to occur at lower temperatures. The substance acted on by the enzyme is called a **substrate**.

PROPERTIES OF ENZYMES

1 Made by living cells.
2 Protein in nature, sometimes incorporating vitamins.
3 Act as **catalysts**.
4 Responsible for one specific reaction.
5 Can also catalyse the reverse reaction, depending on concentration of substrate.
6 Rise of temperature increases rate of reaction at low temperatures.
7 Work fastest at a particular temperature (the optimum).
8 Work most efficiently at a particular pH (the optimum).
9 Can be inhibited by heavy metal ions, e.g. silver nitrate, cyanide.
10 Destroyed (denatured) by heat, e.g. by boiling.
   (For details of enzyme experiments see p.38.)

CONDENSATION AND HYDROLYSIS

Two of the simple reactions vital to life which are catalysed by enzymes are condensation and hydrolysis.

Condensation reactions are involved in the formation of a complex substance from simple ones with the removal of water, e.g. synthesis:

$$\text{amino acids} \xrightarrow[\text{condensation}]{\text{enzyme}} \text{protein} + \text{water}$$

Complex insoluble substances are usually used as storage products in cells because they do not upset the osmotic balance within cells.

Hydrolysis reactions are involved in the splitting of a complex substance into simple substances by the addition of water, e.g. digestion:

$$\text{starch} + \text{water} \xrightarrow[\text{hydrolysis}]{\text{enzyme}} \text{sugars}$$

Simple soluble substances are the form in which food materials are translocated (moved around) the body in solution in water. Enzymes are therefore necessary to convert one form into the other.

complex insoluble substance	enzymes (hydrolysis) →	small simple soluble substances	enzymes (condensation) →	complex insoluble substance
plant storage organ		transport system		growing region

EXPERIMENT TO INVESTIGATE THE EFFECT OF AQUEOUS AMYLASE SOLUTION IN THE BREAKDOWN OF STARCH

Method

A freshly made up sample of aqueous amylase solution (saliva) is divided into two equal parts and one part is thoroughly boiled (boiling breaks down protein and therefore destroys the enzyme amylase).

The unboiled saliva is added to an equal volume of 1% starch solution in a test tube labelled **A**. The boiled saliva is added to an equal volume of 1% starch solution in a test tube labelled **B**. (This is a controlled experiment. **A** is the control.)

Both test tubes are left for 10 minutes in a water bath at 37°C. A few drops of solution are removed from test tube **A** and added to 1–2 drops of dilute iodine/potassium iodide solution. The result is recorded. To the rest of the solution in **A**, an equal quantity of Benedict's solution is added and boiled. The result is recorded. These tests are repeated for the contents of test tube **B**.

Results

Test-tube **A** With iodine solution: brown colour of iodine remained.
         With Benedict's solution: brick-red precipitate formed.
Test-tube **B** With iodine solution: blue-black coloration formed.
         With Benedict's solution: original blue colour remained.

Conclusion

There is no starch present in **A** at the end of the experiment. Reducing sugar is now present in **A**. Starch is still present in **B**, but there is no reducing sugar. In test tube **A** starch has been changed into reducing sugar by the action of amylase on starch. In test tube **B** the enzyme amylase has been destroyed (denatured) by the boiling. No starch breakdown has occurred.

Since all other conditions in the two test tubes are identical, the differences in the two tubes must result from the presence of active amylase in **A**.

EXPERIMENT TO INVESTIGATE THE EFFECT OF TEMPERATURE ON ENZYME ACTIVITY

Method

Six test tubes labelled **A–F** are set up containing equal quantities of 1% starch solution. Test tube **A** is placed in a water bath at 10°C. Test tubes **B–F** are placed similarly in water baths at 10°C intervals up to 60°C. All the test tubes are left in the water baths for 10 minutes until their temperatures equal those of the water baths.

Equal quantities of amylase solution are added to all test tubes **A–F** and shaken. At 30-second intervals a few drops of each mixture are removed and added to iodine solution on a white tile. The times for the blue-black colour of starch/iodine to disappear for each test tube are recorded. After 10 minutes no further results are recorded.

Results

A blue-black colour remained for test tubes **A**, **E** and **F**. A graph is drawn showing the effects of temperature on the activity of amylase solution – see Fig 2.20.

Fig 2.20

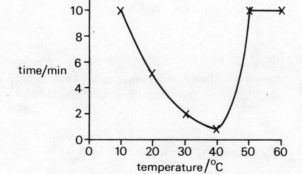

test tube   **A**   **B**   **C**   **D**   **E**   **F**

Conclusion

Enzyme activity increases from 10°C to an optimum at 40°C. It then falls off rapidly at temperatures higher than 40°C.

EXPERIMENT TO INVESTIGATE THE EFFECT OF pH ON ENZYME ACTIVITY

Method

Three test tubes labelled **A**, **B** and **C** are set up containing equal quantities of 1% starch solution. Buffer pH solutions are added to each test tube to make the pH of the contents 4, 7 and 11 respectively. All three test tubes are added to a water bath at 37°C and the same volume of amylase solution added to each test tube. (These volumes of enzyme solutions being equal to the volumes of 1% starch solution present in each test tube.)

At 30-second intervals a few drops of each mixture are removed and added to iodine solution on a white tile. The times for the blue-black colour of starch/iodine to disappear for each test tube are recorded. After 10 minutes no further results are recorded.

Results

A blue-black colour remains for test tubes **A** and **C**. A graph is drawn showing the effects of pH on the activity of amylase solution – see Fig 2.21.

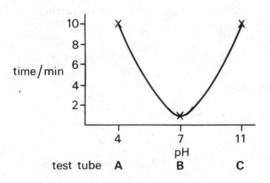

Fig 2.21

Conclusion

Amylase activity is greatest at a pH of 7. There is no activity at an acidic pH (pH 4) or at an alkaline pH (pH 11).

EXPERIMENT TO INVESTIGATE THE BREAKDOWN OF STARCH IN A POTATO TUBER AND A GERMINATING FRENCH BEAN SEED

Method

Label a starch agar plate **A**. Cut a cube of potato of sides 1 cm and then cut it into two halves. Boil one of the cut pieces for two minutes and let it cool. Place the boiled and unboiled potato on to the surface of plate **A** about 2 cm apart. Cover with the lid.

Label a starch agar plate **B**. Cut a soaked French bean seed and an unsoaked French bean seed in half longitudinally. Place the four half bean seeds on the surface of the starch agar at equal distances apart. Cover with the lid.

Leave plates **A** and **B** in an incubator at 37°C for two days. Mark the position of each material carefully before removing them from the surface of the agar. Cover both plates with iodine solution and leave for one minute. Wash the iodine solution away and examine the plates.

Results

The following results are obtained at the positions of the materials:

A   Boiled potato: blue-black colour.
      Unboiled potato: no blue-black colour.
B   Unsoaked French bean: blue-black colour.
      Soaked French bean: no blue-black colour.

Conclusion

The absence of a blue-black colour indicates that no starch is present in the agar. Unboiled potato and germinating French bean seeds break down starch but boiled potato and dried French bean seeds do not break down starch. Since boiling interferes with the ability of potato to break down starch it appears that an enzyme in potato is responsible for this reaction. Absence of water in the dried French bean seeds also appears to interfere with the action of enzymes.

CLASSIFICATION

Each type of plant and animal is identified by two names, e.g. the blackbird is called *Turdus merula*. The first name indicates that the blackbird belongs to the genus *Turdus* and the second name indicates the species to which the blackbird alone belongs. This system of classification which gives all organisms two names is called the **binomial system** (*bi* = two, *nomen* = name) and it was introduced by Carl Linnaeus in the eighteenth century.

Closely related organisms may belong to the same genus, e.g. the song thrush, *Turdus philomelos* also belongs to the genus *Turdus*, but only one type of organism can belong to any species. The blackbird and song thrush have many similarities, hence they belong to the same genus; but they are classified into separate species because they cannot interbreed and produce fertile offspring.

Animals and plants are further classified into larger groups containing many more types of closely related organisms.

Table 2.5 The basis of classification

Group	Example	Characteristics
Kingdom	*Animalia*	Organisms feeding on ready-made food.
Phylum	*Vertebrata*	Animals with a backbone.
Class	*Aves*	Animals with constant body temperature, feathers, wings and hard-shelled eggs.
Order	*Passeriformes*	Perching birds.
Family	*Turdidae*	Thrush-like in appearance.
Genus	*Turdus*	Songbirds.
Species	*merula*	Blackbird.

VARIETY OF ORGANISMS

There are a great many plants and animals which are grouped together for convenience. They have the main features shown in Table 2.6.

Table 2.6 The main classification groups

Group	Characteristics
Viruses	Non-cellular, totally parasitic.
Bacteria	Cell wall, no nucleus.
Fungi	No chlorophyll; mycelium of hyphae; spores.
Algae	No stem, root or leaves.
Mosses	Simple leaves and stem.
Ferns	True roots, stems and leaves.
Flowering plants	Flowers; fruits containing seeds.
Monocotyledons	One seed leaf, parallel veins.
Dicotyledons	Two seed leaves, branching veins.
Protozoans	Single-celled animals.
Annelids	Segmented worms.
Molluscs	Chalky shell, muscular foot.
Arthropods	Exoskeleton, segmented body, jointed limbs.
Insects	Three body regions, wings, three pairs of legs.
Crustaceans	Two pairs of antennae.
Arachnids	Four pairs of legs.
Myriapods	Appendages on all segments.
Vertebrates	Spinal cord protected by vertebrae.
Fish	Scales, gills and fins.
Amphibians	Moist skin; aquatic and terrestrial life cycle.
Reptiles	Dry scaly skin, soft-shelled eggs.
Birds	Feathers, wings, hard-shelled eggs.
Mammals	Hair, mammary glands.

KEYS

A key is a means of identifying organisms by observing common external features such as number of legs, presence of wings, etc. Internal features, hairiness, size and colour should not be used in preparing a key.

Keys which require the user to choose one description from a choice of two descriptions are called **dichotomous keys**, e.g.:

3 pairs of legs – insect
4 pairs of legs – arachnid

KEY WORDS ▶

Movement
Assimilation
Respiration
Reproduction
Irritability
Growth
Excretion
Nuclear membrane
Chromosomes
Tissue
Organ
Organ system
Radicle
Root cap
Root hair
Growing point
Vascular tissue
Xylem
Phloem
Endodermis
Cortex
Exodermis
Tap root
Root tuber
Plumule
Terminal bud

Axil
Lateral bud
Node
Internode
Vascular bundle
Cambium
Fibres
Pith
Cortex
Epidermis
Cuticle
Buds
Leaf blade
Palisade
Chloroplasts
Spongy mesophyll
Guard cells
Stomata
Molecules
Diffusion
Osmosis
Selectively
    permeable
    membrane
Water potential

Plasmolysed
Turgid
Active transport
'Carrier molecule'
Photosynthesis
Carbohydrates
Fats
Proteins
Amino acids
Vitamins
Enzymes
Substrate
Catalysts
Condensation
Hydrolysis
Classification
Binomial system
Kingdom
Phylum
Class
Order
Family
Genus
Species
Dichotomous key

SPECIMEN EXAMINATION QUESTIONS

1   Fig 2.22 below shows an animal cell, such as a cheek cell.

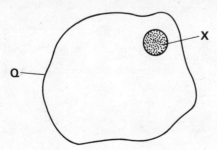

Fig 2.22

(a)   (i) Name the part labelled Q.   (1 mark)

(ii) Name the part labelled X which is the site of genetic material.   (1 mark)

(b)   Draw in and label THREE extra structures that would change this animal cell into a diagram of a typical, green, plant cell.

(3 marks)   [MEG]

2   (a)   Complete the drawing in Fig 2.23 of an epidermal cell of a leaf as you would see it using a school microscope. Draw the internal structures in correct proportion to one another. Label the completed diagram.

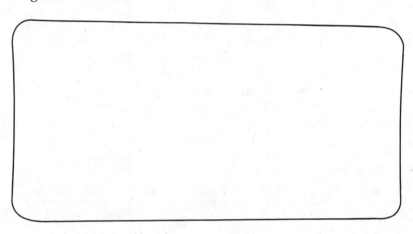

Fig 2.23

(b)   State any TWO differences between this cell and an animal cell.   (5 marks)   [WJEC]

3   Fig 2.24 shows sections of three different cells, A, B and C. They are not drawn to the same scale.

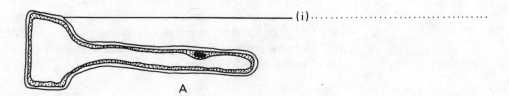

(i)..

A

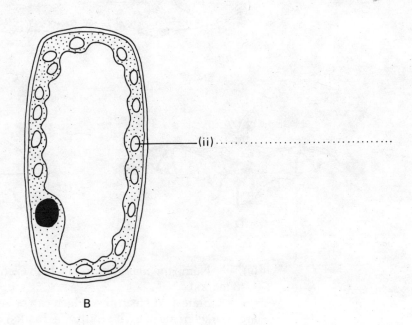

(ii)..

B

Fig 2.24

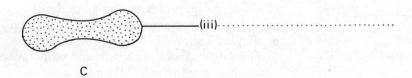

(iii)·...

C

(a)   Label parts (i), (ii) and (iii).   (3 marks)
(b)   A and B are plant cells; C is an animal cell. Give TWO features shown in the diagrams that support this statement.   (2 marks)
(c)   State precisely where in a plant or animal you would expect to find cells A, B and C.   (3 marks)

(d   State ONE way in which the structure of each of the cells A and B helps it to carry out its main functions.   (2 marks)

(e)   (i) Name ONE substance likely to pass through cell A on its way to cell B in a living plant.   (1 mark)

(ii) Name ONE substance produced in cell B which is found in high concentration in cell C.   (1 mark)   [LEAG]

4   Fig 2.25 shows three vertebrate animals. For each of the animals shown, answer the following questions.

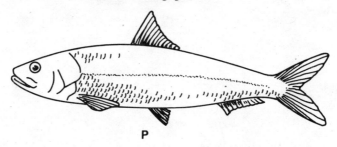

P

Q

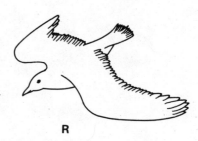

R

Fig 2.25

(a)   Name the main group to which each animal belongs.
    (3 marks)

(b)   State TWO features, which can be seen in the diagram, which are characteristic of each group.   (3 marks)   [MEG]

5   (a)   Name TWO major groups of vertebrates which maintain a constant body temperature.   (2 marks)

(b)   Describe one way in which you would distinguish between:
    (i) a bird and a reptile;
    (ii) a reptile and an amphibian;
    (iii) an amphibian and a fish.   (3 marks)   [NEA]

6   Fig 2.26 shows SIX invertebrate animals. Use the key opposite to identify each of the animals and write the letter (A, B, C, D, E or F) of each animal in the table below.

DRAWING	1	2	3	4	5	6
Animal (A, B, C, D, E, F)						

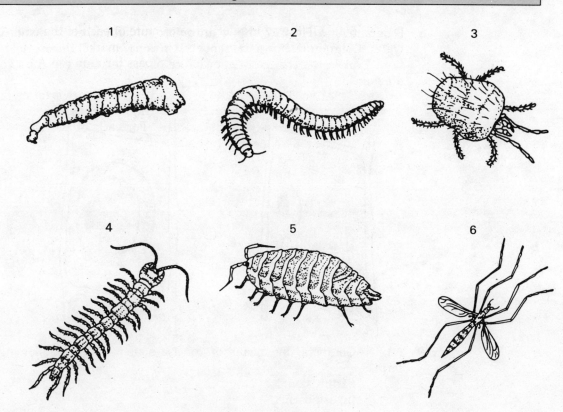

Fig 2.26

(1)	More than 4 pairs of legs	Go to 2
	4 pairs of legs or less	Go to 4
(2)	More than 15 body segments	Go to 3
	Less than 15 body segments	Animal A
(3)	Two pairs of legs on each body segment	Animal B
	One pair of legs on each body segment	Animal C
(4)	No legs can be seen	Animal D
	Legs can be seen	Go to 5
(5)	4 pairs of legs	Animal E
	3 pairs of legs	Animal F
		(3 marks)
		[NEA]

7 Some of the characteristics of four British swallow-like birds are shown in Table 2.7. Construct a simple branching key, which will enable the species below to be identified.

[SEG]

Table 2.7

Species	Tail	Appearance of under-parts	Coloured breast-band
Sand martin	Notched	Light	Present
House martin	Notched	Light	None
Swift	Notched	Dark	None
Swallow	Forked	Light	Present

8   Diagram A in Fig 2.27 shows an onion epidermal cell in distilled water. Diagram B shows the same cell in concentrated glucose solution. Explain the change in appearance of the cell between the two diagrams.

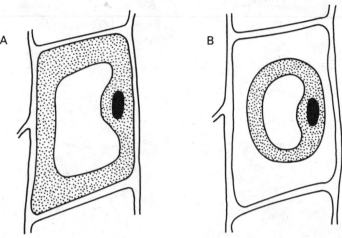

Fig 2.27

9   (*a*)   Compare, by means of concise statements, the following terms:
              (i) diffusion;
              (ii) osmosis;
              (iii) active uptake.   (9 marks)
    (*b*)   It is biologically important that certain substances enter or leave organisms through the following structures. Explain what the substances are, why they enter or leave and how the structures are adapted to the purpose they fulfil:
              (i) root hairs;
              (ii) leaves;
              (iii) villi.   (11 marks)   [*MEG*]

10   In an osmosis investigation using potato, six cylinders of potato were cut to a length of EXACTLY 50 mm.
    Three of the cylinders were put in water.
    Three of the cylinders were put in 30% sugar solution.
    After two hours the cylinders were taken out and dried. They were put on 2 mm graph paper to measure their lengths (see Fig 2.28).

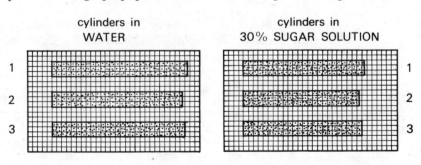

Fig 2.28

(*a*)   Find the length of the three cylinders from each of the liquids. (2 marks)

(*b*)   Find the mean length of the cylinders in each liquid after 2 hours.   (2 marks)

(*c*)   At the start the cylinders were all 50 mm long. Why did the cylinders in the 30% sugar solution change in length?   (1 mark)

(*d*)   After 2 hours the cylinders from the sugar solution would feel different from those that had been in water. What would be the difference in feel?   (1 mark)   [*NEA*]

11 Many people now use biological washing powder rather than ordinary washing powder.

(*a*)   Name the substance obtained from living creatures which is contained in biological washing powder but not in ordinary washing powder.   (1 mark)

(*b*)   Name **one** kind of stain which is best removed by using biological washing powder.   (1 mark)

(*c*)   Describe the best way of using biological washing powder to remove stains.   (2 marks)   [*NEA*]

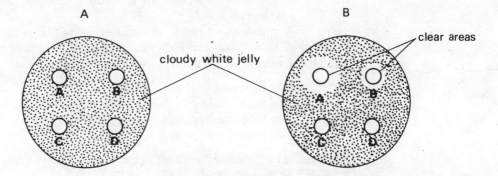

Fig 2.29

12 In an investigation, a cloudy white jelly was prepared by mixing powdered milk protein and molten agar jelly. This mixture was poured into a Petri dish and allowed to cool and set. Small cavities were made in the jelly and various liquids were placed in them as shown in Fig 2.29, Diagram A. After 24 hours at room temperature, the results were as shown in Diagram B.

(*a*)   (i) What type of enzyme is found in both gastric juice (A) and biological detergent (B)?   (1 mark)

(ii) What is the action of this enzyme?   (1 mark)

(*b*)   Why does no clear area appear around detergent D? (1 mark)

(*c*)   Explain why it is usual to soak washing for a few hours in biological detergent before placing it in a washing machine whereas this produces less improvement in cleanliness when it is done with detergent D.   (2 marks)   [*NEA*]

13 (*a*)   A pupil explored the effect of temperature on the digestion of a food by an enzyme and recorded the following:

I tried five temperatures. At 37°C it took two hours for the digestion of the food to be completed but it took only 1½ hours at 45°C. The food wasn't affected at all at 5°C and at 65°C. After five hours all the food was digested at 25°C.

(i) Use this information to complete the following table. Select appropriate headings for the second column of Table 2.8.

Table 2.8

Temperature (°C)	
5	
25	
37	
45	
65	

(ii) What can you conclude about the optimum temperature for the action of this enzyme?

(iii) Use clear labelled diagrams to demonstrate the main steps in an experimental procedure to show the action of amylase on starch.

(b)   A pupil was finding out the effect of temperature on the activity of an enzyme which digests egg white. A little of the enzyme and some acid were placed in each of four test tubes.

One tube was kept at 4°C in the fridge.
One tube was kept at laboratory temperature.
One tube was kept in a water bath at 37°C.
One tube was kept in a water bath at 60°C.

A piece of egg white was placed in each tube. The time taken to digest the egg white was noted.
   Identify TWO factors which will affect the fairness of this test.

(c)   In an experiment, an enzyme caused a reaction which released a gas.
   The volume of gas from the reaction was collected and measured each time the experiment was repeated.
   Six results are shown below.

First result $= 15 \, cm^3$
Second result $= 16 \, cm^3$
Third result $= 13 \, cm^3$
Fourth result $= 15 \, cm^3$
Fifth result $= 16 \, cm^3$
Sixth result $= 14 \, cm^3$

(i) What is the TOTAL volume of gas collected from the six experiments?
(ii) What is the AVERAGE volume of gas collected per experiment?   [SEG]

NUTRITION

CONTENTS

Autotrophic nutrition The nutrition of green plants; the building up of complex organic substances from simple inorganic ones.

Heterotrophic nutrition The taking in of complex organic food materials which are broken down, absorbed and then rebuilt into the tissue of the animal.

Ingestion The intake of complex organic food into the body.

Digestion The breakdown of large complex insoluble molecules into simple small soluble molecules.

Absorption The uptake of soluble food substances into living cells.

Assimilation The utilization of food substances within the cell.

Egestion The elimination of undigested waste from the body.

Secretion The production of chemical substances by a cell or a gland.

Nutrition supplies:

1 the raw materials for growth, repair and synthesis of essential substances;
2 the fuel from which energy is released to build new tissues, and to perform all essential life processes.

AUTOTROPHIC NUTRITION

Green plants produce carbohydrates by **photosynthesis**. These can be converted to fats or, by combining with mineral salts, form amino acids and vitamins. Because of this ability to make organic food materials, green plants manufacture the food on which all other forms of life, including human life, depend.

PHOTOSYNTHESIS

All green parts of the plant which are exposed to light can carry out photosynthesis (see p.57).

The process can be represented by the following equation:

$$\text{carbon dioxide} + \text{water} \xrightarrow[\text{chlorophyll}]{\text{sunlight}} \text{sugars} + \text{oxygen}$$

$$6CO_2 + 6H_2O \longrightarrow C_6H_{12}O_6 + 6O_2$$

The reactions are controlled by enzymes.

Chlorophyll absorbs light energy which is converted to chemical energy, which in turn is used in the reaction. Sugars are produced in the leaf, and oxygen is released into the atmosphere by diffusion. The sugar is changed to starch immediately and stored temporarily in the leaf. At night the starch is hydrolysed by enzymes back to sugar and carried away in the phloem. It may travel to:

1 growing points, to be used to provide energy, and in the production of new cell walls;

2 storage organs or seeds, to be redeposited as starch. Starch is stored as starch grains in the cytoplasm of cells and, being insoluble, does not cause osmotic problems in the cells.

RAW MATERIALS

Adequate supplies of the following are necessary for the formation of carbohydrates by photosynthesis:

1 carbon dioxide;
2 water;
3 light; and
4 chlorophyll.

Carbon dioxide

This is present in the atmosphere in a concentration of 0.04% and enters the leaf by diffusion through the **stomata** (see p.107). As it is used up in the leaf cells, a **diffusion gradient** is set up from the atmosphere to the air spaces of the leaf. Carbon dioxide diffuses through the stomata into the leaf, dissolves in the moisture on the surface of the cells and diffuses to the **chloroplasts** where photosynthesis takes place. The spongy mesophyll layer has many air spaces to help diffusion (see p.30).

Water

This is absorbed by osmosis through the root hair cells. It passes up in the **xylem** of root and stem, and out through the veins of the leaf (see p.122). Use of this water in photosynthesis causes more water to be drawn along the veins to the palisade cells.

Light

The maximum available light reaches the site of photosynthesis because:

1 leaves on a plant are arranged so that the maximum leaf surface is exposed to the sun;

2 the leaf is held at right angles to the direction of the sunlight so that the upper surface receives maximum light;

3 most chloroplasts are in the closely packed upper layer of cells (palisade layer);

4 the chloroplasts in some plants move to the upper parts of the cells in dim light;

5 chlorophyll reflects green light and absorbs red and blue, the wavelengths most valuable in photosynthesis;

6 the enormous surface area/volume ratio of the lamina exposes a very large area of chlorophyll-containing cells to the light.

Specimen question Use information concerning carbon dioxide, water, light and leaf structure (p.54) to answer the following question.

Explain how the leaves of flowering plants are adapted to perform their functions. (7 marks) [*ULSEB*]

EXPERIMENTS DEMONSTRATING PHOTOSYNTHESIS

EXPERIMENT TO INVESTIGATE THE EVOLUTION OF OXYGEN IN PHOTOSYNTHESIS

Apparatus
See Fig 3.1.

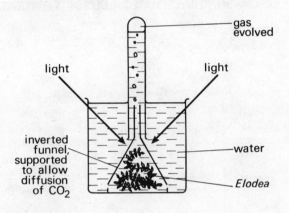

Fig 3.1

Method
Elodea is exposed to sunlight for several hours.

Result
A gas is evolved which ignites a glowing splint.

Conclusion
The gas given off by a green plant in sunlight is oxygen.

EXPERIMENT TO INVESTIGATE THE PRESENCE OF STARCH IN A LEAF

Method
A leaf from a plant which has been exposed to sunlight for 6 hours is detached and:

1   dipped into boiling water for 5 minutes to remove the cuticle;
2   boiled in ethanol to remove the chlorophyll (this is done in a water bath to avoid danger of fire);
3   dipped in boiling water to soften the leaf;
4   spread on a white tile;
5   covered with dilute iodine solution for 1 minute; and
6   washed to remove the iodine solution.

Result and conclusion

A blue-black coloration demonstrates the presence of starch. This test is used in experiments to investigate the conditions required for photosynthesis. The presence of starch in a leaf indicates that photosynthesis has occurred.

In the following experiments one variable in turn is omitted to demonstrate its necessity in photosynthesis. In each case a **control experiment** is performed in which all variables are present. All leaves used are **destarched** before the experiment by keeping the plant in the dark for 48 hours.

EXPERIMENT TO INVESTIGATE THE NECESSITY FOR LIGHT IN PHOTOSYNTHESIS

Apparatus
See Fig 3.2.

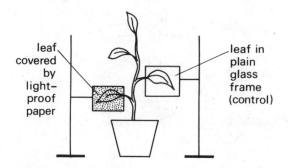

leaf covered by light-proof paper

leaf in plain glass frame (control)

Fig 3.2

Method

A plant is destarched for 48 hours and set up as shown in Fig 3.2. The plant is left in the sun for 6 hours and two leaves detached and tested for starch as described above.

Result

Control leaf: blue-black colour with iodine.
Paper-covered leaf: no blue-black colour.

Conclusion

Absence of starch in the experimental leaf indicates that light is necessary for starch production.

EXPERIMENT TO INVESTIGATE THE NECESSITY FOR CARBON DIOXIDE IN PHOTOSYNTHESIS

Apparatus
See Fig 3.3.

Method

One leaf of a destarched plant is enclosed in a conical flask containing

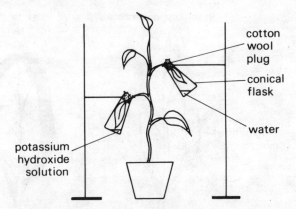

cotton
wool
plug

conical
flask

water

potassium
hydroxide
solution

Fig 3.3

a little potassium hydroxide solution (see Fig 3.3). This absorbs carbon dioxide and provides a carbon dioxide-free atmosphere in the flask. Another leaf is similarly enclosed in a flask containing water. This is the control. The plant is left in sunlight for 6 hours and the leaves are then detached and tested for starch.

Result
Control leaf: blue-black colour with iodine.
CO_2-free leaf: no blue-black colour.

Conclusion
The presence of starch in the control leaf, and the absence of starch in the experimental leaf, indicate the necessity for carbon dioxide.

The role of carbon dioxide in photosynthesis can be demonstrated by supplying a plant with carbon dioxide containing carbon-14 (a radioactive isotope of carbon). The radioactive carbon appears in a number of organic compounds, including carbohydrates, fats and proteins.

EXPERIMENT TO INVESTIGATE THE NECESSITY FOR CHLOROPHYLL IN PHOTOSYNTHESIS

Apparatus
See Fig 3.4.

Method
A sketch is made of the chlorophyll-free areas on a variegated leaf which have been destarched (see Fig 3.4). The leaf is left on the plant and exposed to sunlight for several hours. It is then tested for starch and the result compared with the original sketch.

Result
The original green areas give a blue-black colouration with iodine. The white areas do not stain blue-black.

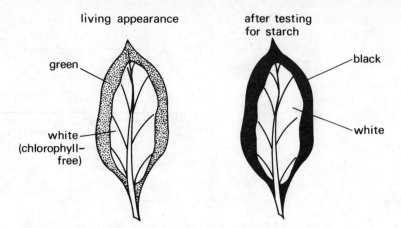

living appearance   after testing for starch

green   black

white (chlorophyll-free)   white

Fig 3.4

Conclusion

Starch is only present in the original green areas of the leaf. Therefore photosynthesis only occurs in the presence of chlorophyll.

Specimen question The following question is typical of many dealing with this topic. You must be certain that you understand how to demonstrate the conditions for photosynthesis, and don't forget to include a control.

How would you demonstrate that carbon dioxide is necessary for photosynthesis to occur?   (8 marks)   [JMB]

EXPERIMENT TO COMPARE THE PRODUCTION OF SUGAR BY ILLUMINATED AND NON-ILLUMINATED IRIS PLANTS

Some plants, e.g. iris, store sugar as well as starch in their leaves, and this can be tested using Benedict's reagent.

Two iris plants are taken, one which has been kept in the dark for 4 days, and the other which has been exposed to light for 4 days. Because this is a comparative experiment, it is important that the quantities of leaf used from each plant, and the volumes of solutions used in both tubes are the same. A cork borer is an easy way of making sure that the same area of leaf is taken from both plants.

An area of leaf is taken from the 'dark' plant by cutting five discs with a cork borer and dropping them into boiling water to remove the cuticle. After 2 minutes the discs are removed and ground with sand in a mortar, to release the contents. $10 \, cm^3$ of water are added. The mixture is filtered into a test tube labelled 'Dark'.

A similar leaf sample is taken from the plant exposed to light, by cutting five discs and treating in the same way. The tube is labelled 'Light'.

$5 \, cm^3$ Benedict's reagent are added to each tube and the tubes are placed in a boiling water bath for 2 minutes.

The colour change in each tube is recorded.

Table 3.1 Results of experiment

Results

	Result with Benedict's reagent
'Dark' tube	Clear blue
'Light' tube	Red precipitate

Conclusions

The clear blue colour of Benedict's reagent in the tube labelled 'Dark' shows that no reducing sugar is present.

The red precipitate in the tube labelled 'Light' shows the presence of reducing sugar.

The presence of sugar only in the plant exposed to light demonstrates the necessity of light for the production of sugar by the iris plant.

RATE OF PHOTOSYNTHESIS

This depends upon many factors.

1. The amount of light falling on the plant.
2. The leaf surface area and amount of chlorophyll.
3. The number of stomata allowing carbon dioxide into the leaf, and whether they are open or closed (they are generally open in daylight and closed in darkness).
4. The temperature – the optimum temperature is about 30°C.
5. The amount of carbon dioxide in the atmosphere (usually 0.04%).

Any one of these factors may limit the rate at which a plant can photosynthesise, provided all other factors are in excess. In a temperate climate light is often the **limiting factor**. The rate of photosynthesis can be increased by increasing the light available. In a sunny climate carbon dioxide availability may limit the rate. If the rate of photosynthesis is determined under a series of different light intensities and the results plotted, the graph in Fig 3.5 shows that the rate rises sharply and then flattens out. An increase in light intensity does not increase the rate further. Some other factor, probably carbon dioxide or temperature, is acting as a limiting factor at this level of light intensity. Repeating the experiment under different conditions, e.g. increased carbon dioxide, can affect the rate of photosynthesis as shown on the graph.

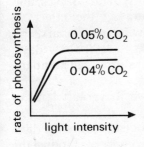

Fig 3.5 Rate of photosynthesis

Specimen question Name three external factors which affect the rate of photosynthesis. (3 marks) [*JMB*]

INCREASING THE RATE OF PHOTOSYNTHESIS

It is often commercially important to increase the rate of photosynthesis in greenhouse plants, where the environment can be controlled. A temperature of 30°C, optimum light conditions and an increase in the carbon dioxide available will all ensure that the rate of photosynthesis is not being limited by any external conditions. The plants will therefore photosynthesise at their maximum rate.

SYNTHESIS OF OTHER PLANT MATERIALS

Plants manufacture fats, vitamins and proteins from the carbohydrates formed in photosynthesis. The necessary additional elements are obtained from **mineral salts** in the soil. These salts enter the root hairs in solution in (but independently of) the water which passes into the root. Salts are present in the soil water in the form of electrically charged particles called **ions**. Plants will absorb ions they need, against a diffusion gradient if necessary, by using energy in **active transport** to pass the ions through the selectively permeable cell membrane and into the cell. They travel in water up the xylem to the leaf, where they are used in the formation of proteins and vitamins.

Two elements which are particularly important to the plant are:

▶ **nitrogen** (nitrates and ammonium salts), for formation of amino acids and proteins; and

▶ **magnesium**, for the formation of chlorophyll.

The effect of a deficiency of a particular element, such as nitrogen or magnesium, on growth can be shown by **'water culture'** experiments.

Similar barley seedlings are grown in a series of solutions. One element is missing from each solution but in all other respects the solution offers the complete mineral needs of the plant. In addition, one plant is grown in a complete solution – the control. The solutions and containers are sterilized to prevent fungal growth. After a few weeks the seedlings are examined to determine the effect of deficiency of individual elements. The following results may be observed.

1   The seedling in the complete culture solution is sturdy, tall and dark green. The other seedlings are smaller.

2   Those lacking magnesium are yellow, because they cannot make chlorophyll.

3   Very little growth occurs in plants lacking nitrogen because they are unable to make protein, the main part of new protoplasm. Production of new cells at the growing points of stem and root therefore stops.

FERTILIZERS

Fertilizers may be added to soil to supply plants with the mineral salts which they need. They may be in a slow-acting organic form, usually animal manure or compost, which releases the salts gradually as it decomposes, or they may be specially manufactured inorganic fertilizers, which add a controlled amount of chemicals to the soil.

Nitrogen fertilizers are important for most crops because nitrogen is used by plants to form protein, the raw material of new protoplasm, necessary for growth.

Care must be used, in applying artificial fertilizers, not to apply too much. A high concentration of salts in the soil draws water *out* of the roots of plants by osmosis, causing dehydration and death.

Problems can also be caused if large quantities of artificial fertilizers are washed into streams by heavy rain. The water-plants are stimulated into excessive growth and the streams become blocked, affecting drainage and causing death of fish.

HETEROTROPHIC NUTRITION

All animals feed on ready-made organic food, as they are unable to build organic materials from simple inorganic molecules. They are therefore dependent on green plants for their food, either directly, or through a food chain (see p.283).

The characteristics of heterotrophic nutrition are:

1 **ingestion** – the intake of complex organic food by animals;
2 **digestion** – the breakdown of this into small simple soluble molecules;
3 **absorption** – the uptake of these simple soluble molecules into living cells;
4 **assimilation** – the utilization of these simple soluble molecules to provide energy and produce new protoplasm;
5 **egestion** – the removal of undigested waste food materials.

CLASSES OF FOOD SUBSTANCES

CARBOHYDRATES

Carbohydrates contain carbon, hydrogen and oxygen. There are three types, each built up by combination of simple sugar units.

1 Those used for storage are usually large complex insoluble molecules such as starch (plants) and glycogen (animals).
2 Complex sugars (maltose, sucrose) have smaller molecules and are soluble.
3 Simple sugars – both **1** and **2** must be broken down to simple sugars, e.g. glucose, before they can be absorbed.

PROTEINS

Proteins are long chain-like molecules made of many amino acids combined, end to end. They contain carbon, hydrogen, oxygen, nitrogen and sometimes sulphur. During digestion, proteins are split up into amino acids, which are absorbed and then built up into the animal's protein.

FATS (LIPIDS)

Fats contain carbon, hydrogen and oxygen. The molecule consists of fatty acids combined with glycerol. When fat is digested, the glycerol and fatty acids are released.

VITAMINS

Vitamins are substances required in minute amounts for the normal working of the body. Lack of them causes the appearance of deficiency diseases.

You need to know details of only two.

Vitamin C

Lack of vitamin C causes the disease **scurvy**. Gums bleed, teeth become loose and small blood vessels bleed beneath the skin and in internal organs. The disease was first noticed in sailors on long sea voyages, where no fresh fruit was available.

Vitamin D

Because of its importance in calcium uptake and bone development, lack of vitamin D is serious in young children, causing weak deformed bones, and stunting growth. The condition is known as **rickets**.

Vitamin deficiency diseases can be cured by giving the vitamin, but in the case of rickets, treatment must be started early to prevent permanent deformity.

MINERAL SALTS

Mineral salts are present in most foods, particularly milk, fruit and vegetables.

Iron is particularly important because it is necessary for the formation of haemoglobin which carries oxygen around the body. Lack of iron affects haemoglobin production, causing anaemia with tiredness and shortness of breath.

Calcium is vital for bone and teeth formation and is particularly important in young children and pregnant women. Softening of bones and tooth decay may occur when calcium is deficient in the diet.

TESTS FOR FOOD SUBSTANCES

Table 3.2 Chemical tests for food substances

Food	Test	Result
Starch	Add 1–2 drops dilute brown **iodine/potassium iodide** solution to a starch suspension	Intense blue-black coloration
Reducing sugar, e.g. glucose, maltose	Add an equal quantity of blue **Benedict's reagent** to a glucose solution and boil	Brick-red precipitate
Protein	**Biuret test** – add an equal quantity of 5% sodium hydroxide solution to a solution of protein; shake; add 2 drops of 1% copper sulphate	A violet coloration develops
Fat	1 Rub into filter paper 2 Dissolve in ethanol; pour solution into water	Makes a grease spot Milky emulsion

VITAMIN C ESTIMATION

The amount of vitamin C in different fruit juices can be compared using a blue dye, dichlorophenol-indolephenol (DICPIP for short), which is decolourized by vitamin C. The object of the test is to see how many drops of fruit juice are needed to decolourize a standard amount of DICPIP. The more vitamin C the fruit juice contains, the less will be needed.

1 cm^3 of a 0.1% solution of DICPIP is placed in each of a number of test tubes.

Exactly 2 cm^3 of fresh lemon juice is drawn up into a syringe without the needle, and the juice allowed to fall, one drop at a time, into the first tube of DICPIP until it becomes colourless. The amount of juice needed is recorded.

The experiment is repeated with a different fruit juice and a fresh tube of DICPIP, and the result recorded. The vitamin C content of a number of fruit juices, cordials and fruit drinks can be compared in this way.

NUTRITION IN MAN

The following classes of food are essential in order to maintain health in Man (see Table 3.3):

▶ Carbohydrates
▶ Fats
▶ Proteins
▶ Vitamins
▶ Mineral salts
▶ Water
▶ Roughage

Table 3.3 Food requirements of Man

Food	Function	Sources
Carbohydrates	Release of energy	
Starch		Flour products, potato
Complex sugars, e.g. sucrose, maltose		Cane sugar
Simple sugars, e.g. glucose		Honey, fruit
Proteins	Growth and repair of tissues	
1st class		Meat, milk, eggs
2nd class		Peas, beans
Fats	Storage; release of energy (contains twice as much energy as the same weight of carbohydrate)	Milk, cream, cheese, butter, plant oils
Vitamins		
C	Health of skin and blood vessels	Fresh citrus fruits
D	Uptake of calcium; bone development; healthy teeth	Fish liver oil, butter, action of sunlight on skin
Mineral salts		
Sodium	Constituents of	
Potassium	blood and cells	
Calcium	Bone and teeth formation	Milk, fruit and vegetables
Iron	Haemoglobin formation	
Iodine	Thyroid gland function	
Phosphorus	Bones, teeth, ATP, DNA	
Water	Constituent of cells and body fluids; solvent for chemicals taking part in all living processes; transport medium	Most food contains a high proportion of water
Roughage (dietary fibre)	No food value; stimulates muscle in alimentary canal; may absorb harmful substances from colon	Fruit and vegetable fibres

DIET IN MAN

A **balanced diet** supplies the necessary classes of food in adequate amounts and correct proportions to maintain healthy active life and, if necessary, growth. It must supply not only the necessary chemical constituents, but also sufficient energy for the needs of the body (see p.36). The main energy-releasing foods are carbohydrate and fat.

Average daily energy requirements vary according to:

▶ **sex** – adult man = 12 000 kJ; adult woman = 9600 kJ;
▶ **activity** – physically demanding job, e.g. coal-miner = 50 000 kJ.
▶ **age** – children require more in proportion to body size = 9000 kJ.

The amount of energy-giving foods in the diet should match these requirements.

The type of food required varies too:

▶ **children and pregnant women** – extra protein and vitamins;
▶ **nursing mothers** – extra fluid and protein, usually supplied by milk;
▶ **babies** – milk, an almost perfect food, lacks iron, but usually sufficient is stored in baby's body from birth;
▶ **elderly people** and those in sedentary occupations – more fresh fruit and vegetables, for vitamins and roughage, and less carbohydrate and fat.

FOOD ADDITIVES

Substances added to food as colourings, flavourings or preservatives must be tested for safety, and only then are allowed by law. There is evidence, however, that some permitted additives cause allergies or are otherwise harmful to some people; natural food without additives is generally regarded as better for health.

ALCOHOL

Alcohol has a calming effect on the body, reducing anxiety and giving a feeling of well-being. It does, however, speed up the heart and raise blood pressure, and taken in excess will cause liver damage.

Over a long period, cirrhosis of the liver may develop, with serious loss of liver function and eventual death. Alcohol is addictive, and in some people addiction prevents them from working or, through irresponsible or criminal behaviour, results in a prison sentence.

STARVATION AND FOOD SUPPLIES

STARVATION AND MALNUTRITION

In **starvation** the diet provides too little food to provide energy for normal life. This causes weight loss, and lowered mental and physical efficiency. There may be enough joules to maintain life, but not enough for normal activity.

In **malnutrition** there may be adequate energy foods in the diet, but inadequate protein or vitamins. In the tropics, diets often contain too much cassava, maize, yams and banana because they are cheap and easy to grow. Such a diet is deficient in protein, and in babies and young children may result in the disease **kwashiorkor**, a serious disease of malnutrition.

In industrialized countries, malnutrition may occur from unwise eating of 'convenience foods' and ignorance of the need for a balanced diet, rather than as a result of poverty. There is often a tendency for the diet to contain too much carbohydrate and fat and too little fresh vegetable food.

Too much carbohydrate and fat will give rise to **obesity**, with its resulting strain on the heart and blood vessels. There may be a link between the consumption of large amounts of animal fats and sugar, and coronary heart disease (see p.133). A diet with insufficient natural roughage, as contained in wholemeal products and fresh fruit and vegetables, will give rise to constipation because of lack of stimulation of the muscles of the intestine.

WORLD FOOD SUPPLIES

Extreme climatic conditions, especially drought and floods, particularly in the tropics, have always caused periods of famine in some areas. In the last 400 years, since the importance of clean water and disposal of sewage has been realized, two important causes of infection and death have been almost removed. This, together with control of most epidemic diseases, e.g. smallpox, tuberculosis, diphtheria, etc., has resulted in a seven-fold increase in the human population. This has put enormous strain on the world resources for food production, and some areas perpetually have large numbers of people starving or barely surviving, despite better methods of food production and communication.

The only alternative to a check on human populations by death from starvation is to limit the birth rate, so that the food available is sufficient for those who need it.

HUMAN ALIMENTARY CANAL

The digestive system is a muscular tube running from mouth to anus (see Fig 3.6), and specialized to perform different functions in different regions (see Table 3.4).

Table 3.4 Functions of different parts of human digestive system

Specialized part	Function
Mouth cavity	Ingestion, mastication
Pharynx	Swallowing
Oesophagus	Links pharynx to stomach
Stomach	Food storage and digestion of protein
Duodenum	Digestion and absorption
Liver (bile)	Emulsification of fats
Pancreas (pancreatic juice)	Digestion of fat, protein, starch
Ileum	Completion of digestion and absorption of food
Colon	Absorption of water
Rectum	Formation and storage of faeces
Anus	Egestion

Fig 3.6 The alimentary canal in Man

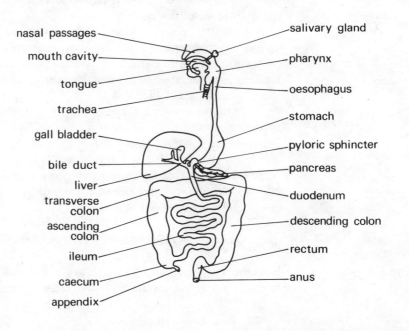

Digestion occurs by mechanical and/or chemical breakdown. Large insoluble molecules, such as starch and protein in the diet, are broken down by digestion to form small soluble molecules which can be absorbed into the bloodstream and transported.

MECHANICAL/PHYSICAL DIGESTION

Food is ingested through the mouth, where the teeth (see Fig 3.7) play a large part in preparation of the food for digestion. **Mastication** is the mechanical breakdown of food by the teeth, aided by the tongue and jaw muscles.

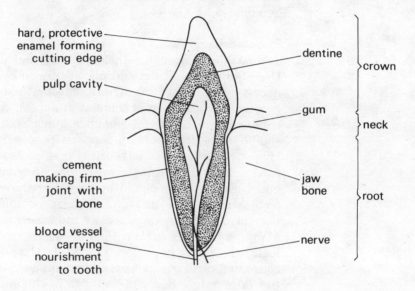

Fig 3.7 VS human canine tooth

It is always worth learning Fig 3.7. It is simple and is a fairly common question in examinations.

Specimen question Make a labelled diagram to show the structure of a mammalian tooth. (8 marks)   [*ODLE*]

Types of teeth

There are four types of teeth present in humans.

▶   **Incisors** – present at front of mouth for biting.
▶   **Canines** – 'eye' teeth (developed as fangs in carnivores).
▶   **Premolars** ⎱ Cheek teeth with double roots, used for chewing,
          ⎰ grinding or crushing.
▶   **Molars**

All mammalian teeth except molars are represented in the milk dentition present in the young animal. The milk teeth are pushed out as the permanent teeth develop.

Dental Decay

About 98% of people living in western countries have some degree of dental decay (**dental caries**). It is caused by bacterial action on food, particularly refined sugar, on the surface of teeth and between teeth and gums. Bacteria ferment the sugar, producing acids which attack the calcium salts in the teeth, causing cavities and making it easier for further invasion of the teeth to occur.

Formation of cavities eventually leads to invasion of the dentine and pulp cavity by bacteria, which cause an abscess to form, leading to toothache, loss of teeth and general ill-health. The bacteria form a whitish covering called **plaque** on the teeth which inflames the gums and may cause bleeding. The resistance of teeth to decay is probably hereditary.

Prevention of Decay

Several things improve the health of teeth and gums.

1　**Diet**. Sufficient calcium and phosphate, and vitamins D and C are necessary for the growth of healthy teeth. Crisp fruit and vegetables, especially when eaten at the end of a meal, remove food from the gaps between teeth and stimulate gums and teeth. Refined sugar should not be eaten between meals as it encourages bacterial growth.

2　**Hygiene**. Teeth should be brushed after meals and at night to remove food scraps. The brush action should be vertical and away from the gums. Dental floss should be used to remove food from between teeth where plaque may form. Regular six-monthly visits to the dentist will identify any cavities early and minimize damage to the teeth. Many toothpastes contain fluoride which replaces minerals in the teeth which may have been eroded. In some areas, fluoride, in the concentration of one part per million, is added to drinking water, and this does reduce decay in the teeth of children. There is, however, public controversy over whether water should be treated with additives in this way, thus forcing the population to take in added fluoride without choice.

CHEMICAL DIGESTION

The chemical process involved is hydrolysis, and **enzymes** increase the rate of this reaction, e.g.:

$$\text{starch} + \text{water} \xrightarrow[\text{(enzyme)}]{\text{amylase}} \text{maltose}$$

Enzymes are produced by glands opening into the alimentary canal, resulting in extra-cellular digestion, i.e. digestion outside the cells, in the cavity of the mouth, stomach and intestine.

When digestion is complete, all carbohydrates have been broken down to simple sugars, e.g.:

$$\text{starch} \xrightarrow{\text{salivary amylase}} \text{maltose} \xrightarrow{\text{maltase in duodenum}} \text{glucose}$$

All proteins have been broken down to amino acids and all fats to fatty acids and glycerol.

Mouth cavity

Following ingestion, the food is broken down into small pieces by the teeth, exposing a large surface area to the action of digestive enzymes.

The food is mixed with saliva from three pairs of salivary glands. This:

1 moistens and lubricates food for swallowing;
2 dissolves soluble food;
3 digests cooked starch by the action of salivary amylase, to form maltose.

Swallowing

The food is formed into an oval mass called a **bolus** by the action of the tongue, and pushed backwards against the roof of the mouth. This starts a reflex action which results in the bolus being pushed into the oesophagus by the contraction of the walls of the pharynx. To prevent food from entering the respiratory passages, the soft palate closes the opening into the nasal passages and the epiglottis closes the larynx.

The walls of the oesophagus convey the bolus to the stomach by **peristalsis**. This is a wave-like muscular action involving the longitudinal and circular muscles of the oesphagus (see Fig 3.8).

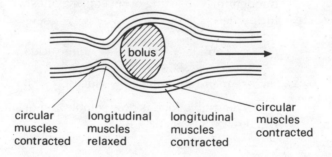

Fig 3.8 Peristalsis in the oesophagus

Stomach

This is a J-shaped organ with muscular walls and a glandular lining. **Gastric glands** open into the stomach and discharge gastric juice which contains:

1 **hydrochloric acid** – stops salivary amylase action and provides the correct pH for pepsin action;
2 **pepsin** – hydrolyses protein to polypeptides.

The stomach has the following functions:

1 digestion of protein;
2 formation of a creamy **chyme** by the churning action of stomach muscles;

3 temporary storage of food, which is passed on to the duodenum in small portions for further digestion.

  The lower opening of the stomach can be closed by a ring of muscle called the **pyloric sphincter**. After a meal, it opens at intervals to allow small amounts of chyme through to the duodenum.

Duodenum

This comprises the first 12 inches of the small intestine. Secretions from three glands mix with food here. They are all alkaline and provide the correct pH for the digestive enzymes.

1 **Bile** – greenish-yellow colour, produced by the liver, concentrated in the gall bladder, passed to the duodenum by the bile duct when food is present. It contains sodium hydrogencarbonate, which neutralizes stomach acid, and bile salts, which **emulsify** fats and activate the enzyme lipase.

2 **Pancreatic juice** – produced by the pancreas, enters duodenum by the pancreatic duct, contains three enzymes which have the following effects:

 (a) $\text{starch} + \text{water} \xrightarrow{\text{amylase}} \text{maltose}$

 (b) $\text{fat} + \text{water} \xrightarrow{\text{lipase}} \text{fatty acids} + \text{glycerol}$

 (c) $\text{protein} + \text{water} \xrightarrow{\text{protease}} \text{peptides and amino acids}$

3 **Duodenal enzymes** – produced by glands in the wall of the duodenum, consisting of several enzymes which complete digestion, including:

 (a) $\text{peptides} + \text{water} \xrightarrow{\text{peptidase}} \text{amino acids}$

 (b) $\text{maltose} + \text{water} \xrightarrow{\text{maltase}} \text{glucose}$

 All digestible food is now soluble and of small molecular size, and can now be absorbed.

Ileum

This is the longest part of the small intestine, and the site of absorption of digested food into the circulatory system. The efficiency of uptake is increased by **villi** – finger-like projections from the already-folded lining of the ileum. These give an enormous surface area for absorption.

 Other features of the villi which increase the rate of absorption are shown in Fig 3.9.

 The digested food is distributed round the body in the bloodstream and absorption is only complete when it has entered the cells of the body (see p.71) where assimilation occurs. Fats absorbed into the **lacteals** enter the lymphatic system, and eventually reach the bloodstream.

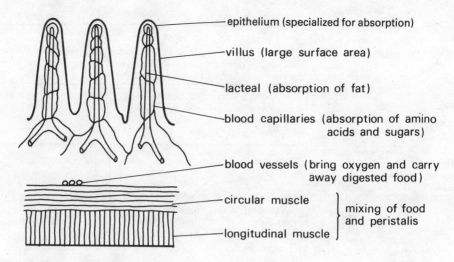

epithelium (specialized for absorption)

villus (large surface area)

lacteal (absorption of fat)

blood capillaries (absorption of amino acids and sugars)

blood vessels (bring oxygen and carry away digested food)

circular muscle ⎫
longitudinal muscle ⎭ mixing of food and peristalis

Fig 3.9 Part of the ileum wall

Specimen question Name any four substances which are absorbed from the digested food in the small intestine. (4 marks) [O & C]

Colon

The main function of the colon is the absorption of water from the fluid contents. This leaves a semi-solid mass of faeces which is moved into the rectum by 'mass peristalsis' before **defaecation**.

Rectum

After further water absorption, the contents of the rectum, consisting largely of undigested cellulose and other plant fibres, bacteria and dead cells, form the faeces. These are eliminated at intervals through the anus by the process of egestion.

ASSIMILATION OF FOOD

Sugars taken up by cells may be used to produce energy in cell respiration.

Excess sugars may be stored in the liver as glycogen, or converted to fat in the liver, and stored under the skin.

Amino acids are converted into body protein (for new tissues or repair).

Excess amino acids are broken down by the **liver** as they cannot be stored. This is called **deamination** and results in the production of **urea** which is excreted by the kidney (see p.160).

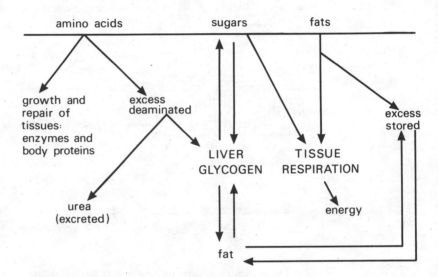

Fig 3.10 Utilization of food – a summary

FUNCTIONS OF THE LIVER

1 Control of constant blood sugar level. Excess sugar in the diet is converted to glycogen (insoluble) under the influence of insulin. When sugar is required to supply energy it can be converted back to glucose (pp. 155/187).

2 Removal of lactic acid from the blood and its conversion to glycogen.

3 Conversion of fat to glycogen. This process is reversible, depending on diet and energy needs of the body.

4 Formation of plasma proteins – albumen, globulin, fibrinogen and prothrombin.

5 Formation of urea from excess amino acids which cannot be stored.

6 Storage of vitamins A, B_{12}, D (p.62).

7 Storage of iron – old red blood cells are removed from circulation and their haemoglobin is broken down. Iron is stored and the rest excreted as bile pigments.

8 Formation of bile (see p.70).

9 Detoxication of poisons.

10 Production of body heat – main source of this because of liver's size and activity.

Notice that most of these functions involve food substances, and the first seven are arranged according to their association with carbohydrates, fats, proteins, vitamins and mineral salts.

KEY WORDS ▶			
Autotrophic	Scurvy	Molars
Heterotrophic	Rickets	Dental caries
Photosynthesis	Mineral salts	Plaque
Chlorophyll	Roughage	Enzymes
Carbon dioxide	Iodine/potassium	Salivary amylase
Stomata	iodide	Bolus
Diffusion gradient	Benedict's reagent	Peristalsis
Chloroplasts	Biuret test	Hydrochloric acid
Water	Balanced diet	Pepsin
Xylem	Malnutrition	Chyme
Light	Starvation	Pyloric sphincter
Control experiment	Obesity	Bile
Destarched	Alimentary canal	Emulsify
Limiting factor	Pharynx	Pancreatic juice
Mineral salts	Oesophagus	Amylase
Ions	Stomach	Lipase
Active transport	Duodenum	Protease
Water culture	Liver	Maltase
Fertilizers	Pancreas	Ileum
Ingestion	Ileum	Villi
Digestion	Colon	Lacteal
Absorption	Rectum	Colon
Assimilation	Anus	Defaecation
Egestion	Mastication	Rectum
Carbohydrates	Incisors	Liver
Proteins	Canines	Deamination
Fats (lipids)	Premolars	Urea
Vitamins		

SPECIMEN EXAMINATION QUESTIONS

1 Photosynthesis is the process by which green plants make food materials.

(a) Complete the equation which summarizes the process:

$$\text{carbon dioxide} + \text{(i)} \xrightarrow[\text{from sunlight}]{\text{energy}} \text{glucose} + \text{(ii)} \qquad \text{(2 marks)}$$

(b) What part does chlorophyll play in the process of photo-synthesis? (1 mark)

(c) Why is photosynthesis so essential to animal life? Suggest TWO reasons. (2 marks)

(d) The presence of starch is often taken as an indication that photosynthesis has been taking place in leaves. Fig 3.11 indicates the steps taken in testing a leaf for starch.

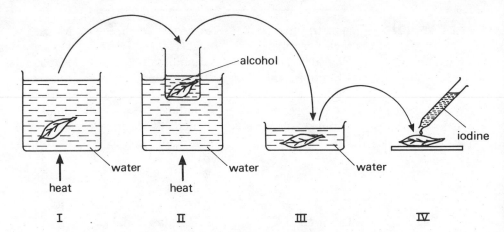

Fig 3.11   I   II   III   IV

(i) What is the purpose of stage I?

(ii) What is happening to the leaf in stage II?

(iii) What evidence would be obtained from stage IV which would indicate the presence of starch.   (3 marks)

[NISEC]

2   (a)   Read the following passage.

Photosynthesis is the process whereby plants use the light energy of the sun to produce food. The food produced today is the basis of all life on this planet and without photosynthesis plant and animal life would die out. The food produced in times past has been reshaped to form fossil fuels. These fossil fuels are now being extracted from beneath the ground and seas, and their energy is used in factories, offices and homes.

(i) What is the main theme of this passage about photosynthesis?

(ii) State TWO key points made in the passage.

(b)   A pupil was studying the effect of light on starch production in geranium leaves. A geranium plant had been destarched by keeping it in the dark for 24 hours. One leaf was covered by a small black polythene bag, whilst another leaf was left uncovered.

The plant was placed in bright light for 24 hours and then both of the leaves mentioned above were tested for starch.

(i) Identify ONE way in which this was not a fair test.

(ii) Describe how you would change the procedure to make it a fair test.   [SCE]

3   The graph in Fig 3.12 shows how much sugar is produced by a green plant over a period of several days, under natural conditions.

(i) Suggest ONE factor in the environment to explain why less sugar is produced during day 2.   (1 mark)

(ii) Draw a line on the graph to show how much sugar would be produced if the plant was kept under bright light all the time. Label the line X.   (1 mark)   [MEG]

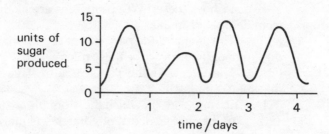

Fig 3.12

4   Lettuces may be grown in 'tunnels' covered with clear polythene and in air to which extra carbon dioxide has been added.
    (*a*)   Give TWO reasons why the use of clear polythene tunnels may result in better growth of lettuces. Explain your reasons. (4 marks)
    (*b*)   Explain why, when extra carbon dioxide is added to the air, lettuces grow better.   (2 marks)
    (*c*)   Suggest TWO reasons why it could be a disadvantage to grow lettuces in polythene tunnels.   (2 marks)   [*LEAG*]

5   Fig 3.13 shows a section through a human canine tooth which has begun to decay.

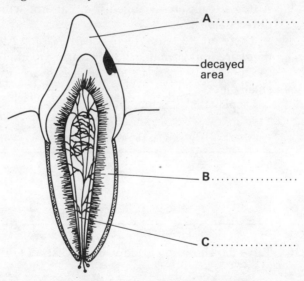

Fig 3.13

(*a*)   Name, on the diagram the parts labelled A, B and C. (3 marks)
(*b*)   (i) Explain how the combination of bacteria in the mouth and the eating of sugary foods may bring about dental decay. (2 marks)
           (ii) State TWO reasons why it is important that the decay should not reach part C.   (2 marks)
(*c*)   Modern toothpastes (i) contain fluoride salts and (ii) are alkaline.

Explain how these TWO properties are likely to protect the teeth from decay.   (2 marks)   [*MEG*]

6   (*a*)   The liver and the pancreas have important roles to play in the digestion of food. Describe these roles in detail.   (10 marks)

(*b*)   The liver and the pancreas also have roles beyond that of digestion.

Describe any ways in which these organs are involved in:

(i) the storage of carbohydrates;   (4 marks)

(ii) the excretion of wastes.   (6 marks)   [*MEG*]

7   (*a*)   How would you carry out a test on a breakfast cereal to show it contained sugar?   (3 marks)

(*b*)   What colour change would you expect during the test if sugar was present in the cereal?   (1 mark)

(*c*)   State ONE precaution which must be taken to carry out the test safely.   (1 mark)   [*MEG*]

8   An artificial diet was fed to a group of rats. It contained carbohydrates, protein, fat and mineral salts only. The animals had as much water as they needed.

(*a*)   Name TWO mineral salts and explain why the rats needed them.   (4 marks)

(*b*)   The rats did not remain fully healthy on the diet. What important group of chemicals is missing from the diet?   (1 mark)

9   A dog's teeth are arranged in a pattern, with different teeth doing different jobs.

There are 12 biting teeth called *incisors*. At the side of the mouth there are four *canines* used for tearing food. The teeth at the back of the mouth, 16 *premolars* and 10 *molars*, are used for slicing food into small pieces.

Display this information in the same style as Table 3.5.

Table 3.5

Type of teeth	The job performed by these teeth	The number of these teeth present

10   Table 3.6 shows the food value of a school lunch eaten by a 16-year-old girl.

Table 3.6

Food eaten	Protein in g	Carbohydrate in g	Fat in g	Iron in mg	Vitamin C in mg
Sausages	9	5	24	1	0
Chips	8	70	20	2	20
Baked beans	10	20	1	3	4
Apple pie	5	60	25	1	1
Ice cream	2	20	12	0	0
Fizzy drink	0	30	0	0	0

(a)   (i) In this meal, which food gave the girl most protein?
(1 mark)
(ii) Name ONE other food not eaten in this meal which is rich in protein.   (1 mark)
(iii) Why does the girl need protein?   (1 mark)

(b)   (i) The total energy value of this meal is 6600 kJ. In one day the girl needs 9600 kJ. If she ate this meal, how many MORE kJ would she need in that day?   (1 mark)
(ii) What would happen if she eats much more than 9600 kJ of food every day?   (1 mark)
(iii) A lot of energy comes from carbohydrate and fat. Name the TWO foods in this meal which gave her the most energy. (2 marks)

(c)   The girl needs 14 mg of iron and 25 mg of vitamin C each day to keep healthy.
(i) How much of her daily iron needs did this meal give her? (1 mark)
(ii) How much of her daily vitamin C needs did this meal give her?   (1 mark)
(iii) What will happen if she does not have enough iron and vitamin C?   (2 marks)

(d)   Why should she eat fibre (roughage) every day?   (1 mark)

[LEAG]

11 (a)   Table 3.7 shows the percentage of overweight British people in different age groups in 1981.

Table 3.7

Age group	Percentage overweight	
	Men	Women
20–4	22	23
25–9	29	20
30–9	40	25
40–9	52	38
50–9	49	47
60–5	54	50

Source: Report of Royal College of Physicians, 1983

Use the table to answer the following questions.
(i) Which sex in which age group has the smallest percentage overweight?   (1 mark)
(ii) Which age group has a greater percentage of women than men who are overweight?   (1 mark)
(iii) Which age group has the greatest percentage difference between men and women who are overweight?   (1 mark)

(b)   (i) What is the main substance stored in the body which forms the extra weight?   (1 mark)
(ii) In or around which organ is this substance likely to be found in large amounts?   (1 mark)

(iii) Give an example of ill health that overweight people are more likely to suffer from.   (1 mark)

(c)   (i) Explain how your body loses weight when it is at rest. (3 marks)

(ii) Why do you lose more weight when you take exercise than you lose at rest?   (2 marks)

(d)   Doctors recommend a diet which includes cereals and bread with a high fibre content, vegetables and fruit but which contains only a little fried food and only a little sugar. Give a different reason in each case why doctors recommend:

(i) a diet that includes cereals and breads with a high fibre content;   (1 mark)

(ii) a diet that includes vegetables and fruit;   (1 mark)

(iii) a diet that includes only a little fried food;   (1 mark)

(iv) a diet that includes only a little sugar.   (1 mark)

[SEG]

12   Fig 3.14 shows the structure of a single villus.

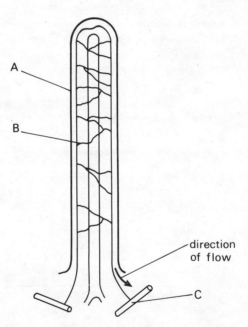

Fig 3.14

(a)   Where would you expect to find this structure in the gut? (1 mark)

(b)   Name TWO chemicals passing through part C after a meal. (2 marks)

(c)   (i) What is part B called?   (1 mark)

(ii) Why is it important in the villus?   (1 mark)

(d)   Name the blood vessel connecting structure C to the liver. (1 mark)

(e)   Suggest ONE advantage of blood going to the liver from the villus before going to the whole body.   (1 mark)   [MEG]

RESPIRATION

CONTENTS

Contents

Respiration The liberation of energy by the breakdown of food molecules.

Energy The capacity to do work.

Fermentation The process of anaerobic respiration in yeasts and some bacteria.

Ventilation The production of a sustained flow of air over a gaseous exchange surface.

Inspiration The passage of air containing oxygen into an organism by muscular movement.

Expiration The passage of air containing carbon dioxide out of an organism by muscular movement.

Diffusion The movement of molecules down a concentration gradient from a region of their high concentration to a region of their low concentration.

Metabolic rate The rate at which respiration occurs in living organisms.

Compensation point The point at which the rates of photosynthesis and respiration are equal.

Carcinogen A chemical substance which changes a healthy cell into a cancer cell.

Allergy An unusual reaction shown by living cells to repeated exposure to a foreign substance.

ENERGY

Energy cannot be created or destroyed. It may occur in many forms, e.g. heat, light, sound, electrical, chemical, mechanical, and these can be changed from one form into another, i.e. they are interconvertible, e.g.:

$$\text{light} \xrightarrow{\text{photosynthesis}} \text{chemical} \xrightarrow[\text{and respiration}]{\text{Feeding, digestion}} \text{mechanical}$$
$$\text{(sun)} \qquad\qquad \text{(sugars} \qquad\qquad \text{(muscle contraction}$$
$$\text{in plants)} \qquad\qquad \text{in animals)}$$

All living cells require a continual supply of energy in order to carry out a variety of processes vital to life. These include:

1 mechanical contraction of muscle (movement);
2 chemical synthesis of substances;
3 growth and division of cells;
4 active transport of substances into and out of cells;
5 electrical transmission of nerve impulses;
6 maintenance of a constant body temperature (birds and mammals).

The above are forms of work carried out by living organisms.

All the energy used by living organisms comes from the sun in the form of light waves. The only organisms capable of trapping the light energy supply are the plants which carry out photosynthesis. Light energy from the sun cannot be stored, so plants convert this into chemical energy, as shown below.

The light energy is used to convert carbon dioxide and water into glucose. The energy is stored in the chemical bonds holding the atoms together in these molecules (see p.36).

$$\text{carbon dioxide} + \text{water} \xrightarrow[\text{chlorophyll}]{\text{light energy (sunlight)}} \text{glucose} + \text{oxygen}$$

$$6CO_2 \qquad\qquad +6H_2O \qquad\qquad C_6H_{12}O_6 \;\; +6O_2$$

(chemical energy)

Plants are able to store this manufactured food as starch or sugars. Plants provide energy for all other forms of life. They are the primary producers that form the basis of all food chains (see p.283).

This energy cannot be used by plants or animals for any of the processes vital to life until it is released from the food molecules in which it is stored. The process by which energy is released from food substances is called **respiration**.

RESPIRATION

Respiration is a characteristic feature of all living organisms. There are two forms of respiration.

1 **Aerobic** respiration – respiration in a supply of oxygen.
2 **Anaerobic** respiration – respiration in the absence or a reduced supply of oxygen.

Furthermore, a distinction has to be made between the following.

1 **Cell respiration** – otherwise known as internal respiration.
2 **Gaseous exchange** – otherwise known as external respiration.

AEROBIC RESPIRATION

This occurs in most organisms and depends upon a constant supply of oxygen. It is basically a chemical reaction which may be represented as follows.

$$\text{carbohydrate} + \text{oxygen} \xrightarrow{\text{enzymes}} \text{carbon dioxide} + \text{water} + \textbf{energy}$$

(used for **work**)

The energy released comes from the breakdown of glucose molecules in the **presence of oxygen**.

EXPERIMENT TO INVESTIGATE HEAT PRODUCTION DURING RESPIRATION IN SEEDS

Apparatus
See Fig 4.1

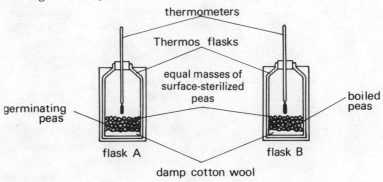

Fig 4.1

Method
Germinating peas require energy released by respiration. Some energy is released as heat and a rise in temperature in the apparatus is used to indicate that respiration is occurring.

The apparatus is set up as shown in Fig. 4.1. Surface sterilization in sodium hypochlorite solution prevents bacterial and fungal growth. Boiling the peas in flask **B** destroys all enzymes involved in respiration. Flask **B** is necessary as this is a controlled experiment.

Results

Table 4.1 Results of experiment to investigate heat production during respiration

| Day | Temperature (°C) | |
	Flask A	Flask B
1	21	20
2	22	19
3	25	20
4	25	20

Conclusion
No heat is released in flask **B** as no respiration occurs. The fluctuation in temperature in flask **B** probably results from a fluctuation in room temperature. The rise in temperature in flask **A** results from heat produced by germinating peas during respiration.

Details of the above experiment and the one on p.84 may be used in answering the question given on p.108.

EXPERIMENT TO INVESTIGATE THE HEAT ENERGY RELEASED DURING COMBUSTION OF A PEANUT

Apparatus
See Fig 4.2.

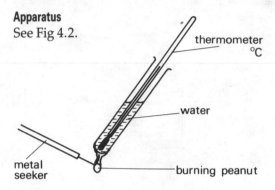

Fig 4.2

Method
20 cm³ of water is added to a test tube. A piece of peanut is cut until it weighs 1 g. The peanut is firmly attached to a sharp metal seeker. The temperature of the water is measured and recorded. The peanut is placed in the flame of a bunsen burner until it begins to burn. The burning peanut is held under the test tube until all the peanut has burned away. The water is stirred gently with the thermometer and the highest temperature recorded. The experiment is repeated with another 20 cm³ of water and another 1 g of peanut. The mean temperature rise of the water is recorded.

Results

Mean rise in water temperature	$= x°C$
Volume of water	$= 20\ cm^3$
Mass of water	$= 20\ g$
Mass of peanut	$=\ 1\ g$
Heat energy to raise 1 g water 1°C	$= 4.2\ kJ$
Heat gained by water from burning 1 g peanut	$= 20 \times x \times 4.2\ kJ$

Conclusion
1 g of peanut releases x kJ of energy, calculated as shown above.

EXPERIMENT TO INVESTIGATE THE REMOVAL OF OXYGEN FROM THE ATMOSPHERE DURING AEROBIC RESPIRATION

Apparatus
See Fig 4.3.

Method
The apparatus is set up as shown in Fig 4.3. Gas jar **A** contains 40 germinating peas and gas jar **B** contains 40 boiled peas. Both batches of peas are surface-sterilized by placing them in a mild disinfectant for 5 minutes. The glass covers of the gas jars make a good seal and the

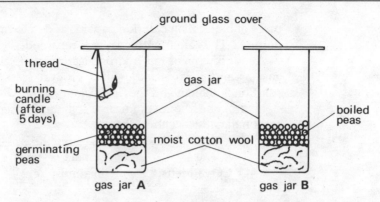

Fig 4.3

gas jars are left in a warm room for 5 days. A small lighted candle is then attached to a piece of cotton. The lid of jar **A** is quickly removed, a burning candle is inserted into the jar and the glass plate is replaced (as shown in Fig 4.3).

The number of seconds for which the candle burns is recorded and the procedure repeated for gas jar **B**. (Remember, a burning candle requires oxygen to burn.)

Results
Candle burns in gas jar **A** = 6 s
Candle burns in gas jar **B** = 15 s

Conclusion
The germinating peas in gas jar **A** remove oxygen from the air in the gas jar. This oxygen is used up in respiration. Germinating peas carry out respiration, boiled peas are dead and do not carry out respiration.

EXPERIMENT TO INVESTIGATE THE PRODUCTS OF THE COMBUSTION OF FOOD USING COBALT CHLORIDE PAPER AND HYDROGENCARBONATE INDICATOR

Apparatus
See Fig 4.4.

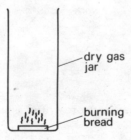

Fig 4.4

Method
A small piece of dried bread is held in the flame of a bunsen burner until the bread begins to burn. The burning bread is then dropped into a clean dry gas jar. As soon as the burning stops the gas jar is sealed with a ground glass plate. The gas jar is allowed to cool. A

piece of blue cobalt chloride paper is added to the gas jar and left for 2 minutes. The colour of the paper is recorded.

About 50 cm^3 of red hydrogencarbonate indicator is added to the gas jar and it is sealed with a ground glass plate. The indicator solution is shaken and the final colour recorded.

Hydrogencarbonate indicator solution is used to show changes in carbon dioxide levels as follows:

$$\text{yellow} \xleftarrow{\hspace{2cm}} \text{red} \xrightleftharpoons{\hspace{2cm}} \text{purple}$$

yellow	red	purple
as	normal CO$_2$ level	as
CO$_2$ added	in atmosphere	CO$_2$ removed

Results
Blue cobalt chloride paper turns red.

Red hydrogencarbonate indicator turns yellow.

Conclusion
The results with cobalt chloride paper shows that water is present. The result with hydrogencarbonate indicator shows that carbon dioxide is present. Therefore, when dry bread burns in air, water and carbon dioxide are released.

CELL RESPIRATION (TISSUE OR INTERNAL RESPIRATION)

Raw materials enter the cell, respiration occurs and waste products are removed (see Fig 4.5). Inside the cell, enzymes break down the glucose molecules in a series of stages. Each stage is controlled by a different enzyme and a small amount of the total energy of the molecule is released (see Fig 4.6).

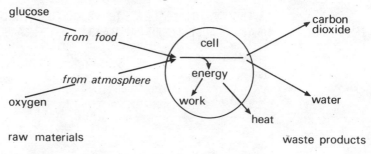

Fig 4.5 Summary of cell respiration

The overall reaction may be represented as:

$$C_6H_{12}O_6 + 6O_2 \xrightarrow{\text{enzymes}} 6CO_2 + 6H_2O \quad 2880\text{ kJ}$$

| glucose | oxygen | | carbon dioxide | water | energy |

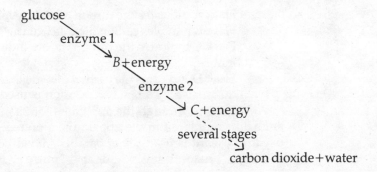

Fig 4.6 Release of energy in respiration

The amount of energy released by an organism in a given time is known as the **metabolic rate**. Wherever energy is transferred from one compound to another or used in work, some is lost as heat energy. This is usually considered as lost or wasted energy but homoiothermic animals (birds and mammals) can control their heat loss and use it in order to maintain a constant body temperature (see p.153).

The removal of the waste products of respiration from the cell is called excretion (see p.156).

EXPERIMENT TO INVESTIGATE THE RELEASE OF CARBON DIOXIDE FROM PLANTS AND ANIMALS USING HYDROGENCARBONATE INDICATOR

Apparatus
See Fig 4.7.

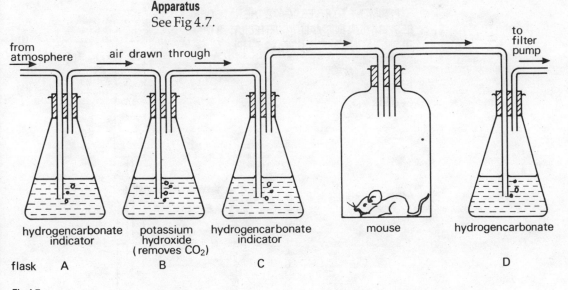

Fig 4.7

Method
The apparatus is set up as in Fig 4.7. Hydrogencarbonate indicator is used to show changes in carbon dioxide levels in the flasks (see p.86 for details of hydrogencarbonate test). The hydrogencarbonate indicator in all flasks is red at the beginning of the experiment.

Flask **A** indicates the carbon dioxide level of atmospheric air.
Flask **B** removes carbon dioxide from air.
Flask **C** indicates the carbon dioxide level of air passing **to** the mouse.
Flask **D** indicates the carbon dioxide level of air passing **from** the mouse.

Air is passed through the apparatus for 30 minutes. Instead of an animal being placed in the apparatus, a potted green plant could be used. If a plant is used the apparatus should be kept in darkness to eliminate photosynthesis and air should be passed through the apparatus for a minimum of 4 hours.

Results

The original red colours of the hydrogencarbonate indicator solutions are now:

Flask **A** – red
Flask **C** – purple
Flask **D** – yellow

Conclusions

Flask **C** shows that air passing to the mouse contains less carbon dioxide than atmospheric air. The result from flask **D** shows that the mouse has released carbon dioxide. This carbon dioxide is a waste product of respiration.

EXPERIMENT TO INVESTIGATE THE RATE OF RESPIRATION IN SMALL INVERTEBRATES OR GERMINATING SEEDS USING A SIMPLE RESPIROMETER

Apparatus
See Fig 4.8.

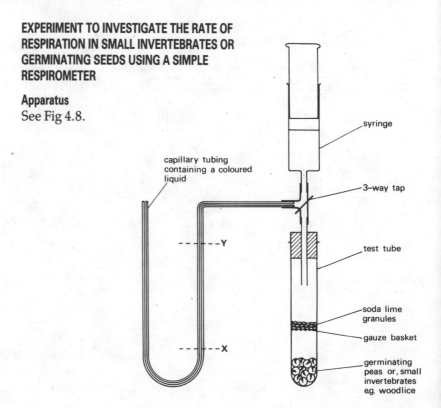

capillary tubing containing a coloured liquid

syringe

3–way tap

test tube

soda lime granules

gauze basket

germinating peas or, small invertebrates eg. woodlice

Fig 4.8

Method

The apparatus is set up as shown in Fig 4.8. Twelve peas are soaked in water for 48 hours, dried and weighed. The mass of the germinating peas is recorded. The peas are placed in the large test tube, along with a gauze basket containing soda lime granules to absorb any carbon dioxide in the test tube. The test tube is then placed in a beaker of water (not shown in Fig 4.8) at room temperature. This acts as a water bath.

The syringe and three-way tap are manipulated so that the level of the liquid in the capillary tubing is at position X. The three-way tap is adjusted so that the air in the test tube is continuous with the air in the capillary tubing and closed off from the syringe. The time taken for the level of the liquid in the capillary tubing to rise from X to Y is recorded.

The level is returned to X, and in each case the experiment is repeated five times.

Results

The mean time, x minutes, for the level of the liquid to rise y cm from X to Y is calculated. Assuming that the volume of oxygen used by the respiring peas is represented by the distance, in centimetres, from X to Y it is possible to calculate the rate of respiration of the peas in centimetres of oxygen per gram of pea per minute.

Conclusion

The rate of respiration of these germinating peas is y cm O_2 per g per min.

ANAEROBIC RESPIRATION

The breakdown of glucose in the absence of oxygen occurs in some fungi, bacteria and skeletal muscle during vigorous exercise. It is not as efficient as aerobic respiration in terms of energy production. The waste products vary, as shown below, and may be economically important.

ANAEROBIC RESPIRATION IN YEAST (FERMENTATION)

This process is important in the baking and brewing industries. Single-celled yeasts grow and divide very rapidly and obtain their energy by breaking down sugars, as shown below:

$$C_6H_{12}O_6 \rightarrow 2C_2H_5OH + 2CO_2 + 210\,kJ$$

glucose   ethanol   carbon   energy
dioxide

The waste products are ethanol and carbon dioxide. Carbon dioxide is used to make dough rise and the alcohol produced by brewer's yeast is used in beer and wine making.

EXPERIMENT TO INVESTIGATE CARBON DIOXIDE PRODUCTION BY YEAST DURING ANAEROBIC RESPIRATION

Apparatus
See Fig 4.9.

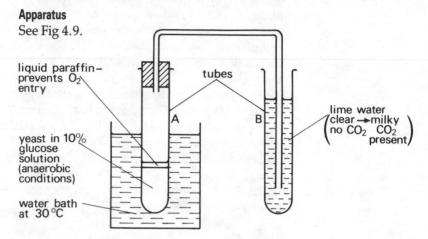

Fig 4.9

Method
A yeast and glucose solution is made up using boiled water (contains no air), set up as shown in Fig 4.9 and left for 2 hours.

Results
The limewater turns milky as gas produced in Tube **A** bubbles through it.

Conclusion
The gas produced by the yeast cells during the anaerobic breakdown of glucose contains carbon dioxide.

EXPERIMENT TO INVESTIGATE THE RATE OF ANAEROBIC RESPIRATION USING A YEAST/DOUGH MIXTURE

Apparatus
See Fig 4.10.

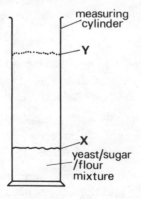

Fig 4.10

Method

A mixture containing equal quantities of glucose and yeast is added to water at 40°C to make a 10% glucose/yeast mixture. A known volume of this mixture is stirred into five times the same volume of plain flour to produce a dough mixture. The dough is added to a measuring cylinder and the height **X** recorded. The measuring cylinder is placed in a water bath kept at 40°C and the height reached by the dough recorded at 5-minute intervals for 30 minutes. The height **X–Y** represents the volume change of the dough. The volume from **X** to **Y** (cm^3) is divided by the time taken (min) to calculate the rate of respiration of the yeast.

A graph of volume (y axis) was plotted against time (x axis). See p.316 for details of plotting a graph.)

Results

The volume of the dough increases steadily during the 30-minute period due to carbon dioxide production.

Conclusion

The rate of anaerobic respiration using a yeast/dough mixture is z cm^3 per minute.

ANAEROBIC RESPIRATION IN SKELETAL MUSCLE

During vigorous activity oxygen supply to the cells becomes insufficient, despite faster breathing. Anaerobic respiration occurs at the same time as aerobic respiration and supplies extra energy for muscle contraction. **Lactic acid** accumulates and an **oxygen debt** is incurred:

$$glucose \rightarrow lactic\ acid + energy$$

The lactic acid enters the bloodstream and passes to the liver, where it is converted to glucose as the oxygen debt is repaid. The glucose is returned to the muscle and stored as glycogen (see Fig 4.11).

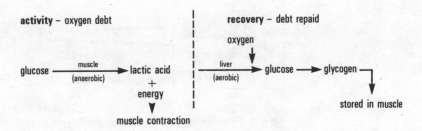

Fig 4.11 Anaerobic respiration in skeletal muscle – a summary

Specimen questions The above information is required in answering the following questions.

1   Give the name of the substance which accumulates in the muscles of man during vigorous exercise. (1 mark)
2   Why must the rate of breathing remain fairly high for some time after the period of exercise is over? (1 mark)   [SCE]

AEROBIC AND ANAEROBIC RESPIRATION COMPARED

Table 4.2 Comparison of aerobic and anaerobic respiration

	Aerobic	Anaerobic
Occurrence	Most animal and plant cells	Some fungi and bacteria; skeletal muscle
Energy released per glucose molecule	High (2800 kJ)	Low (210 kJ)
End products	Carbon dioxide, water	Ethanol and carbon dioxide, or lactic acid

Specimen question Give three differences between aerobic and anaerobic respiration. (3 marks)   [O&C]

GASEOUS EXCHANGE (EXTERNAL RESPIRATION)

All aerobic organisms require oxygen for respiration and produce carbon dioxide as a waste product. There is a continual exchange of these gases between the environment and the cell.

The movement of these gases occurs by **diffusion** (see p.32). This is the movement of molecules down a concentration gradient from a region of *their* high concentration to a region of *their* low concentration.

Diffusion gradients are always maintained between environment and cell because cells use up oxygen and produce carbon dioxide (see Fig 4.12).

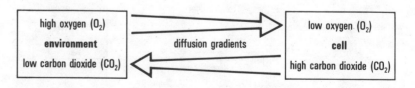

Fig 4.12 Diffusion gradient between a respiring cell and the atmosphere

GASEOUS EXCHANGE SURFACES

Gaseous exchange occurs through a **gaseous exchange surface**. In all cells this is the **cell membrane.**

In small simple organisms, e.g. *Amoeba*, gaseous exchange occurs over the whole outer surface of the organism. As organisms increase in size and complexity two problems arise:

1 the ratio of their surface area:volume decreases and direct diffusion becomes inadequate;
2 the distance between the environment and the cell increases.

Direct diffusion between environment and cell is thus insufficient for gaseous exchange and a transport system is required. A specialized gaseous exchange surface becomes necessary at the point where environment and transport system meet, e.g. the gill.

All gaseous exchange surfaces have the following features which permit diffusion.

1 They are thin.
2 They possess a large surface area.
3 They are permeable to gases.

As animals increase in size, their energy demands increase. More oxygen is required and their gaseous exchange surface must also have the following additional characteristics.

4 They must be well ventilated.
5 They must have a good blood supply containing a respiratory pigment, e.g. haemoglobin (this is most important in birds and mammals since they have a high metabolic rate).

You should learn these five features. They are vital to all answers dealing with gaseous exchange and may themselves form part of a question.

Specimen question Name three characteristics possessed by surfaces involved in respiratory exchange. [*AEB*]

GASEOUS EXCHANGE IN MAMMALS e.g. MAN

Gaseous exchange in Man occurs in the **lungs**. These are suited to exchange of gases in the terrestrial environment. The lungs are positioned inside the body to prevent excess water loss.

The two lungs are situated in the air-tight **thoracic cavity**. This is a sealed cavity protected by the **sternum**, **ribs** and **intercostal muscles** at the front and sides and the **vertebral column** at the back. The muscular diaphragm separates the thorax from the abdominal cavity.

Air enters the nose and mouth and passes through the **pharynx** and **larynx** (voice-box) to the **trachea** (windpipe). Food is prevented from entering the trachea by the **epiglottis** (see Fig 4.13). The trachea is kept open by rings of cartilage and its lining is covered with cilia. Mucus is secreted by the nose and the trachea to keep the surface moist, to warm incoming air and to trap dust and bacteria. Upward beating of the cilia carries the mucus up the pharynx where it is swallowed as phlegm.

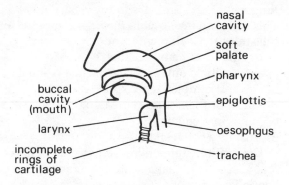

Fig 4.13 Upper part of the respiratory tract

At its base the trachea branches, forming right and left **bronchi**. These branch to form many **bronchioles** which end in structures resembling bunches of grapes, called **alveoli**. Each alveolus is covered by capillaries and this is the site of gaseous exchange (see Fig 4.14).

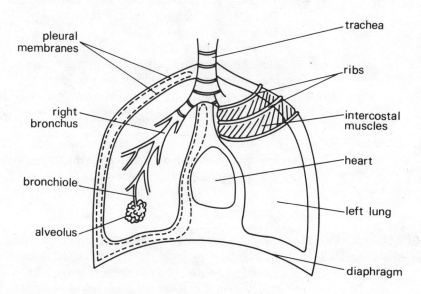

Fig 4.14 Lungs and associated structures.

Pleural membranes cover the lungs and line the thoracic cavity. Between the membranes is the pleural cavity containing pleural fluid to lubricate the lungs during breathing (ventilation) movements.

BREATHING (VENTILATION OF THE LUNGS)

Breathing movements are produced by the contraction and relaxation of the diaphragm and intercostal muscles. This alters the volume of the thorax and produces pressure changes. Air is forced into the lungs when the pressure in them falls below that of the atmosphere. This is **inspiration**. When the pressure in the lungs rises above that of the atmosphere air is passed out in **expiration** (see Fig 4.15).

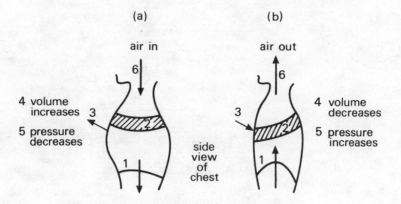

Fig 4.15 (a) Inspiration and (b) expiration in Man

Table 4.3 Process of breathing

	Inspiration	Expiration
1 Diaphragm	Contracts (moves down)	Relaxes (moves up)
2 External intercostal muscles	Contract	Relax
3 Rib cage	Moves up and out	Moves down and in
4 Volume of thorax	Increases	Decreases
5 Pressure of thorax	Decreases	Increases
6 Air moves	Into lungs	Out of lungs

Questions dealing with the topic of breathing occur quite frequently and you should ensure that it is understood.

Specimen question
(*a*)   List in order the parts through which tidal air passes.
(*b*)   Where is residual air found?
(*c*)   Describe the mechanism of inhalation (breathing in).   [*AEB*]

Capacities of lungs – approximate values for adult Man
▶ **Total capacity** – volume of lungs when fully inflated = 5 litres.
▶ **Vital capacity** – volume of air passing in and out of lungs during forced breathing = 4 litres.
▶ **Tidal air** – volume of air passing in and out of lungs during breathing = 0.5 litre at rest.
▶ **Residual air** – volume of air which cannot be removed from lungs by breathing out (mainly in alveoli) = 1 litre.

EXPERIMENT TO INVESTIGATE HUMAN VITAL CAPACITY

Apparatus
See Fig 4.16.

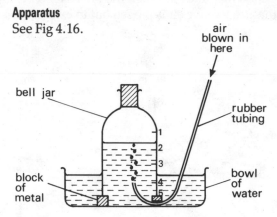

Fig 4.16

Method
One litre of water at a time is added to an upturned bottomless bell jar. The volume occupied by each litre of water is marked on the bell jar. The bell jar is placed upright in a bowl of water, filled with water and sealed with a tight-fitting bung. A length of rubber tubing is placed inside the bell jar, as shown in Fig 4.16.

The subject of the experiment takes a very deep breath and exhales it fully through the rubber tubing. This volume of air displaces an equal volume of water. The volume occupied by the air is recorded. The experiment is repeated three times and the mean volume is calculated.

Result and conclusion
The vital capacity is the volume of air which passes out of the lung during forced breathing. For an average man this volume is about 4 litres.

GASEOUS EXCHANGE AT THE ALVEOLI

There are approximately 700 million alveoli in the lungs. They have the following features.
1 Thin – walls only one cell thick.
2 Large surface area.
3 Permeable to respiratory gases.
4 Well ventilated.
5 Good blood supply.
       The exchange of gases is shown in Fig. 4.17.

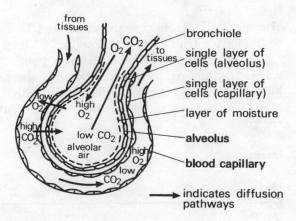

Fig 4.17 Gaseous exchange at the alveolus

The sequence of events is as follows.

1 Oxygen in alveolar air dissolves in moisture lining alveolus.
2 Oxygen diffuses through single-celled alveolar and capillary walls into blood.
3 Oxygen combines with haemoglobin in red blood cells to form oxy-haemoglobin (see p.130).
4 Carbon dioxide, transported as hydrogencarbonate ions in blood diffuses through capillary and alveolar walls into moisture layer.
5 Carbon dioxide diffuses from moisture layer into alveolar air.

Alveolar air composition remains nearly constant, despite continual loss of oxygen to blood and gain of carbon dioxide, because diffusion occurs between it and tidal air in the bronchioles, which constantly bring in oxygen and remove carbon dioxide.

Table 4.4 Approximate composition of breath-in air

	Inspired air	Expired air	Alveolar air
Oxygen	21%	16%	14%
Carbon dioxide	0.04%	4%	6%
Nitrogen	78%	78%	80%
Water vapour	Variable	Saturated	Saturated

EXPERIMENT TO INVESTIGATE THE CARBON DIOXIDE CONTENT AND THE OXYGEN CONTENT OF INHALED AND EXHALED AIR

Apparatus for carbon dioxide
See Fig 4.18.

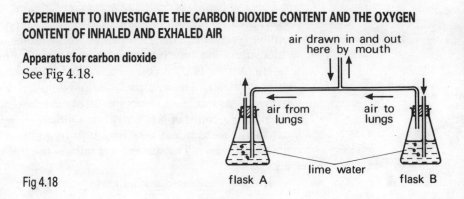

Fig 4.18

Method

The apparatus is set up as shown in Fig 4.18. Breathing in and out is continued for 2 minutes. Any cloudiness in the limewater is recorded.

The limewater in flasks A and B is poured away, the flasks are washed out and red hydrogencarbonate indicator solution is added to both flasks. Breathing in and out is continued for 2 more minutes, after which the colour of the hydrogencarbonate indicator is recorded.

Results

Table 4.5

	Flask A	Flask B
Limewater	Very milky	Slight milkiness
Hydrogencarbonate indicator solution	Yellow	Red

Conclusion

Exhaled air contains more carbon dioxide than inhaled air.

Apparatus for oxygen

See Fig 4.19.

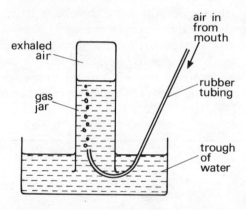

Fig 4.19

Method

A burning candle is added to a gas jar of air and sealed with a ground glass plate as shown in Fig 4.19. The time taken for the candle to go out is recorded. This is repeated three times and the mean time calculated. This time is related to the oxygen content of inhaled air.

The gas jar is then completely filled with water and inverted in a dish of water. The gas jar is held vertically, keeping the opening below the water level. A person is told to take a deep breath, hold the breath for a count of ten, blow out a little air through the mouth then exhale the remainder of the breath through the rubber tubing into the gas jar of water. The water level falls as the gas jar fills with expired air.

The gas jar, sealed with a glass plate, is removed from the dish, a lighted candle introduced and the gas jar sealed again with a glass plate. The time take for the candle to go out is recorded. The experiment is repeated three times and the mean time calculated. This time is related to the oxygen content of exhaled air.

Results

Table 4.6

Air	Mean time for candle to go out (s)
Inhaled air	10.3
Exhaled air	8.7

Conclusion
Inhaled air contains more oxygen than exhaled air.

GASEOUS EXCHANGE AT TISSUES

Oxygenated blood passes from the lungs to the heart via the pulmonary veins. The heart distributes blood around the body to the tissues. Diffusion of gases occurs throughout the body wherever a concentration gradient exists between the blood, tissue fluid and cells. In regions of low oxygen and high carbon dioxide concentrations, oxyhaemoglobin releases its oxygen. This diffuses into the tissue fluid and then into the cells, to be used in cell respiration. Waste carbon dioxide passes back into the blood down its concentration gradient and dissolves in the plasma forming hydrogencarbonate ions (see Fig 4.20).

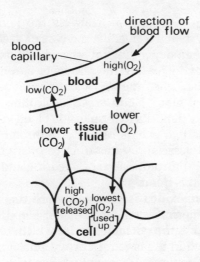

Fig 4.20 Gaseous exchange at the tissues

Specimen question Use the diagrams and notes given in this chapter to answer this question.

With the aid of diagrams, explain how, in a mammal, oxygen:

(*a*) reaches the lungs; (*b*) enters the blood stream; and (*c*) is transported to the liver. (12,8 and 5 marks)   [*ULSEB*]

SOCIAL AND APPLIED ASPECTS OF GASEOUS EXCHANGE

As we breathe in we take into our bodies many materials suspended in air. Some of these may be harmless but many can cause us serious damage. We are becoming increasingly aware of the problems of breathing polluted air. These problems can be considered under the following headings.

1 Smoking
2 Air pollution
3 Airborne transmission of disease
4 Exercise
5 Mouth-to-mouth ventilation

SMOKING

Cigarette smoke contains tars, nicotine, carbon monoxide and ash particles. **Tars** have been shown to contain substances called **carcinogens**, which cause cancer in laboratory animals. Smokers are much more likely to suffer from cancer than non-smokers. Someone who smokes 25 cigarettes per day has a 25 times greater chance of dying from lung cancer than a non-smoker. As the number of cigarettes smoked doubles so does the risk of dying in this way. As yet the way in which cigarette smoke causes cancer has not been demonstrated.

Nicotine is a drug which affects the nervous system and the circulatory system. It can either increase or decrease the activity of the nervous system, depending on other conditions. In general, it acts as a stimulant by increasing the release of adrenaline (see p.187). This speeds up the heart rate and increases blood pressure by causing constriction of many blood vessels. Nicotine also increases the tendency for fatty deposits to form inside blood vessels and causes blood to clot. These two events can lead to **thrombosis** (clotting of blood within blood vessels). Deaths from coronary (heart) thrombosis and cerebral (brain) thrombosis are increasing and smoking is an important factor in this trend.

Carbon monoxide (CO) is a gas which combines with the oxygen-carrying pigment haemoglobin in red blood cells. It forms a compound called **carboxyhaemoglobin** which reduces the amount of oxygen carried in the blood. In heavy smokers this leads to shortage of breath and lethargy. Pregnant women who smoke produce undersized babies and run the risk of having a spontaneous abortion. Both of these situations result from the effects of carbon monoxide in the mothers' and babies' blood.

Ash particles in the smoke irritate the lining of the windpipe and bronchial tubes. The lining produces more mucus and the cilia in these tubes stop beating. The mucus accumulates and can be removed only by coughing. The 'smokers cough' damages the lining of the tubes and allows it to be attacked by bacteria and viruses. **Chronic bronchitis** can result. When this occurs, excessive coughing begins to damage the alveoli. The thin walls of the alveoli break down, decreasing the surface area available for gaseous exchange. Sufferers become very short of breath. This medical condition is called **emphysema.**

There is a very strong correlation between smoking and premature deaths from lung cancer, chronic bronchitis and emphysema. Increasing pressure is being brought to limit, if not ban, smoking in public places in an attempt to reduce the occurrence of such diseases and deaths.

EXPERIMENT TO INVESTIGATE THE TAR CONTENT OF CIGARETTE SMOKE USING A TRAP BETWEEN A CIGARETTE AND AN AIR PUMP

Apparatus
See Fig 4.21.

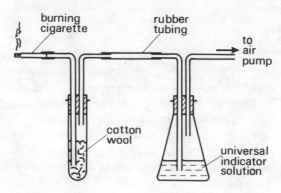

Fig 4.21

Method
The apparatus is set up as shown in Fig 4.21. The speed of the air pump is regulated until a steady stream of smoke is drawn through the apparatus. The cotton wool is used to trap the particles in the smoke. The universal indicator is used to determine the pH of the gases released by the burning cigarette. The experiment is repeated with various brands of cigarettes, both tipped and non-tipped.

Results
The cotton wool is stained brown with the tars released from the burning cigarettes. The universal indicator solution indicates the gases released from the burning cigarettes are acidic. Untipped cigarette smoke turns the cotton wool browner and changes the colour of the universal indicator solution faster.

Conclusions

Untipped cigarettes release more tar and more acidic gases than tipped cigarettes, the tip acting as a filter.

AIR POLLUTION

The smoke produced by burning fossil fuels such as coal and oil contains carbon particles and gases such as carbon dioxide and sulphur dioxide. The fumes produced by car and lorry exhausts contain carbon monoxide, lead compounds and oxides of nitrogen. Smoke particles and carbon monoxide affect the gaseous exchange system, as described above. Lead compounds have a harmful effect on the nervous system and high levels in the air, produced by heavy traffic, can cause brain damage in young children.

A mixture of smoke and fog is called **smog**. It is caused when a layer of cold air is kept close to the ground by a layer of warmer air above it. In December 1952 over 4000 people died in London from respiratory disorders resulting from the smog. Clean air legislation has prevented this from happening again (see p.293).

AIRBORNE TRANSMISSION OF DISEASE

Many disease-causing organisms can be spread from person to person in the tiny droplets of moisture released when we breathe out, cough, sneeze, or even when we talk and laugh. The bacteria causing diphtheria, whooping cough, pneumonia and tuberculosis and the viruses causing common colds, influenza, mumps, measles and polio can all be spread by droplet infection. In conditions of high humidity and overcrowding such as in schools, cinemas, trains and buses the risks of infection are increased. Occasionally viral particles stick to dust particles suspended in the air and these can produce infection when inhaled.

The common cold, spread by viruses, is an infection of the upper respiratory tract. The viruses attack the epithelial lining cells of the nasal cavity causing them to become inflamed, break down and release watery mucus.

Substances called **allergens** can also affect and damage the epithelial cells of the nose, throat, eyes and windpipe. Pollen from flowers and dust, which is fine particles of soil, building materials, dead plant and animal tissues, can be carried in the air. Hay fever, caused by pollen, irritates the nose, eyes and throat causing the cells to release a group of substances called **histamines**. It is these substances which cause congestion of the nose, sneezing, dry throat and watering and itching of the eyes. Hay fever is an allergy illness (see p.81). Drugs called **antihistamines** are used to relieve and in some cases prevent unpleasant reactions to allergens.

EXERCISE

Exercise has a number of extremely beneficial effects on the body (see p.135). Jogging (gentle running) encourages deep breathing. This involves increasing the depth and rate of breathing. The diaphragm and intercostal muscles are made to work harder and the elasticity of the air sacs is increased. Blood flow both to and from the lungs and within the lungs is also improved.

EXPERIMENT TO INVESTIGATE THE EFFECT OF EXERCISE ON BREATHING RATE

Method

The number of breaths taken in during a 1-minute period at complete rest was counted and recorded. This was repeated for three 1-minute periods and the mean breathing rate was recorded.

The subject then ran on the spot very vigorously for 3 minutes. The number of breaths taken in during each minute afterwards was counted over a 10-minute period and recorded.

Results and conclusion

A graph is plotted of the number of breaths per minutes (y axis) against time (x axis) for the mean rest period and for each minute afterwards.

The graph shows how much the breathing rate rises as a result of exercise and the time taken for the breathing rate to return to normal after exercise.

MOUTH-TO-MOUTH VENTILATION

Everyone should learn how and when to apply this. If a person has stopped breathing as a result of shock, heart attack or accident the following should be done.

1 Remove false teeth, damaged teeth or any obstructions in the mouth.
2 Ensure that the person's tongue is forward.
3 Place one hand behind the person's neck and raise the neck so that the head is tilted backwards.
4 Pinch the person's nostrils with the other hand.
5 Take a deep breath, place your mouth over the person's mouth and blow strongly.
6 Take your mouth away and the person will exhale.
7 Repeat stages 5 and 6 about 20 times per minute.
8 If the person's heart has stopped beating, another person should apply heart massage alternating with your mouth-to-mouth ventilation.

Exhaled air may only contain 16% oxygen but this is adequate to sustain gaseous exchange in the unconscious person.

GASEOUS EXCHANGE IN FLOWERING PLANTS

The overall exchange of gases depends upon the light conditions.

During *daylight* flowering plants carry out **photosynthesis** and **respiration**. The rate of photosynthesis is much greater than respiration and supplies all the oxygen for energy release and uses up the waste carbon dioxide from respiration. Net gaseous exchange with the environment involves the uptake of carbon dioxide and release of oxygen.

During *darkness* plants carry out respiration only. They take up oxygen and release carbon dioxide.

COMPARISON OF PHOTOSYNTHESIS AND RESPIRATION

In many ways the two processes are opposite. Photosynthesis traps and stores energy whereas respiration releases the stored energy, as shown in Fig 4.22.

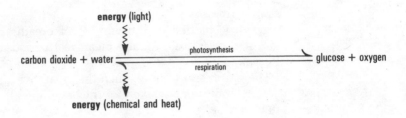

Fig 4.22

▶ All plants and animals respire at all times.
▶ Green plants photosynthesize during daylight hours only.

Specimen question List the differences between photosynthesis and respiration.

EXPERIMENT TO INVESTIGATE THE RELEASE OF OXYGEN AS A BYPRODUCT OF PHOTOSYNTHESIS IN AN AQUATIC PLANT

Apparatus
See Fig 4.23.

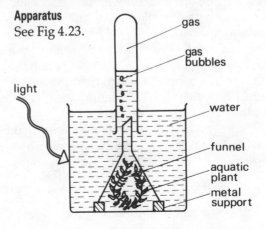

Fig 4.23

Method

An aquatic plant, such as *Elodea*, is placed in water and the apparatus is set up as shown in Fig 4.23. The plant is then kept in strong sunlight for 6 hours and the gas given off is tested for the presence of oxygen with a glowing splint.

The same apparatus as in Fig 4.23 is set up and kept in darkness for the same number of hours as above.

Results

A test tube full of gas is given off by the plant kept in the light but no gas is given off by the plant which is kept in darkness. The gas given off in daylight rekindles a glowing splint.

Conclusion

The gas given off by an aquatic plant in sunlight is oxygen. This oxygen is released as a byproduct of photosynthesis.

COMPENSATION POINT

At two points every 24 hours, gaseous exchange appears to cease. These are the compensation points, and they represent the times at which the rates of photosynthesis and respiration are equal (see Fig 4.24).

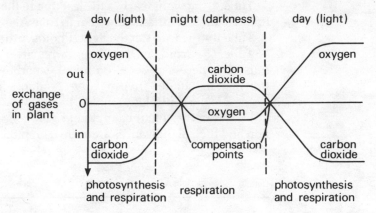

Fig 4.24 Graph comparing photosynthesis and respiration.

EXPERIMENT TO INVESTIGATE THE BALANCE BETWEEN CARBON DIOXIDE PRODUCTION AND ABSORPTION IN PLANTS UNDER LIGHT AND DARK CONDITIONS

Apparatus
See Fig 4.25.

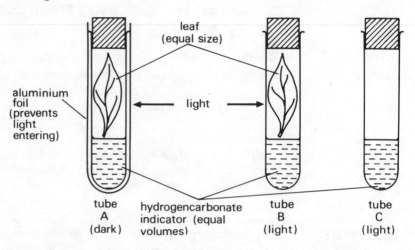

Fig 4.25

Method
The apparatus is set up as shown in Fig 4.25 and left for 2 hours.

Tube **A** – no light reaches the leaf due to the presence of aluminium foil. No photosynthesis can occur in tube **A**.

Tube **B** – the leaf is in the light. Photosynthesis can occur.

Tube **C** – contains hydrogencarbonate indicator solution only. Tube **C** is necessary in a controlled experiment to demonstrate that the material under investigation produces the changes observed. (Tube **B** is the control, not tube **C**.)

Details of the colour changes of hydrogencarbonate indicator solution and their significances are shown on p.86.

Results

Table 4.7

Time (h)	Tube A	Tube B	Tube C
0	Red	Red	Red
2	Yellow	Purple	Red

Conclusion
The presence of the tube **C** shows that changes in colour of the hydrogencarbonate indicator solution result from reactions occurring in the leaves. Carbon dioxide is released in tube **A** by respiration. No photosynthesis occurs in tube **A** in the absence of light. Photosynthesis and respiration occur in tube **B**, but the rate of photosynthesis is greater than respiration and there is a **net** release of oxygen.

STOMATA AND LENTICELS

Gaseous exchange in flowering plants occurs through openings called stomata and lenticels. The structure of the leaf is designed to ensure efficient gaseous exchange (see p.30).

STOMATA

These are tiny pores in the epidermis of leaves and soft green stems of herbaceous plants. The sequence of gaseous exchange is shown in Fig. 4.26.

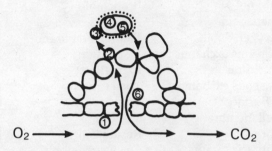

Fig 4.26 Gaseous exchange at the stoma

1 and 2	Oxygen diffuses in through stoma and into intercellular spaces.
3	Oxygen dissolves in moisture surrounding cell and diffuses into cytoplasm.
4	Oxygen used in respiration – maintains concentration gradient.
5 and 6	Carbon dioxide produced by respiration diffuses out along concentration gradient.

LENTICELS

Small openings in bark of woody stems filled with loosely packed cork cells having many intercellular air-spaces (see Fig 4.27). Oxygen and carbon dioxide are exchanged here down their concentration gradients.

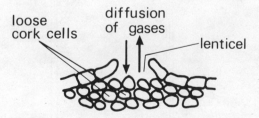

Fig 4.27 Lenticels

KEY WORDS ➧			
Energy	Sternum	Hydrogencarbonate
Aerobic	Ribs	Smoking
Glucose	Intercostal muscles	Tars
Oxygen	Diaphragm	Carcinogens
Carbon dioxide	Pharynx	Nicotine
Water	Larynx	Thrombosis
Metabolic rate	Trachea	Carboxyhaemoglobin
Anaerobic	Epiglottis	Bronchitis
Fermentation	Bronchi	Emphysema
Ethanol	Bronchiole	Smog
Lactic acid	Alveoli	Allergen
Oxygen debt	Pleural membrane	Histamine
Gaseous exchange	Inspiration	Mouth-to-mouth
Diffusion	Expiration	Ventilation
Gaseous exchange	Total capacity	Photosynthesis
Surface	Vital capacity	Compensation point
Cell membrane	Tidal air	Stomata
Lungs	Residual air	Lenticels
Thoracic cavity	Oxyhaemoglobin	

SPECIMEN EXAMINATION QUESTIONS

1   Fig 4.28 shows an experiment to demonstrate that germinating pea seeds release heat. The experiment has been set up for four days.

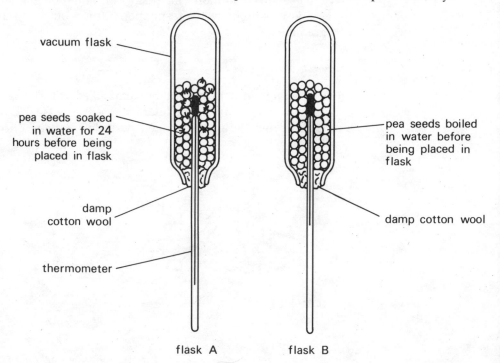

vacuum flask

pea seeds soaked in water for 24 hours before being placed in flask

damp cotton wool

thermometer

pea seeds boiled in water before being placed in flask

damp cotton wool

flask A   flask B

Fig 4.28

(*a*)   Name the living process which has caused the temperature inside flask A to be higher than the temperature inside flask B.

(*b*)   Explain the importance of:

(i) using the same number of pea seeds in each flask;

(ii) soaking the pea seeds in water for 24 hours before placing them in flask A.

(*c*)   (i) The seeds in flask B were rinsed in disinfectant before being placed in the flask. Name a type of organism which might have grown on the surface of the dead peas in flask B if the peas had not been treated in this manner.

(ii) Explain how such organisms might have affected the results.

(*d*)   (i) Complete the following sentence:

The flask with the boiled seeds acts as a . . .

(ii) Explain why it is necessary for the experiment to include flask B.   [*ULSEB*]

2   (*a*)   To investigate the amount of energy present in different foods, a pupil burned a peanut under a test tube of water as shown in Fig 4.29. The temperature of the water was recorded at the start and after the peanut had burned out. The rise in temperature indicated the energy content of the peanut.

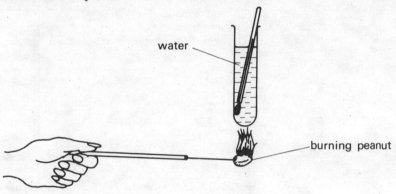

water

burning peanut

Fig 4.29

If the pupil now wished to compare the energy content of butter to that of peanuts, state two factors which would affect the fairness of the comparison.

(*b*)   Table 4.8 shows the energy used in kJ/minute for adults in various occupations.

Table 4.8

Occupation	Energy used (kJ/min)
Taxi driver	10
Teacher	12
Postman	22
Construction worker	30

(i) What conclusion can you draw from this data about the physical activity involved in the different occupations?

(ii) Which of the following figures is most likely to be the energy used by a secretary?

12 kJ/min
24 kJ/min
36 kJ/min
(iii) Use the data to calculate the amount of energy used by a postman during his 8–hour working day.   [*SCE*]

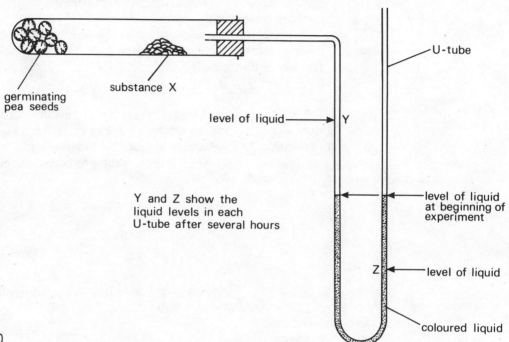

Fig 4.30

3   The apparatus shown in Fig 4.30 was set up with normal air present in the tube surrounding the germinating pea seeds. The liquid levels in the U-tube were then exactly equal.
(*a*)   What physiological process occurring in the seeds accounts for the change in volume of the air after several hours?
(*b*)   (i) What is the purpose of substance *X* in this experiment?
(ii) Name a suitable chemical for substance *X*.
(*c*)   Name TWO possible changes in the environment surrounding the test tube that could bring about movement of the liquid in the U-tube.

4   The apparatus shown in Fig 4.31 is used to investigate whether a person breathes out more carbon dioxide than is breathed in. The drawing is not complete.
(*a*)   Complete the figure by drawing in the correct arrangement of the glass tubing inside each test tube.
(*b*)   Name a suitable carbon dioxide indicator which could be used in this apparatus.

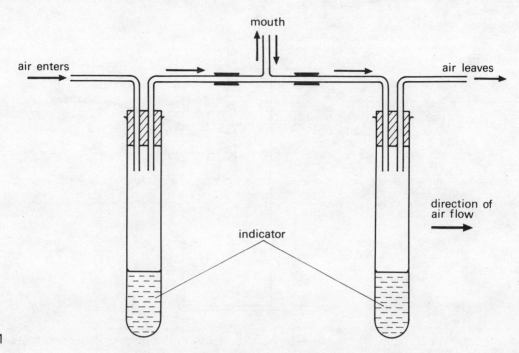

air enters → mouth ↑↓ air leaves

direction of air flow

indicator

Fig 4.31

(c)   When a person breathes IN several times through the mouth-piece, what would be observed in:
(i) test tube **A**;
(ii) test tube **B**?
(d)   When a person breathes OUT several times through the mouthpiece, what would be observed in:
(i) test tube **A**;
(ii) test tube **B**?   [*LEAG*]

5   Three samples of air were collected in gas jars from the sources shown in Table 4.9 below. A glass plate was used to cover the open end of the jar. The plate was removed and a lighted candle was then lowered into the gas jar as shown in Fig 4.32. The time for the flame to be extinguished was recorded. This was repeated four times for each sample of air. The results are shown in Table 4.9.

Table 4.9

Sample	Sample take from	Time for candle flame to be extinguished (s) Results
A	Air in the laboratory	23 20 17 20
B	A student exhaling after exercise	6 7 8 7
C	Glass chamber above an aquatic plant brightly illuminated	26 24 27 23

(a)   Calculate the mean time for the candle flame to be extinguished for samples **A**, **B** and **C**. (3 marks)
(b)   Name the gas which permits combustion of the candle wax in the gas jar. (1 mark)

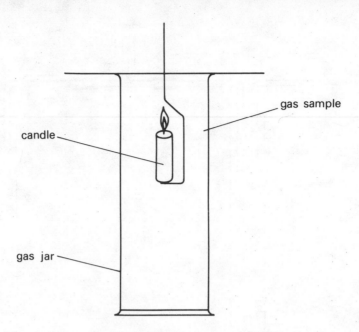

Fig 4.32

(c)   (i) Which ONE of the three samples contained most of this gas? (1 mark)
(ii) Explain your answer in (c) (i) above. (3 marks)
(d)   Account for the burning time of the candle in sample **B**. (2 marks)
(e)   Name a gas which is present in minute amounts in sample **A**, not present in sample **C** and is present in the largest amount in sample **B**. State its percentage volume in sample **A** and sample **B**. (3 marks)

[*LEAG*]

6   Chronic bronchitis is a disease as a result of which people suffer from a persistent cough and shortness of breath.
    The graphs in Fig. 4.33 show the percentages of smokers and non-smokers, aged between 35 and 69, who suffer from chronic bronchitis in towns A and B. Town A is an industrial town with a high level of air pollution. Town B is a small seaside town with a low level of air pollution.
    (a)   Study the graphs in Fig 4.33 and complete Table 4.10. (2 marks)

Table 4.10

	% of people suffering from chronic bronchitis
(i) Smokers aged 55–64 in town A	
(ii) Smokers aged 55–64 in town B	
(iii) Non-smokers aged 55–64 in town A	
(iv) Non-smokers aged 55-64 in town B	

(b)   What evidence is there to suggest that smoking is more important than air pollution in causing chronic bronchitis? (2 marks)

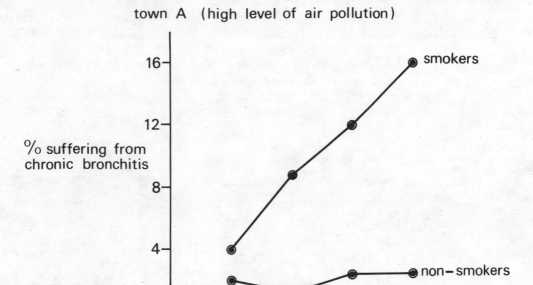

town A (high level of air pollution)

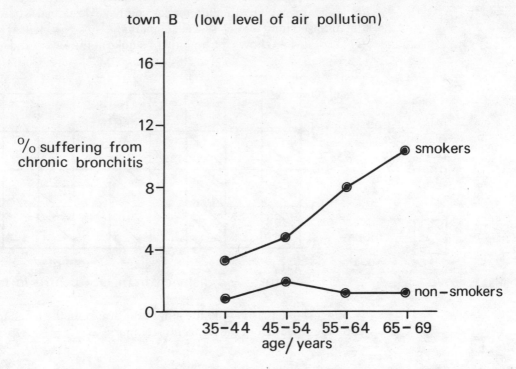

town B (low level of air pollution)

Fig 4.33

(c) What evidence is there to suggest that air pollution is ONE factor which increases the chance of people suffering from chronic bronchitis? (1 mark) (*d*) Name TWO other effects heavy smoking has on the human breathing system (2 marks) [*MEG*]

7 Fig 4.34 shows a small part of the lung from a healthy person and from a person suffering from the effects of air pollution. Both are drawn to the same scale.

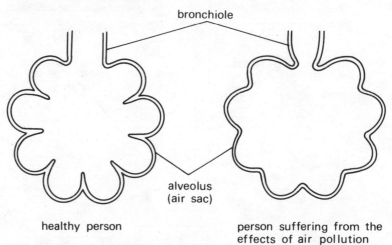

bronchiole

alveolus (air sac)

Fig 4.34

healthy person

person suffering from the effects of air pollution

(*a*) Write down TWO differences which can be seen on the diagrams between the healthy lung and the diseased lung. (2 marks)

(*b*) Suggest why the differences you have described would make the diseased lung work less well. (2 marks) [*NEA*]

8 (*a*) Fig 4.35 shows the amount of smoke in the air around a city.

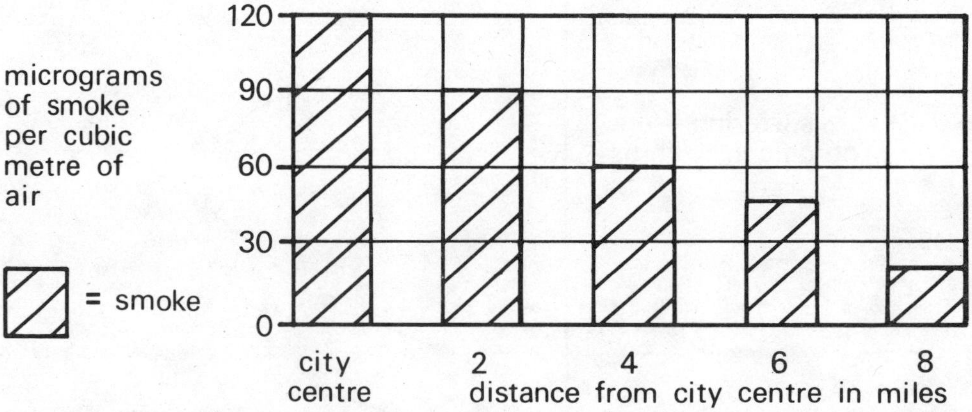

microgram of smoke per cubic metre of air

= smoke

city centre 2 4 6 8

distance from city centre in miles

Fig 4.35

Suggest one reason why the amount of smoke in the air changes as you move away from the city centre. (1 mark)

(b)   Fig 4.36 shows the deaths of men from bronchitis around the SAME city.

number of deaths per 100 000 of population

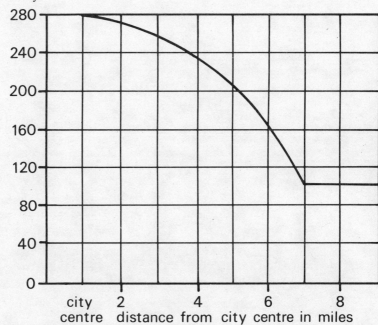

Fig 4.36

Suggest why the numbers of deaths from bronchitis decrease as you move away from the city centre. (1 mark)

(c)   The city council would like to cut down the deaths from bronchitis. Suggest TWO different things which they could do.

(2 marks)   [NEA]

TRANSPORT

CONTENTS

Translocation Movement of substances about the plant.

Transpiration Loss of water vapour to the atmosphere from the surface of the plant.

All living organisms require a continuous exchange of materials between their cells and the environment, e.g. oxygen, carbon dioxide, water, food and waste products. Special structures on their surfaces allow these exchanges to occur. In single-celled organisms, e.g. *Amoeba*, movement of materials by diffusion and osmosis across the cell membrane supplies the needs of the organism.

As organisms increase in size, so do the distances between parts of the body, and between internal tissues and the environment. Movement of materials within those organisms therefore requires a special transport system linking all the cells to the environment.

TRANSPORT IN PLANTS

The xylem and phloem are arranged together in the stem of a plant (see Figs 5.1 and 5.2), and form a number of strands running along the length of the stem connecting the roots to the leaves. These are called the **vascular bundles**, and are responsible for **translocation** of substances about the plant. The **xylem** carries water and dissolved mineral salts from the roots to the leaves. The **phloem** carries organic materials, mainly sugars and amino acids, from the leaves to growing points and storage organs.

Fig 5.1 TS young stem of sunflower

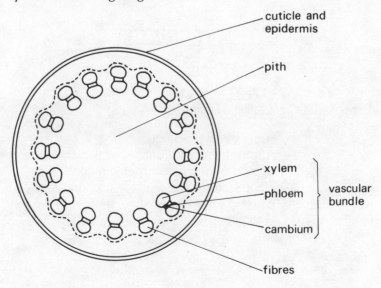

cuticle and epidermis

pith

xylem

phloem

cambium

vascular bundle

fibres

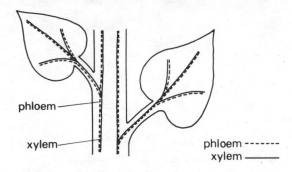

Fig 5.2 LS young stem

WATER TRANSPORT

TRANSPIRATION

The loss of water vapour occurs mainly from the leaves of a plant. The lamina of a leaf is covered by a waterproof cuticle, so nearly all water loss occurs through gaps in the cuticle, the **stomata**, shown in Fig 5.3. Water evaporates from moist cell surfaces into the air in the sub-stomatal air space which becomes saturated with water vapour. Any factors producing a concentration gradient between the air spaces and the atmosphere will cause a continuous loss of water vapour through the stomata

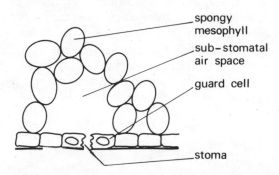

Fig 5.3 VS stoma

Factors affecting transpiration

1 Atmospheric conditions, e.g. wind, high temperature, low humidity, all increase the rate of transpiration.
2 Plant factors, e.g. surface area of leaves, number of stomata and whether open or closed.
3 Water supply.

EXPERIMENT TO INVESTIGATE THE EFFECT OF ATMOSPHERIC CONDITIONS ON TRANSPIRATION RATE

Apparatus

See Fig 5.4.

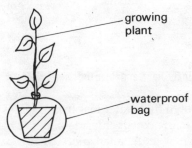

Fig 5.4

Method

A well-watered potted plant is set up, as shown in Fig 5.4. The plant is systematically left under conditions of high and low light intensity, wind, temperature and humidity for 3 hours. The plant is weighed before and after this period in each case and the results recorded.

Results

The mass of water lost for high values of light, wind and temperature is greater than for low values. In the case of humidity, loss in mass is lower for the high humidity value.

Conclusion

Assuming that all losses in mass are due to loss of water vapour, then transpiration increases with rising light, wind and temperature levels and decreases with rising humidity. Increase in mass due to photosynthesis is relatively small and may be ignored.

WATER LOSS FROM LEAVES

Since water loss occurs mainly through the stomata, it will be influenced by the degree of opening of these pores. The stoma is guarded by two sausage-shaped **guard cells** with thickened inner walls. They are the only epidermal cells with chloroplasts.

When light is available for photosynthesis the concentration of sugar in the guard cells decreases their water potential, they take in water and become turgid. As the cell increases in volume the thickening on the inner wall causes the outer wall to curve more, opening the stoma. Therefore in light the stoma opens (see Fig 5.5 (a)). In the dark, the cell loses water, and the pore closes, reducing water loss (see Fig 5.5 (b)).

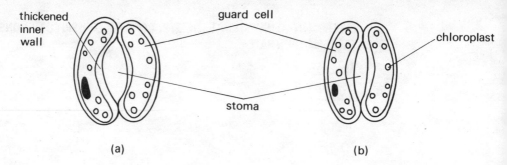

Fig 5.5 Stoma (a) in the light, and (b) in the dark

It can be shown that water loss from a leaf is related to the presence of stomata by using cobalt chloride paper. This is pale blue when dry and pink when wet. A small piece of the paper is enclosed under glass on both sides of a leaf (see Fig 5.6). It is found that it turns pink more quickly on the surface bearing stomata.

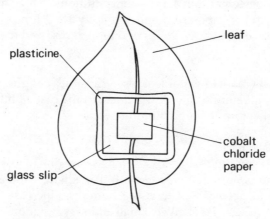

Fig 5.6 Demonstrating water loss from a leaf

It can also be shown that water loss is faster through open stomata. When water is lost from the mesophyll cells, their cell sap becomes more concentrated and they become less turgid. This increases their tendency to take in water. Water passes by osmosis (see p.32) from neighbouring cells into them. These cells in turn draw water from their neighbours, and in this way water passes across the leaf from the xylem vessels of the veins to the stomata.

The xylem forms a continuous system through the leaves, stem and root of the plant. When water is withdrawn from the xylem in the leaf, water passes up the vessels of the stem and root in a continuous stream. Such long narrow columns of water can remain unbroken because of the large forces of attraction between the molecules of water, and between the water and the sides of the vessels.

EXPERIMENT TO INVESTIGATE THE SITE OF WATER TRANSPORT IN A STEM

Method
A piece of celery is cut and left in a dilute solution of the red dye eosin for 3 hours. Transverse sections of the stem are cut and examined under the microscope.

Results
The only tissue containing the dye and showing up red is the xylem.

Conclusion
Water is transported through the stem in the xylem.

WATER UPTAKE BY ROOTS

Just behind the tip of each root is a region bearing numerous delicate **root hairs**. These die as the root grows on, but are replaced by new ones so that a band of hairs always exists at the same distance behind the root tip.

Each hair is an elongated epidermal cell with a *thin* cellulose wall. It is in close contact with the soil particles. The root hairs give a very large surface area for the absorption of water and salts.

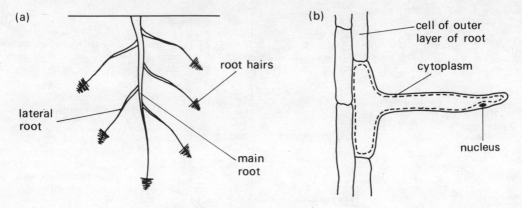

Fig 5.7 (a) Tap root. (b) Root hair cell

Near the tip of the root the water passing along the xylem is replaced by water from neighbouring cells. This loss of water increases the osmotic potential of their sap, and they draw water from neighbouring cells. Water passes across the root through successive cells of the cortex, until finally it is drawn from the root hair. Loss of water from the root hair causes water to enter it from the soil if it is available.

The vascular or conducting tissue of the root forms a central core (see Fig 5.8). The xylem which conducts water also provides mechanical strength. This arrangement gives the root strength to resist the pulling strains which result from movement of the aerial part of the plant.

The xylem is arranged in the shape of a star alternating with the phloem. A well-defined **endodermis** surrounds the vascular tissue. A wide **cortex**, which often contains storage tissue, separates the endodermis from the outer **exodermis**, which in a young root will bear the root hairs.

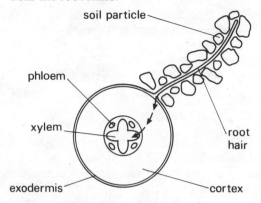

Fig 5.8 TS of root to show passage of water across the root

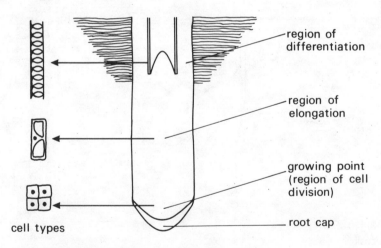

Fig 5.9 LS root tip to show vascular tissue

Root pressure is a force generated by the root of a plant which uses energy. It causes water to rise up the stem, particularly in spring when the absence of leaves on a tree means that there is no transpiration. If the stem of a potted plant, e.g. a vine, is cut off, and a manometer fitted as in Fig 5.10, root pressure may be measured after a few hours.

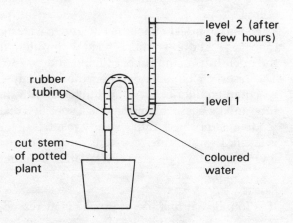

Fig 5.10 Demonstration of root pressure

Factors affecting water uptake

1 Rate of transpiration (which depends upon other factors, see p.120).
2 Temperature.
3 Water potential of soil water.
4 Availability of soil water.
5 State of turgor of plant.
6 Root pressure.

Some of these factors may be demonstrated by using a **potometer**. NB This apparatus does not directly demonstrate transpiration, but water uptake.

EXPERIMENT TO INVESTIGATE THE EFFECT OF VARIOUS FACTORS ON WATER UPTAKE USING A POTOMETER

Apparatus
See Fig 5.11.

Fig 5.11 The potometer

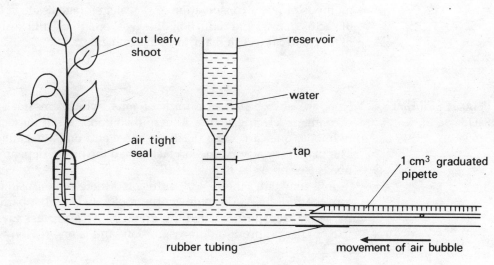

Method

The stem of a leafy shoot is cut under water to prevent air entering the xylem. The apparatus is filled with water, and the shoot fixed into the open tube using rubber tubing and wax to make an airtight seal. The reservoir tap is closed and the apparatus left for 15 minutes to reach an equilibrium. An air bubble is introduced into the capillary tube and its passage timed along a specified distance on the scale. The reading is repeated until a steady result is obtained. The temperature is taken. Readings are repeated, varying the conditions, e.g. high and low temperature, moving air, variation in humidity.

Results

It is found that the rate of uptake is increased by high temperature, moving air, low humidity. It is decreased by low temperature, still air, high humidity and darkness.

Conclusions

In general, conditions which affect transpiration rate will affect uptake in the same way.

WILTING

If the rate of water loss by transpiration from a plant is greater than the rate of water uptake, the tissues will lose their turgor (see p.202). The result will be a loss of rigidity in the plant stem and leaves, as the support of soft tissues is largely due to the pressure of water inside the cells. The plant will droop and is said to have **wilted**.

In normal circumstances the tissues will recover when water uptake is again adequate, and the plant will stand erect again. If water loss is severe and prolonged, however, the tissues may be permanently damaged and the plant may die.

In plants living in conditions of restricted water supply, such as sand dunes or deserts, the leaves or stems often show special methods of **water conservation**, e.g. water storage tissue in the stems of cactus plants, and reduction of leaves, or a thick cuticle and rolling of leaves to protect stomata, as in marram grass.

UPTAKE OF MINERAL SALTS

Salts are absorbed in the form of **ions**, which are small particles carrying an electric charge. When in solution, a salt dissociates into two ions, one carrying a positive charge and one a negative charge. The plant may absorb one ion faster than the other, depending on its needs (see pp.35, 60).

Ions may enter the root by diffusion if there is a diffusion gradient into the root hair. Alternatively the root may absorb a particular ion by **active transport**, against the gradient. This process involves the use of energy, produced in respiration, and is one reason why roots need oxygen.

After entering the root, the salts travel in dilute solution in water in the xylem to the growing points and to the leaves, where they are necessary for protein synthesis. 'Ringing' experiments on stems, i.e. removing the bark and phloem (see Fig 5.12), show that the transport of salts is not affected. Therefore they must travel in the xylem.

Fig 5.12 'Ringing' a stem

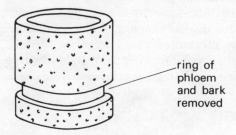

ring of phloem and bark removed

TRANSPORT OF ORGANIC MATERIALS

The movement of sugars and amino acids depends on the presence of living cells in the phloem. If the phloem is killed, translocation of organic material stops.

If a leaf manufactures carbohydrate in an experimental atmosphere containing radioactive carbon dioxide ($^{14}CO_2$), the radioactive sugar can be detected in the phloem both above and below the leaf. If the phloem below the leaf is killed by steam, the radioactive sugar can only be found above the leaf, indicating that the dead phloem has lost the ability to conduct sugar.

If a stem is 'ringed' by removing a complete ring of phloem and bark the passage of organic materials up or down the stem is prevented. This can be shown by the presence of radioactive sugar on one side of the ring only. It cannot pass across the ring in the absence of phloem.

TRANSPORT OF CHEMICALS APPLIED TO LEAVES

Some substances sprayed on to leaves can be absorbed and translocated about the plant, e.g. some pesticides (chemicals which kill pests). A systemic pesticide can be absorbed through the leaves and will be carried in the phloem to all parts of the plant. When, e.g., greenfly suck the sugary solution from the phloem in a shoot of the plant, they will take in the poison and die.

TRANSPORT IN ANIMALS

The components of an efficient circulatory system are:
1 a system of closed vessels (arteries, veins and capillaries);
2 a pump (the heart) with valves to ensure a one-way flow;
3 a circulatory fluid (blood).

BLOOD

Blood consists of about 55% fluid plasma and 45% cells. Plasma is a straw-coloured fluid consisting largely of water, with dissolved substances:

1 salts – hydrogencarbonates, phosphates, chlorides, sulphates, of sodium, calcium, potassium;
2 food substances – mainly glucose, fats and amino acids;
3 blood proteins – albumen, globulin and fibrinogen;
4 excretory substances, mainly urea;
5 hormones circulating from the glands which secrete them.

The blood cells are suspended in the **plasma**.

BLOOD CELLS

Red blood cells (erythrocytes)

Minute, biconcave disc-shaped cells (5 million per mm^3 blood) containing haemoglobin which carries oxygen from lungs to tissues. Shape and size gives them a very large surface area/volume ratio, ideal for rapid exchange of oxygen with the plasma. They have no nucleus and consequently a short life-span of about 3 months. They are destroyed by the liver and constantly replaced by cells in the bone marrow.

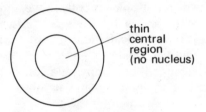

thin
central
region
(no nucleus)

Fig 5.13 A red blood cell

White blood cells (leucocytes)

There are about 8000–10 000 white cells per mm^3 blood (see Fig 5.14). They play a vital part in the defence of the body against disease (see p.139).

Phagocytes (phagocytic white cells) Ingest bacteria with pseudopodia and destroy them.

Lymphocytes Produce chemicals called antibodies which destroy or neutralize the disease organisms.

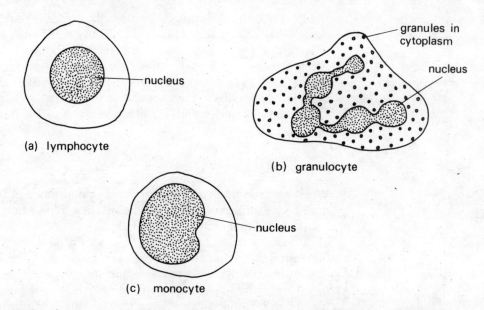

Fig 5.14 Types of white blood cell: (a) Lymphocyte. (b) Granulocyte. (c) Monocyte

Table 5.1 Types of white blood cell

White blood cells	Site of formation	Nucleus	Cytoplasm	Function
Lymphocyte	Lymph nodes	Round	No granules	Release of antibodies
Granulocyte	Bone marrow	Lobed	Contains granules	Phagocytosis
Monocyte	Bone marrow	Kidney-shaped	No granules	Phagocytosis

Platelets (thrombocytes)

These are very small fragments of cytoplasm without a nucleus. They are formed in the bone marrow and are vital for blood clotting.

BLOOD CLOTTING

Damage to a blood vessel causes release of an enzyme from platelets, starting a chain of reactions which result in a clot (see Fig 5.15).

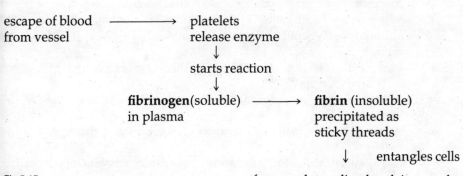

Fig 5.15

Blood will clot if it contacts any rough surface. The inside of blood vessels is normally very smooth, but if fatty substances are laid down in rough patches on the inside of vessels, blood may clot there, and either narrow the vessel more, or break off and lodge in another vessel, blocking it completely. Drugs called **anti-coagulants** are given to patients with this tendency.

Formation of a clot within a blood vessel is called **thrombosis** (see pp.100, 133).

BLEEDING

When an artery or a vein is damaged, blood flows out because it is under pressure, particularly in the arteries. Blood from a cut artery spurts out in time with the pulse beat, and is bright red (oxygenated). Flow from a cut vein is slower and steady and the blood is dark bluish-red (deoxygenated).

Clotting is a defence mechanism to stop the body losing too much blood and, when bleeding occurs, clotting is speeded up if the flow of blood can be stopped or slowed down. This is the principle behind the treatment of bleeding. Details of how to deal with bleeding may be found in any good manual of first aid.

FUNCTIONS OF BLOOD

1 Transport.
2 Homeostasis.
3 Temperature regulation.
4 Defence.

Transport

1 Oxygen from the lungs to the tissues. The red blood cells contain **haemoglobin** which picks up oxygen from the air in the lungs (see p.97)

$$haemoglobin + oxygen \rightleftharpoons oxyhaemoglobin$$

Oxygenated blood containing oxyhaemoglobin is carried to the tissues. Here, the lower oxygen concentration and high carbon dioxide concentration causes the unstable oxyhaemoglobin to give up oxygen to the cells. Haemoglobin is a respiratory pigment and, because of its affinity for oxygen, it increases the amount of oxygen the blood can carry.

2 Carbon dioxide from the tissues to the lungs as sodium hydrogen-carbonate (see pp.97, 99).
3 Absorbed food (glucose, fats, amino acids) from the intestine to the tissues.
4 Waste products from the tissues, e.g. urea from the liver, to the kidneys.
5 Hormones from endocrine glands to the tissues on which they act.

Homeostasis

The blood temperature, osmotic pressure, acidity and levels of substances such as sugar, hormones and salts, are kept at constant levels by the various processes of homeostasis. Thus the body tissues are supplied with a fluid of constant composition.

Temperature regulation

1 The blood distributes heat from active organs, which release much heat (liver, muscles), to the rest of the body.
2 By variations in the amount of blood flowing to the skin the amount of heat lost from the body can be changed according to the body temperature and external conditions (see p.153).

Defence against disease

1 Phagocytic action of white cells.
2 Antibodies produced from lymphocytes (see pp.128, 129).
3 Clotting (see p.129).

BLOOD GROUPS

Human blood can be any one of four types, depending on the presence or absence of two substances A and B on the red blood cell membranes. Other substances called anti-A and anti-B circulate in the plasma of some groups and can cause red blood cells to stick together in clumps if blood from different groups is mixed. Because of this effect A and anti-A never occur together naturally, and B and anti-B never occur together naturally.

When a patient needs a blood transfusion, his blood is carefully matched against the blood of the donor to check that it is **compatible**, i.e. that mixing the two bloods will not cause this clumping of red blood cells (with the resulting blockage of blood vessels and danger to the patient).

The features of each blood group are shown in Table 5.2. Blood groups are genetically controlled (see p.255).

Table 5.2 Blood groups in Man

Blood group	Substance on cell	Substance in plasma
A	A	Anti-B
B	B	Anti-A
AB	A and B	Neither anti-A nor anti-B
O	Neither A nor B	Anti-A and anti-B

CIRCULATION OF THE BLOOD

The **heart** is a four-chambered muscular pump forcing blood round a closed system of vessels. Valves ensure that blood flows in only one direction.

In a mammal the blood passes through the heart twice during each circulation of the body: once when returning from the lungs to the left side of the heart; and once returning from the body to the right side. This is called a **double circulation** (see Fig 5.16). The heart is divided down the middle to separate the oxygenated blood from the lungs from the deoxygenated blood returning from the body.

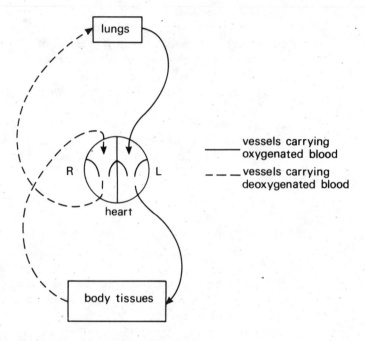

Fig 5.16 Double circulation in a mammal

The simplified diagram (Fig 5.17) shows the basic features of the structure of the heart. An accurate fully labelled drawing of the heart should be learnt (see Fig 5.18) – you may be expected to draw or label one.

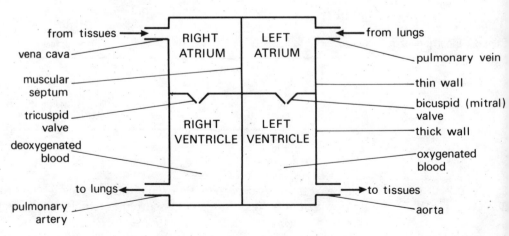

Fig 5.17 Diagrammatic representation of a mammalian heart

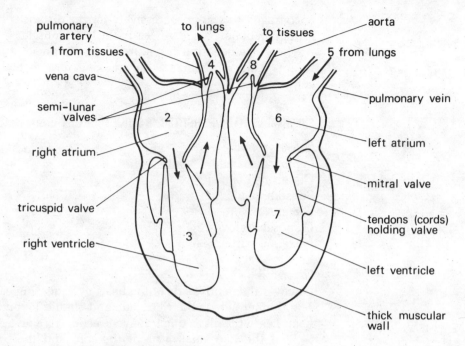

Fig 5.18 The mammalian heart

ACTION OF THE HEART (CARDIAC CYCLE)

The heart contracts rhythmically at an average of 70 beats per minute. Both atria (auricles) beat at the same time, followed by both ventricles. The sounds of the heart beat are caused by the closing of valves, produced by changes in pressure in the blood as the heart beats. The thick muscular walls of the ventricles produce a high pressure in the blood in the arteries leaving them. The functions of the various parts are annotated in Fig 5.17 and the path taken by blood during the cardiac cycle is shown by the numbers in Fig 5.18.

BLOOD SUPPLY TO THE HEART

The heart muscle is supplied with oxygen from the blood in the **coronary arteries**, which leave the aorta just above the semi-lunar valves, and run through the muscle of the heart wall, especially the ventricles.

Because the heart works continuously throughout life, it needs a constant oxygen supply, and it is important that the coronary arteries are kept open to maintain a good flow of blood carrying oxygen. Sometimes these arteries become narrowed, related perhaps to a high fat/sugar diet or smoking, and there is then a danger of **coronary thrombosis** occurring. A blood clot blocks the narrow artery, cutting off the blood supply to an area of heart muscle and causing severe pain and damage to the heart muscle. After recovery, the patient is encouraged to walk progressively longer distances to stimulate the formation of new blood vessels in the heart muscle.

There has been much research into the cause of heart disease in recent years, and links with smoking and diet are of particular concern.

EXPERIMENT TO INVESTIGATE THE STRUCTURE OF THE MAMMALIAN HEART

Materials needed
Lamb's heart.
Dissecting dish.
Scissors.
Forceps.
Disposable gloves.
Pasteur pipette.

Preparation
Discover the ventral side of the heart by squeezing each side in turn. The thinner side is the right side and should be on your left as the heart lies in the dissecting tray, ventral (lower) side up.

Find the two small atria at the top, and the coronary arteries running over the surface of the ventricles. Draw the heart to show as much as you can of its external features.

Opening the heart

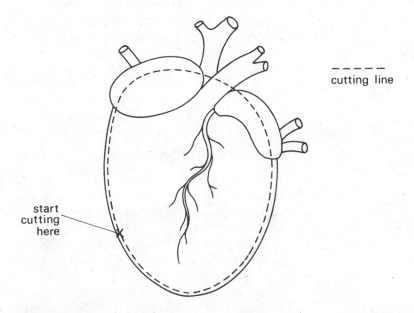

Fig 5.19 Opening up the heart

Cut along the equivalent of the dotted line in Fig 5.19, in order to free the ventral (upper) part of the heart from the lower. When you finish the cut, the upper and lower parts will still be joined by the thick wall of muscle (the septum) which separates right from left. Cut through this and lift off the upper part. You will now see the four chambers and main valves. Using Fig 5.18, identify as many parts as you can.

Feel the very smooth lining of the heart with your finger, and the strength of the cords holding down the mitral and tricuspid valves.

Identify the pulmonary artery and aorta and find the semi-lunar valves at their vase. Using the Pasteur pipette, squirt water against the valve from the ventricle and see what happens. Now squirt water on to the valve from the artery and see what happens. Write a note about the action of the valve.

Draw your dissection to show as much of the structure as you can.

EXPERIMENT TO INVESTIGATE THE EFFECT OF EXERCISE ON THE PULSE RATE AND RATE OF BREATHING

Draw a copy of Table 5.3 to record your results.

Table 5.3

1 Time (min)	2 Activity	3 Pulse rate (beats/min)	4 Breathing rate (breaths/min)
1	Rest		
2–3	Exercise		
4	Rest		
5	Rest		
6	Rest		
7	Rest		
8	Rest		
9	Rest		
10	Rest		

Work in pairs. The subject should be seated. Check that you can find your partner's pulse by feeling with two fingers on the inside wrist behind the thumb. Using a stop-clock, count the pulse for 30 seconds, while your partner counts his own breathing rate. Double both results to get the rate per minute, and enter in the table in columns 3 and 4 opposite minute 1.

Your partner now takes 2 minutes of exercise by running on the spot, and sits down again. Take the pulse and breathing rates as before for each of minutes 4–10 and enter in the table after doubling.

Change places and repeat the experiment.

Plot two graphs, of your partner's pulse and breathing rates, using time in minutes on the horizontal (x) axis and rate per minute on the vertical (y) axis.

Questions

1   What do you notice about the change in:
    (*a*)   pulse rate; and

(b)   breathing rate;
immediately after exercise?

2 Describe what happens to the breathing rate during the 7-minute period after exercise. Why is the breathing rate still above the resting rate, even though the subject is sitting down.

3 Describe what happens to the pulse rate after exercise. How does this change affect the blood pressure, and the rate at which blood moves to the muscles? Name two substances needed by muscles during exercise.

BLOOD SUPPLY TO THE ORGANS OF THE BODY

All organs are supplied with blood through an artery. After the exchange of materials between the blood and the tissue cells in the capillaries of the organ, the blood is collected into veins and returned to the heart.

The main blood vessels of the circulatory system are shown in Fig 5.20.

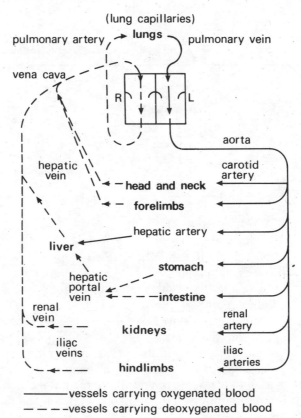

—————vessels carrying oxygenated blood
— — — —vessels carrying deoxygenated blood

Fig 5.20 Circulation and the main vessels in a mammal

BLOOD VESSELS

There are three main types of blood vessels. You should be familiar with their structural similarities and differences and their functions within the circulatory system.

Table 5.4 Comparison of arteries, veins and capillaries

Arteries	Veins	Capillaries
Wall thick	Wall thin	Wall one cell thick
Thick muscle layer	Thin muscle layer	No muscle
Elastic fibres	No elastic fibres	No elastic fibres
Carry blood away from heart	Carry blood towards heart	Link artery and vein
Blood flow rapid	Blood flow slow	Blood flow slowing
Low volume	Increased volume	High volume
High pressure	Low pressure	Falling pressure
No valves	Valves present	No valves
Pulse (wave of pressure due to heartbeat)	No pulse	No pulse
Blood oxygenated (except pulmonary artery)	Blood deoxygenated (except pulmonary vein)	Mixed oxygenated and deoxygenated blood

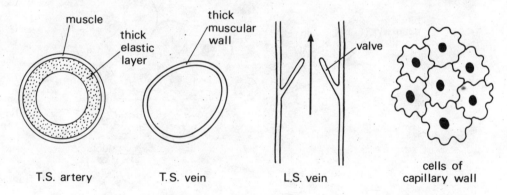

Fig 5.21 Blood vessels: (a) TS artery (b) TS vein (c) LS vein (d) Cells of capillary wall

Arteries break up into **arterioles** which lead to **capillaries**. These lead to **venules** which join up to form **veins**. The elastic walls of the arteries convert the irregular blood flow from the heart into a steady flow to the tissues. The capillaries are the site of exchange of substances between the blood and the tissues. Because they are so numerous, and their walls are thin and permeable, small-molecule substances can diffuse freely through the walls between the blood and the tissues. Blood is returned to the heart in veins by pressure produced by contraction of the skeletal muscles pressing on them from outside, and by breathing movements.

**EXCHANGE OF
SUBSTANCES BETWEEN
THE BLOOD AND THE
TISSUES**

In mammals all living cells are bathed in a fluid called **tissue fluid**. It forms a link between the blood and the cells. Materials (substances) moving between them must pass through tissue fluid but can only enter and leave the circulatory system through capillaries. (Why? See Table 5.4.)

Tissue fluid is formed at the arterial end of the capillaries where the high blood pressure forces fluid out through the thin walls of the capillaries into spaces between the cells. It is similar to plasma in containing oxygen, glucose and amino acids, but does not contain protein molecules because they are too large to pass through capillary walls. The cells absorb oxygen and food by diffusion and active transport, utilize them and pass waste products (and some protein) out into the tissue fluid.

At the venous end of the capillaries, some fluid flows back through the capillary walls carrying carbon dioxide and waste from cells into the blood (see p.99).

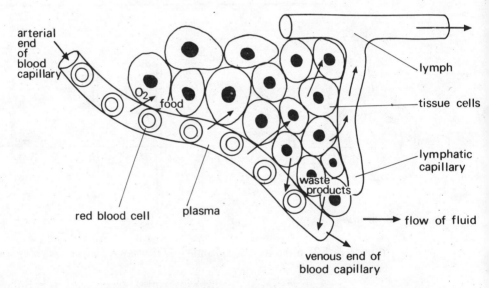

Fig 5.22 Exchange of substances between blood and tissues – formation of lymph

LYMPH

FORMATION OF LYMPH

Not all the fluid which leaves the capillary network is returned to the bloodstream. Some filters into small lymph capillaries and becomes lymph.

COMPOSITION OF LYMPH

It is similar to tissue fluid but contains some protein molecules. It is a watery solution of salts, sugars, amino acids, and contains proteins, fat droplets and some white blood cells, mainly lymphocytes.

LYMPHATIC SYSTEM

A system of vessels containing lymph supplies all parts of the body. The larger lymphatic vessels are similar to veins in structure and contain valves to direct the flow of lymph. At intervals along the vessels lie **lymph glands** or **nodes** in which the lymph flows through narrow channels lined with phagocytic cells. These ingest and destroy any bacteria present in the lymph. Lymph nodes often occur in groups, e.g. in the neck and abdomen. Other areas of lymphatic tissue occur in the tonsils and intestinal lining. The **lacteals** of the villi are part of the lymphatic system (see p.71).

All lymph drains into two main lymphatic ducts which join the veins of the neck where the fluid, originally filtered from the blood, is returned to it.

FUNCTIONS OF LYMPHATIC SYSTEM

1 Transfer of substances between tissues and blood.
2 Absorption of fat.
3 Destruction of bacteria by phagocytes.
4 Production of lymphocytes.

DEFENCE OF THE BODY AGAINST DISEASE

1 The prevention of entry into the body of disease organisms (**pathogens**) is by:
    (*a*)   impermeable epidermis of skin;
    (*b*)   healthy mucous membranes of nose and throat;
    (*c*)   cilia lining nose and trachea;
    (*d*)   bacteriocidal fluid in tears and nasal secretions;
    (*e*)   clotting of the blood.
2 The destruction of organisms occurs when:
    (*a*)   acid in gastric juice kills bacteria;
    (*b*)   phagocytic cells ingest bacteria – this is accomplished by the lymph nodes, the granulocytes and monocytes of blood, and by cells in the liver and spleen;
    (*c*)   through immunity.

IMMUNITY

The ability to resist pathogens may be active or passive.

Active immunity involves the production by the organism of antibodies. Pathogenic organisms entering the body act as **antigens**. They stimulate lymphocyctes to produce and release specific chemical substances called **antibodies**. These react with the antigen and destroy it or neutralize its effects. The ability to produce this antibody at a later date protects against a second attack by the same pathogen.

This natural immunity can be supplemented artificially in some cases by **immunization** (**vaccination**). Immunization is the introduction of antigens into the body by mouth or injection. Attenuated (weak) pathogens, heat-killed pathogens, or toxoids (destroyed bacterial toxins) may be used as antigens. Vaccination is a more effective and permanent form of immunization, e.g. measles, smallpox.

Passive immunity results from one organism containing antibodies derived from another organism, e.g. via placenta from mother to foetus, or injection of serum. It provides only short-term immunity but is useful in preventing epidemics.

KEY WORDS ▶

Vascular bundles	Leucocytes	Aorta
Translocation	Lymphocyte	Semi-lunar valves
Xylem	Granulocyte	Coronary arteries
Phloem	Monocyte	Coronary thrombosis
Stomata	Platelets	Arteries
Guard cells	Fibrinogen	Arterioles
Root hair	Fibrin	Capillaries
Endodermis	Anti-coagulant	Venules
Cortex	Thrombosis	Veins
Exodermis	Haemoglobin	Tissue fluid
Root pressure	Double circulation	Lymph
Potometer	Vena cava	Lymph glands
Wilting	Auricles	Lacteals
Water conservation	Tricuspid valve	Pathogens
Ions	Right ventricle	Immunity
Active transport	Pulmonary artery	Antigens
Blood	Pulmonary vein	Antibodies
Plasma	Left auricle	Immunization
Compatible	Mitral valve	Vaccination
Erythrocytes	Left ventricle	

1   Fig 5.23 shows two weight potometers set up with different types of plants.

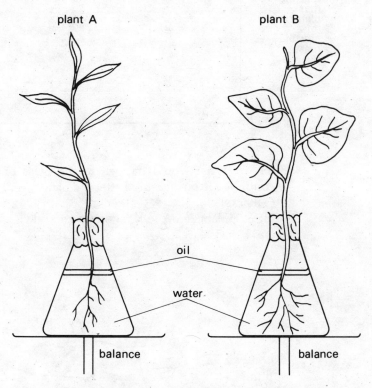

Fig 5.23

(a)   What do weight potometers measure? (1 mark)
(b)   Draw the axes of a graph as in Fig 5.24. On the graph draw two lines to show the change of mass you would expect for each potometer. The starting mass is already shown. Be sure to label the lines 'plant A' and 'plant B'. (2 marks)

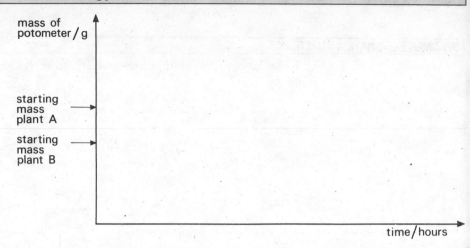

Fig 5.24

(c)　　What would happen to the mass of both potometers if it continued to be measured after the plants were put in the dark? (3 marks)　　　　　　　　　　　　　　　　[MEG]

2　Fig 5.25, labelled A to K, shows a ventral view of a mammalian heart and blood vessels.

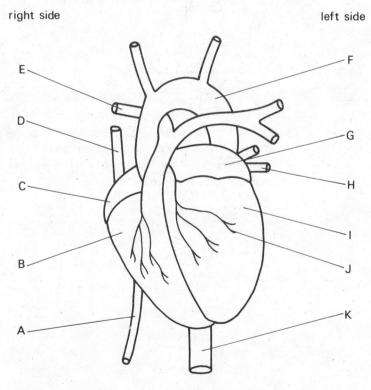

Fig 5.25

(a)　　State PRECISELY where the blood in D and E would go to next. (2 marks)

(b)   Write the letter of the part which contracts to send blood to the brain. (1 mark)

(c)   (i) What effect may heavy smoking have on J? (1 mark)

(ii) How may this affect the heart as a whole? (1 mark)

[*LEAG*]

3   Fig 5.26 shows a mammalian heart.

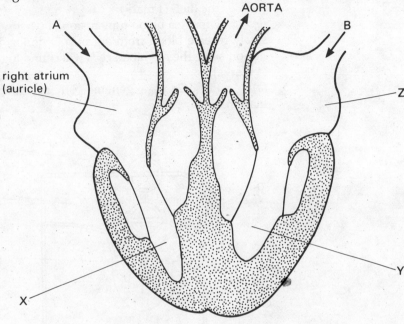

Fig 5.26

(a)   Name the chambers in the heart labelled X and Y. (2 marks)

(b)   Name the two blood vessels labelled A and B which bring blood to the heart. (2 marks)

(c)   State two differences in the composition of the blood in blood vessels A and B. (2 marks)

(d)   Why is the wall of the heart thicker in chamber Z than in chamber X? (2 marks)

(e)   (i) Through which blood vessels does the heart muscle receive its own blood supply? (1 mark)

(ii) Why should a blockage in these vessels cause a 'heart attack'? (4 marks)   [*NISEC*]

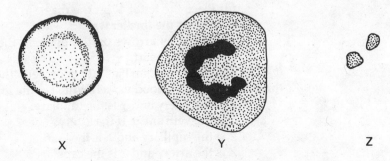

X   Y   Z

Fig 5.27

4 Fig 5.27 shows three types of structure (X, Y and Z) collected from healthy human blood.

(a) Give the letter of the structure which:

(i) increases in number at a site of bacterial infection, such as a pimple or boil; (1 mark)

(ii) will be reduced in number when there is a lack of iron in the diet. (1 mark)

(b) During a blood transfusion, a person with blood group A can safely receive blood from a group O donor, but not from a group B donor, since the red blood cells will clump together. Explain this. (4 marks)   [NEA]

5 (a) Fig 5.28 is a general plan of the circulatory system in a mammal.

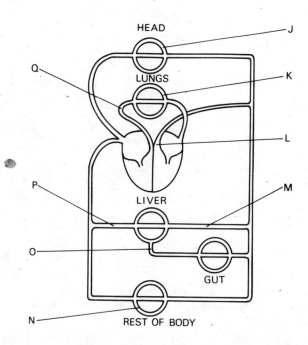

Fig 5.28

(i) Using the letters given on the diagram, identify the following parts of the circulatory system:
the hepatic artery;
the pulmonary artery.

(ii) Place the letter V on the diagram to indicate the ventricle which has the thicker wall.

(iii) Show by arrows on the diagram the circulation of blood through the heart.

(b) The diagrams in Fig 5.29 represent the appearance of the three main kinds of blood vessel. Which of the following is correct?

X is the artery and Y is the capillary.
Y is the vein and X is the artery.
Z is the capillary and X is the vein.
Z is the artery and Y is the capillary.   [SCE]

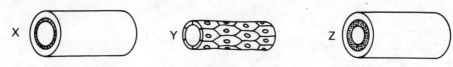

Fig 5.29

6   Fig 5.30 represents the relationship between blood capillaries, cells and lymph vessels (lymphatic capillaries).

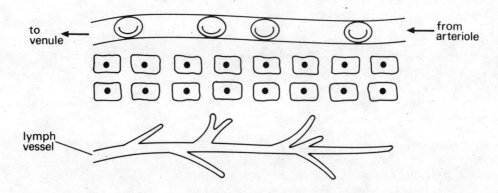

Fig 5.30

(a)   Label, on the figure, blood plasma, tissue fluid and lymph and indicate, with appropriate arrows, the direction of movement of these fluids in and between the capillaries, cells and lymph vessels. (4 marks)

(b)   (i) List four substances that move between the blood capillaries and the tissue fluid. (2 marks)
(ii) Explain the use made of ONE of these substances by the surrounding cells. (2 marks)

(c)   (i) Distinguish between clotting and clumping (agglutination) of blood. (2 marks)
(ii) Explain why a transfusion of group A blood to a group B patient is inadvisable. (1 mark)   [MEG]

HOMEOSTASIS, TEMPERATURE REGULATION, EXCRETION AND OSMOREGULATION

CONTENTS

Homeostasis The maintenance of a constant internal environment, despite changes in the external environment.

Excretion The removal from the body of the waste products of cell metabolism. (Do not confuse with egestion or secretion.)

Metabolism The chemical processes occurring in living organisms.

Ultra-filtration The passage of small molecules from the capillaries of the glomerulus of the kidney as a result of the high blood pressure within them. This process does not require energy.

Selective reabsorption The uptake of molecules required by the body, from the kidney tubules into the bloodstream. Energy is required for this process.

Osmoregulation The process by which a constant balance of osmotic pressure is maintained in the body of an organism.

Dialysis Selective diffusion of small molecules through a selectively permeable membrane.

HOMEOSTASIS

Homeostasis usually includes maintaining normal levels of salts, glucose, hormones, excretory products, pH value, osmotic pressure and, in birds and mammals, a constant body temperature.

The conditions under which cells work most efficiently are described as **optimum**. A change in pH or temperature may affect the enzymes in the cell and alter its metabolism. Each cell is responsible for its own 'internal environment', but it depends on a constant composition of the fluids surrounding it to function normally. Maintenance of a constant internal environment is an active process and uses energy. Its advantage is that it makes the functioning of the body independent of changes in the external environment. The maintenance of a constant body temperature in mammals is a good example of homeostasis.

TEMPERATURE REGULATION

SKIN

The largest organ in the body is the skin and one of its main functions in mammals is temperature regulation. Before considering this, its structure should be fully understood (see Fig 6.1). A knowledge of Fig 6.1 is important. Questions are often based on a similar diagram.

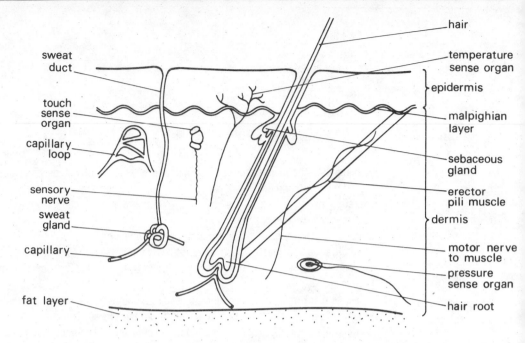

Fig 6.1 Mammalian skin

The skin consists of two layers, the **epidermis** and the **dermis.**

EPIDERMIS

This is a protective layer made up of stratified epithelial cells. These cells are continuously produced from the **Malpighian layer** which forms the boundary with the dermis. As new cells are produced, they move upwards through the epidermis because of the production of new cells from below.

A waterproof substance, **keratin**, is laid down in these cells, which become more flattened, lose their nuclei and finally die. They are eventually lost from the surface of the skin by friction. This constant replacement of cells is responsible for the ability of the skin to heal rapidly and to resist constant friction. The keratin waterproofs the epidermis, preventing loss of water from the surface of the living tissues below.

The epidermis is pierced by pores, which are the openings of sweat glands, and by the hair follicles. In some mammals most of the skin surface is covered by hair, which is insulating and which sometimes helps to camouflage the animals.

DERMIS

The dermis is the deeper layer of the skin, containing hair follicles, blood vessels, sweat glands, muscles and nerves. Beneath the dermis is a layer of fatty tissue. This protects delicate organs from blows, and acts as an insulator.

Hair follicles contain the shaft of the hair which is produced by the hair root at the base of the follicle. The upper part of the hair projects through the epidermis. Blood capillaries bring nourishment to the hair root. Opening into the hair follicle from the side are **sebaceous glands** which secrete an oily fluid, **sebum.** This keeps the follicle free from dust and bacteria, and spreads as a thin film over the surface of the hair. Attached to the base of the follicle is an **erector pili muscle.** This is attached to the underside of the epidermis at its other end, and when it contracts (shortens) it pulls the hair upright.

Sweat glands are coiled tubular glands lying in the dermis, with a long slender duct which carries sweat to the opening (pore) on the surface of the skin. The water, salts and urea which make up sweat are brought to them by capillaries.

The blood vessels of the dermis bring nourishment and oxygen to the tissues, and some play an important part in temperature regulation. There are many **capillary loops** just below the epidermis for this purpose (see Fig 6.3).

Motor nerves stimulate the glands and muscles, and sensory nerves run from skin sense organs to the brain.

SENSE ORGANS

The skin is a barrier between the body and the environment, and it is vital that changes in the environment can be detected rapidly. This is done by five types of sense organ – for heat, cold, pain, touch and pressure. The impulses from the heat and cold receptors are important in the regulation of body temperature.

EXPERIMENT TO INVESTIGATE THE EFFECTS OF CLOSE, SIMULTANEOUS STIMULI ON ARM AND FINGERTIP

Method
Working in pairs, the experimenter uses a pair of compasses to stimulate the skin of the subject's upper arm with either one point or two.

Starting with the compass points about 5 cm apart, the two points are pressed simultaneously on to the subject's skin; occasionally only one point is used. The subject cannot see the experiment, and each time is asked whether he/she can feel one point or two. The distance between the points is gradually reduced until the shortest distance is found at which the subject can accurately judge the number of points used.

The experiment is repeated on the fingertip. This enables a comparison to be made between the two skin areas as to the shortest distance at which identification of the number of points can be accurately made.

Results
The fingertips are much more sensitive to touch than the arm.

Conclusion
Sense organs are very close together on the fingertips. This makes perception of close stimuli much easier.

TEMPERATURE REGULATION IN MAMMALS

Mammals and birds have a constant body temperature. They are said to be **homoiothermic**. All other animals are **poikilothermic**, i.e. their body temperature varies with that of the environment, and with their degree of activity (see Fig 6.2).

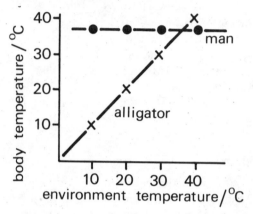

Fig 6.2 Relationship between body temperature and environmental temperature in Man and alligator

ADVANTAGES OF A CONSTANT BODY TEMPERATURE

1. Activity in animals depends on chemical changes (metabolism). Enzymes influence the rate of chemical change and are affected by temperature. A constant body temperature therefore allows animals to be equally active in winter, summer, day and night.
2. A constant body temperature makes an animal independent of the temperature of the environment. For example, polar bears, penguins and seals can inhabit very cold regions.

CONTROL OF BODY TEMPERATURE

Maintenance of a constant temperature depends on balancing heat production and heat loss, so that:

heat lost from body = heat gained by body

The hypothalamus in the brain controls temperature regulation. Nerves leave the hypothalamus and control the reactions of blood vessels, skin and muscles, to regulate heat gain and loss.

Heat production

The source of body heat is tissue respiration. When carbohydrate is broken down in the cells to release energy for movement and other vital processes, about one third of the energy is released as heat. This heat is circulated around the body by the bloodstream. The liver and muscles produce most heat, and the faster they work, e.g. during exercise and fever, the more heat they produce. Some heat is absorbed from the sun.

Heat loss

Heat is constantly lost from the skin by **convection**, **conduction** and **radiation**, and by evaporation of sweat from the skin and water from the lungs.

Some heat loss also takes place in expired air, faeces and urine. In man, in temperate regions, radiation is responsible for nearly half the heat loss from the skin. In very hot weather or during strenuous exercise, sweating is more important.

Sweat glands are supplied by blood capillaries, from which they extract water, salts and urea which together form **sweat.** The water evaporates from the surface of the skin taking **latent heat** and so cooling the body. In furry animals, e.g. the cat, sweat glands are restricted mainly to bare areas such as feet.

Heat produced by cells is carried to the skin by the circulating blood. The blood vessels of the skin (**cutaneous** vessels) play a vital part in temperature regulation. The blood flowing through them is cooled as heat escapes to the cooler air or water surrounding the animal.

Vasodilation

When the capillaries are dilated (enlarged – Fig 6.3(*a*)) the blood flow is increased, the skin becomes warm and red and more heat is lost.

Vasoconstriction

When the capillaries are constricted (narrow – Fig 6.3(*b*)) the blood flow is decreased, the skin becomes cool and pale and heat loss is reduced.

A thorough understanding of the role of these blood capillaries is recommended.

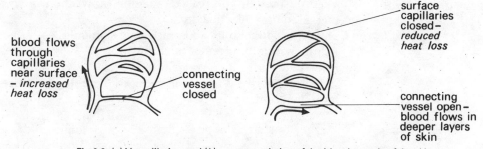

blood flows through capillaries near surface – *increased heat loss*

connecting vessel closed

surface capillaries closed – *reduced heat loss*

connecting vessel open – blood flows in deeper layers of skin

Fig 6.3 (*a*) Vasodilation and (*b*) vasoconstriction of the blood vessels of the skin

Specimen question As a result of vigorous exercise, the body of a man becomes hot and changes take place in the blood passing through the capillaries of the skin. Describe the changes and indicate their effects.

(*UCLES*)

INSULATION

All homoiothermic animals have some form of insulation in or on the skin, to cut down heat loss.

Fat layer

This is particularly thick in cold regions, e.g. blubber in whales in Antarctic seas.

Hair in mammals

The air trapped between the hairs is a good insulator. A thicker coat traps more air and is therefore warmer. Furry animals have a thicker coat in winter.

The thickness of the fur layer can be increased by contraction of small muscles at the base of the hairs – pulling them upright, so that more air is trapped between them. (In Man, this causes 'goose flesh'.) Beneath the outer feathers of birds there are many soft down feathers which trap air and so form a good insulating layer.

REGULATORY MECHANISMS

A rise in body temperature above the normal value, e.g. in Man 37 °C, produces the following responses.

1 Increased sweating.
2 Vasodilation – increased radiation, convection and conduction.
3 Reduced muscular activity.
4 Fewer clothes and reduced artificial heating.
5 Hair lies flat against skin.

Failure of above produces heat stroke, **hyperthermia**, then heat death.

A fall in body temperature below the normal value produces the following responses.

1 Sweating stops.
2 Vasoconstriction – decreased radiation, convection and conduction.
3 Increased muscular activity.
4 Shivering – involuntary contraction of skin muscles.
5 Additional clothing and artificial heating.
6 Hair stands on end – 'goose flesh'.

Failure of above results in reduced 'core' temperature, **hypothermia**, then cold death.

HYPOTHERMIA

If the body continues to lose heat faster than it gains heat, body temperature drops dangerously and hypothermia results. The subject becomes tired and weak and eventually becomes unconscious. Unless the body temperature is carefully restored to normal quite soon, heart failure may result. Exposure in cold wet conditions, particularly in a chilling wind, can cause hypothermia, but elderly people sitting inactively in inadequately heated rooms are equally at risk. It is important that elderly people, especially those who live alone, should be encouraged to make deliberate efforts to keep warm and to eat properly in cold weather. The expense of fuel and food is often a factor in hypothermia cases.

Out of doors, adequate protective clothing should always be worn in potentially exposed places. This should include several layers of warm clothing, topped by a windproof outer layer. The 'survival bags' made of aluminium foil, carried by some expeditions, surround the body with a windproof layer and enclose a layer of still air which is warmed by the body, thus reducing heat loss.

REVISION: FUNCTIONS OF MAMMALIAN SKIN

1 Protection against:
   (a)   loss of water;
   (b)   entry of disease organisms;
   (c)   friction;
   (d)   ultra-violet light (melanin);
   (e)   loss of heat (fat layer and hair).
2 Forms a flexible, slightly elastic covering for body, maintaining shape of body.
3 Temperature regulation by sweating, vasodilation and vasoconstriction.
4 Formation of vitamin D by action of sunlight.
5 Replacement of cells from Malpighian layer for rapid repair.
6 Contains sense organs of touch, heat, cold, pain and pressure.

THE LIVER AND HOMEOSTASIS

The liver is an important **homeostatic** organ. All absorbed food substances pass through the liver before reaching the tissues. This enables their levels to be regulated. (Summary of liver functions on p.72.)

REGULATION OF BLOOD SUGAR LEVEL

The level of sugar (mainly glucose) in the blood is maintained by two hormones, **insulin** and **adrenaline.**

A large amount of sugar enters the blood after a meal containing carbohydrate has been digested and absorbed. Blood sugar level rises, and insulin from the pancreas is secreted into the bloodstream to reduce the level. Insulin stimulates the change from glucose to glycogen, which is then stored in the liver. It also encourages the breakdown of sugar to produce energy in the muscles. Thus the extra sugar is either stored or used up. Between meals, adrenaline causes the slow release of sugar from liver glycogen, to replace that being used by the tissues.

BREAKDOWN OF HARMFUL SUBSTANCES

The liver is also important in homeostasis, in breaking down poisonous substances such as alcohol and drugs, a process called **detoxication.**

The liver completely destroys some drugs such as short-acting barbiturates; others, e.g. benzoic acid (a food preservative), it converts to substances which can be excreted by the kidney.

The liver can be damaged by alcohol, chloroform, carbon tetrachloride (dry-cleaning fluid), but it can generally resist such damage if it has a sufficient store of glycogen and amino acids. Severe damage only occurs if the intake into the body of such toxic substances is very high.

EXCRETION

The removal of waste products of metabolism is a vital part of homeostasis since it prevents the accumulation of substances which are toxic or would eventually interfere with the normal function of body cells.

EXCRETORY PRODUCTS OF ANIMALS

There are three main excretory products in animals – carbon dioxide, water and nitrogenous compounds.

Carbon dioxide and water are formed as a result of tissue respiration.

$$\text{glucose} + \text{oxygen} \rightarrow \text{carbon dioxide} + \text{water} + \text{energy}$$

In mammals, the main nitrogenous waste product is **urea.** It is soluble, and relatively non-toxic. Urea is derived from excess or unusable protein in the diet and from the breakdown of damaged and dead cells. This protein is broken down into amino acids and **deaminated** by the liver. The amino group ($-NH_2$) is removed from the amino acids and converted into urea:

$$\text{protein} \rightarrow \text{amino acids} \xrightarrow[\text{(liver)}]{\text{deamination}} \text{amino group} \rightarrow \text{urea}$$

Most waste products containing nitrogen are toxic (poisonous) so must be eliminated quickly and efficiently.

MAMMALIAN EXCRETORY ORGANS

The main organs of excretion in a mammal are the lungs, skin, liver and kidneys.

LUNGS

Carbon dioxide is excreted by the lungs. It diffuses out of the blood into the air in the alveoli of the lungs and is breathed out with the expired air. Some water is lost in this way.

SKIN

Large quantities of sweat are secreted by the skin. The main purpose of this is loss of heat during evaporation, as part of the temperature-regulating mechanism of the body. However, some excess water, salts and urea are excreted in the sweat.

LIVER

Deamination of excess amino acids occurs here and urea is produced as described earlier. Another main function of the liver is the breakdown of worn red blood cells. The iron in the haemoglobin is used to make new red blood cells and the waste remaining forms **bile pigments**, which are excreted in the bile and lost from the body in the faeces.

Many candidates are confused as to which organ is responsible for urea formation; it is often asked in questions. Remember that it is the liver.

KIDNEYS

The kidneys of a mammal excrete nitrogenous waste, e.g. urea, and excess mineral salts, and are responsible for the osmoregulation of blood.

Structure of the mammalian kidney

The kidneys are two bean-shaped organs lying against the dorsal side of the abdominal cavity. They are dark red in colour because of the large amount of blood they contain. Each kidney is surrounded by a fibrous **capsule** which maintains its shape. Three vessels join the kidney at the **hilum**, which is the indentation.

1 The **ureter** carries urine to the bladder.
2 The **renal artery** carries blood to the kidney.
3 The **renal vein** carries blood away from the kidney (see Fig 6.4).

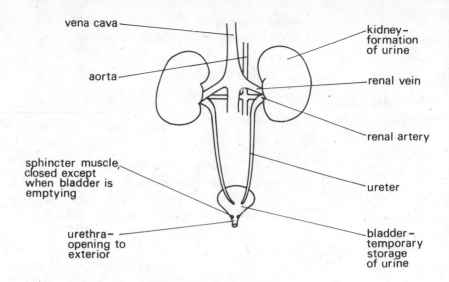

Fig 6.4 The urinary system of a mammal

Internally the kidney is divided into a darker outer **cortex** and a lighter inner **medulla.** In Man, the medulla extends inwards to form 15–16 **pyramids.** The **collecting ducts,** which carry the **urine** towards the ureter, open into the **pelvis** at the tips of the pyramids (see Fig 6.5).

The urine is formed by the **nephrons** or kidney tubules (uriniferous tubules). There are about 1 million nephrons in each kidney in Man. They lie mainly in the cortex.

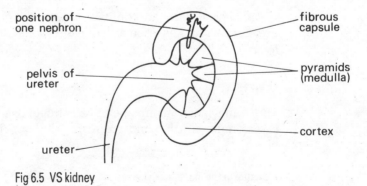

Fig 6.5 VS kidney

Nephron

Each nephron consists of a cup-shaped hollow **Bowman's capsule,** and a long narrow tubule leading to a collecting duct (see Fig 6.6). The tubule is divided into three regions with different functions: **first convoluted tubule, the loop of Henlé** and the **second convoluted tubule.** The nephron is supplied with blood at high pressure by an **arteriole,** which breaks up into a knot of capillaries called a **glom-**

erulus. This lies in the cup of Bowman's capsule. Bowman's capsule and a glomerulus have walls only one cell thick (see Fig 6.7).

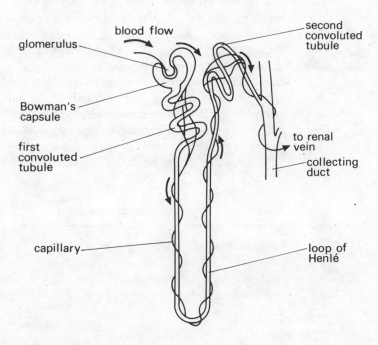

Fig 6.6 A nephron

It is important that you understand the *structure* of the kidney and nephron because only then can you fully appreciate how it functions.

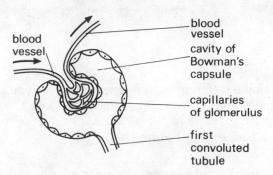

Fig 6.7 Glomerulus and Bowman's capsule

Urine formation

From the Bowman's capsule the arteriole breaks up into capillaries which twine round the nephron, allowing reabsorption of substances to take place from the nephron to the blood. Urine formation takes place in two stages.

1 **Ultra-filtration** in the Bowman's capsule. Blood runs to the glomerulus through an arteriole which supplies blood at high pressure. The blood pressure forces fluid and all dissolved substances with small molecules, e.g. urea, glucose, mineral salts and water, through the capillary walls of the glomerulus and into the cavity of the Bowman's capsule. Proteins are too large to pass out of the blood. This fluid is called **glomerular filtrate.**

2 **Selective reabsorption** in other parts of the nephron. The glomerular filtrate flows along the narrow tubule of the nephron, and substances useful to the body are reabsorbed into the capillaries surrounding the tubule. The excretory materials and excess water left in the tubule are excreted as urine.

    The regions of the nephron absorb different substances, as shown in Table 6.1.

Table 6.1 Details of selective reabsorption

Region	Substances reabsorbed	Notes
First convoluted tubule	Glucose, amino acids, water	Uptake by active transport against concentration gradient; energy required
Loop of Henlé	Water	Important to terrestrial organisms
Second convoluted tubule	Water and salts	Regulation of blood pH and osmoregulation according to water supply to organism (see p.163)

Man eliminates an average of 1500 cm^3 of urine per day. This is mostly water (96%), urea and uric acid (2%) and sodium and potassium salts (2%). Urine passes out of the body as follows:

collecting ducts → pelvis → ureter → muscular bladder → **urethra**
(stored)   (during urination)

Diabetes

People suffering from a lack of the hormone **insulin** have an abnormally high level of glucose in their blood. They suffer from an illness called **diabetes mellitus.** The excess glucose is excreted by the kidney and appears in the urine (see p.155).

EXPERIMENT TO INVESTIGATE THE PRESENCE OF SUGAR AND PROTEIN IN LIQUIDS USING LABSTIX TEST

Method

A reducing-sugar labstix is dipped into the liquid to be tested in a test tube. The colour is allowed to develop and is compared with the colour chart on the labstix label. The percentage of reducing sugar present is recorded.

Using the protein labstix, a second sample of liquid is tested, and the percentage of protein present is recorded after comparing with the colour chart for protein.

Interpretation

If the liquid tested is urine, there should be no glucose or protein present.

Revision: functions of the mammalian kidney

1 Excretion of nitrogenous waste, mainly urea.
2 Elimination of excess amounts of normal substances from the blood, e.g. glucose.
3 Elimination of abnormal substances from the blood, e.g. alcohol, drugs, toxins in disease.
4 Maintenance of the pH of the blood.
5 Maintenance of the osmotic pressure of the blood.
6 Regulation of the salt content of the blood.
7 Elimination of hormones from the blood.

Kidney failure

Because of its important function in homeostasis, the normal functioning of the kidney is vital to life. One normal kidney is usually enough to support health, but if both kidneys fail, their function must be replaced, by either **dialysis** or a **transplant.**

Dialysis

A kidney machine works on the principle of dialysis. The patient's blood is passed through the machine on one side of a dialysis membrane, which allows small molecules to pass through but not large molecules. The blood is separated by the membrane from an artificial 'perfect plasma' solution, which contains the right balance of all the small molecule substances normally present in healthy blood.

As the blood flows through the machine, the fluid flows in the opposite direction on the other side of the membrane. Diffusion of all small molecules such as urea, mineral salts and sugars takes place

Fig 6.8 Basic features of dialysis

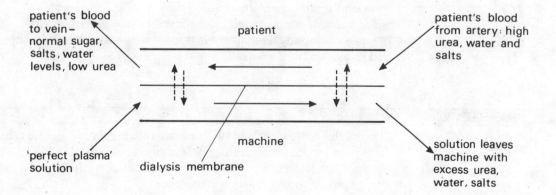

patient's blood to vein – normal sugar, salts, water levels, low urea

patient

patient's blood from artery: high urea, water and salts

'perfect plasma' solution

dialysis membrane

machine

solution leaves machine with excess urea, water, salts

across the membrane between the blood and the solution, so that waste products, especially urea, which are in high concentration in the blood, are removed from it and the concentration of salts, sugars and amino acids is adjusted to that of the 'ideal solution'.

Kidney transplants

A more permanent treatment for kidney failure is to transplant a healthy kidney from a donor into the abdomen of the patient and connect it surgically to the renal artery and vein and ureter, so that it can perform normal kidney function.

The problem with organ transplants is tissue rejection. In this the defence mechanisms of the body identify the transplanted kidney as 'foreign', and reject it. To avoid this, it is vital that the donor's tissues are chemically as similar as possible to the patient's tissues. This is done by 'tissue matching', which is similar to blood group matching for blood transfusions but more complex. At the time of the transplant, and for a short while afterwards, the patient's defence reactions are reduced by drugs so that the transplanted kidney can be accepted. This does mean that for a time the patient is more likely to suffer serious infections, and so must be isolated in a germ-free environment.

EXCRETION IN PLANTS

Plants make their own proteins by combining mineral salts, especially nitrates, with carbohydrates formed in the leaves during photosynthesis. They do not therefore have an excess of unwanted proteins because they only manufacture what they need. There is virtually no nitrogenous excretion in flowering plants.

Waste materials of metabolism can be eliminated as follows.

1 Carbon dioxide formed in respiration is used up during daylight in photosynthesis. During darkness it diffuses out of the leaf through the partially closed stomata.
2 Water formed in respiration may be used by the plant in photosynthesis. Excess is lost by evaporation from the stomata.
3 Oxygen is a product of photosynthesis. In daylight the plant produces an excess of oxygen which diffuses across the leaf and out through the stomata to the atmosphere.
4 Some minor waste materials are deposited as solids inside cells.
5 In some deciduous trees waste is transferred to leaves in the autumn and lost when the leaves fall.

OSMOREGULATION

Living cells are surrounded by a delicate cell membrane, across which osmosis may occur. Since the cell is easily damaged by either excess, or too little, water, it is vital that the fluid surrounding the cells should have a constant osmotic pressure.

For instance, mammalian red blood cells, if placed in a very weak salt solution, will absorb water by osmosis and the delicate cell membrane will burst, thus preventing the cells from carrying oxygen. In the body the red blood cells are surrounded by plasma, whose water potential is constantly regulated, thus protecting the red blood cells from damage.

In very small organisms like *Amoeba*, with no blood or tissue fluids, each cell must maintain its own osmotic balance.

OSMOREGULATION IN PROTOZOA

In *Amoeba*, living in fresh water, there is a tendency for water to enter the cytoplasm by osmosis through the selectively permeable cell membrane (see Fig 6.9(*a*)). If uncontrolled, this would cause the *Amoeba* to swell and, ultimately, to burst.

The amount of water in the cell is controlled by the **contractile vacuole**. Excess water collects in the contractile vacuole and is expelled at intervals through the cell membrane, thus maintaining the osmotic balance (see Fig 6.9(*b*)).

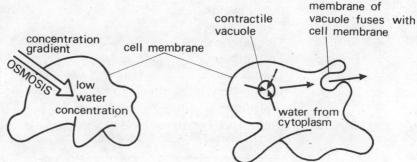

Fig 6.9 Amoeba: (*a*) water entry by osmosis, (*b*) contractile vacuole

OSMOREGULATION IN PLANT CELLS

Plant cells have, in addition to a cell membrane, a strong, slightly flexible cellulose wall. When the cell absorbs water and swells, the cell wall stretches slightly until the cell becomes turgid (see pp.202, 204). At this point, the tension in the cell wall is sufficient to stop the entry of any more water, and the cell is protected from bursting.

OSMOREGULATION IN MAMMALS

The second convoluted tubule of the nephron in a mammalian kidney reabsorbs water from the fluid in the nephron into the blood. The amount of water reabsorbed and the concentration of urine varies according to the need of the body for water.

When the body is short of water, more water is reabsorbed and less is excreted. Thus on a hot dry day, when a lot of water has been lost in sweating, the urine will be concentrated and small in volume.

When there is too much water in the body, the tubule absorbs less and more water is lost in the urine. This variation in the amount of water lost in the urine maintains a constant water balance in the body.

KEY WORDS ▶

Homeostasis	Cutaneous	Pyramids
Excretion	Vasodilation	Collecting ducts
Metabolism	Vasoconstriction	Urine
Epidermis	Hyperthermia	Pelvis
Malpighian layer	Hypothermia	Nephron
Keratin	Insulin	Bowman's capsule
Dermis	Adrenaline	Convoluted tubules
Hair follicles	Detoxication	Loop of Henlé
Sebaceous glands	Urea	Arteriole
Sebum	Deamination	Glomerulus
Erector pili muscles	Lungs	Ultrafiltration
Sweat glands	Skin	Glomerular filtrate
Capillary loops	Liver	Selective
Homoiothermic	Bile pigments	reabsorption
Poikilothermic	Capsule	Active transport
Convection	Hilum	Urethra
Conduction	Ureter	Diabetes
Radiation	Renal	Dialysis
Sweat	Cortex	Osmoregulation
Latent heat	Medulla	Contractile vacuole

1   Fig 6.10 shows a vertical section of human skin.

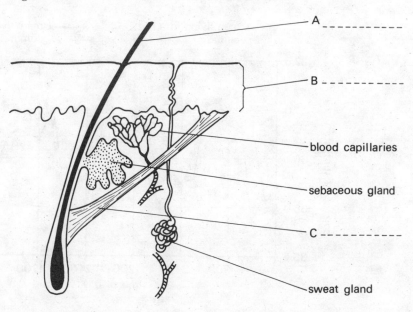

A - - - - - - - - - - -

B - - - - - - - - - - -

blood capillaries

sebaceous gland

C - - - - - - - - - - -

sweat gland

Fig 6.10

(a)   Name the parts A, B and C.   (3 marks)
(b)   After running a race, your skin is wet and your face is hot.
(i) Why is your skin wet and how does this help to cool your body?   (4 marks)
(ii) Why is your face hot and how does this help to cool your body?   (4 marks)
(c)   How do you think the sebaceous glands help to keep hair and skin healthy?   (3 marks)   [LEAG]

2   **EITHER**
(a)   Explain how the skin helps to return body temperature to normal after vigorous exercise.   (14 marks)
OR
(b)   Explain how urea passes from the liver where it is made to the bladder.   (14 marks)   [LEAG]

3 Fig 6.11 shows the mean body temperatures of two groups of men over a period of four days. Both groups did the same work. One group lived in a cool climate, the other in a hot climate.

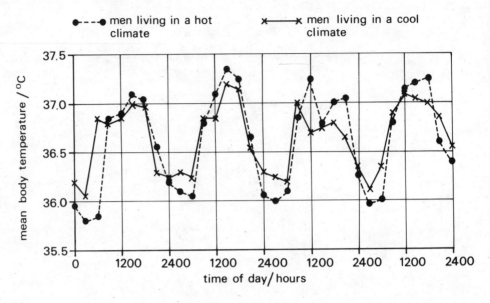

Source: *Man – Hot and Cold* by Otto G. Edholm

Fig 6.11

Write down five things that the graph tells you about changes in body temperature.   (5 marks)   [SEG]

4 Fig 6.12 shows a section through a mammal's kidney.

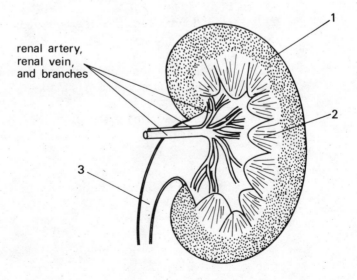

Fig 6.12

(a)   Name the parts 1, 2 and 3.   (3 marks)
(b)   Table 6.2 gives information about the human kidney.

Table 6.2

Rate of blood flow in kidneys	Rate of filtration into kidney tubules (nephrons)	Rate of urine passing out of kidneys
1.2 dm³ per minute	0.12 dm³ per minute	1.5 dm³ per day

(i) What percentage of blood passing into the kidney is filtered into the kidney tubules?   (1 mark)
(ii) Where in the kidney (part 1, 2 or 3 on Fig 6.12) does filtration take place?   (1 mark)
(iii) About 172 dm³ are filtered from the blood into the kidney tubules per day, yet only 1.5 dm³ of urine are excreted. What happens to the other 170.5 dm³   (2 marks)   [SEG]

5   Table 6.3 includes information about the percentages of various substances present in blood plasma, the filtrate in the kidney tubules (nephrons) and in the urine. It also shows concentration factors for substances present in the urine.

Table 6.3

Substances	% in plasma	% in filtrate in nephron	% in urine	Concentration factor
Water	90–3	90–3	95.0	
Protein	7.0	0	0	
Glucose	0.1	0.1	0	
Sodium ions	0.3	0.3	0.35	× 1.0
Chloride ions	0.4	0.4	0.6	× 1.5
Urea	0.03	0.03	2.0	× 60.0
Uric acid	0.004	0.004	0.05	× 12.0
Creatinine	0.001	0.001	0.075	× 75.0
Ammonia	0.001	0.001	0.04	× 40.0

Answer the following questions.
(a)   (i) Which substance, filtered into the kidney tubules, is reabsorbed into the blood?   (1 mark)
(ii) State your reasons, based upon the evidence in Table 6.3. (2 marks)
(b)   (i) Which substance is not filtered from the blood plasma? (1 mark)
(ii) Name ONE example of this substance found in the plasma.   (1 mark)
(iii) State ONE reason why the process of filtration does not occur with this substance.   (1 mark)
(c)   The concentration of substances in the urine is much greater than in either the plasma or in the filtrate. In the case of urea this may be 60 times greater. Account briefly for this increase in solute concentration.   (3 marks)   [MEG]

6   Fig 6.13 illustrates the principle of an artificial kidney machine. The blood of a patient flows on one side of a partially permeable mem-

brane and dialysing fluid flows on the other side. The dialysing fluid has a composition and concentration equal to that of the plasma of a normal person.

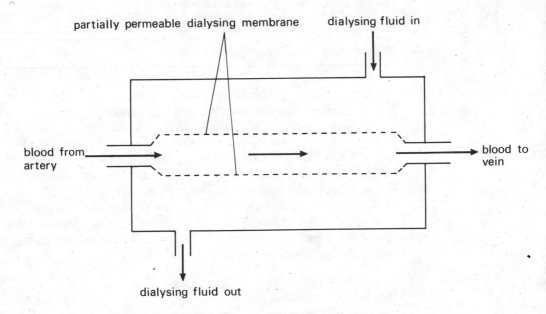

Fig 6.13

(a)   What process causes excess water from the patient to pass into the dialysing fluid?   (1 mark)

(b)   (i) Name an excretory product, other than water, which will pass out of the blood into the dialysing fluid.   (1 mark)
(ii) Name the process by which this occurs.   (1 mark)

(c)   Explain why, in the case of permanent kidney failure, it is more economic and more satisfactory to a patient to be given a kidney transplant rather than treatment with an artificial kidney.   (2 marks)

[*NEA*]

COORDINATION

Irritability The ability, shown by living organisms, to respond to a stimulus.

Homeostasis The maintenance of a constant internal environment, despite changes in the external environment.

Tropism A growth movement (response) by part of a plant in a direction determined by the direction of the stimulus.

Neurone A nerve cell.

Synapse The junction between one nerve cell and another or between nerve cell and effector.

Reflex action and **reflex arc** An involuntary response to a stimulus and the nerve pathway taken from receptor to effector in a specific reflex action.

Receptor A structure capable of converting a stimulus into an electrical impulse.

Effector A structure capable of converting the electrical energy of a nerve impulse into a response.

Drug A chemical substance taken to bring about a change in a natural process in the body.

Hormone A specific chemical substance produced in animals by an endocrine gland. It enters the circulatory system and passes to a cell, tissue or organ, where it produces a specific response.

Gland A structure capable of secreting a chemical substance.

Behaviour The way in which an organism responds to a stimulus.

Taxis The movement of a whole organism in response to a directional stimulus.

IRRITABILITY, STIMULI AND COORDINATION

Irritability is a characteristic of all living organisms. It is the means by which they respond to stimuli in order to maintain the best conditions for life.

Stimuli are produced by changes in the environment, e.g. sound waves, temperature change. Many stimuli are forms of energy. They are detected by specialized regions of organisms called receptors, which may be situated inside or outside the organism. **Receptors** detect stimuli and set up an electrical current which travels as a nerve

Fig 7.1

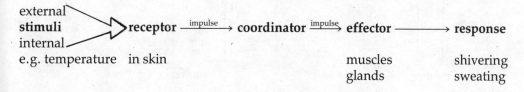

impulse to an effector which produces the appropriate **response** (see Fig 7.1). The type of response and its extent and duration are all directly related to the nature of the stimulus.

Coordination is the process whereby the organism makes the correct response at the correct time to the given stimulus. It has an important role in allowing the organism to adapt to change and increase its chances of survival. Mechanisms of coordination maintain the functioning of organisms at a constant level. These processes are therefore **homeostatic.**

Coordination in plants is controlled by **hormones.** In animals it is under the control of hormones and nerves.

PLANT RESPONSES

This is a favourite topic with examiners, so learn it very well, especially the experimental evidence and the explanation of phototropism and geotropism. A typical question on this topic is given below.

Specimen question How do the shoots (or coleoptiles) of plants respond to light reaching them from one side only? Describe the mechanism by which these changes are brought about.   [*UCLES*]

Fig 7.2 Regions of sensitivity in a shoot

This type of question may be answered by using the following information.

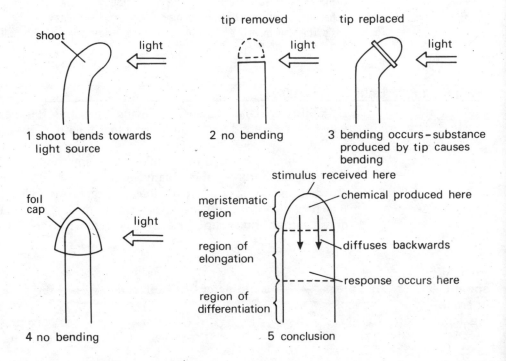

Plants respond to stimuli by the production and/or release of a chemical substance which functions as a hormone. These substances are involved in root and shoot growth, in flowering and leaf-fall and they produce the growth responses made to light and gravity. The commonest plant growth substances are called auxins, e.g. indole acetic acid (IAA). They are produced at the tips of shoots and roots. They stimulate growth by increasing the rate of cell elongation in the region just behind the shoot tip. In the case of root tips, auxins may inhibit growth.

The regions of sensitivity to stimulus and response can be demonstrated by the experiments shown in Fig 7.2.

Plants respond to light, gravity, temperature, water, chemicals and touch. Most responses are bending movements produced by cell elongation in the growth region behind the stem or root tip.

TROPISM

A tropic movement is a growth movement by part of a plant in a direction determined by the direction of the stimulus. This may be *towards* the stimulus (**positive tropism**), or *away from* it (**negative tropism**). The type of tropic movement depends upon the nature of the stimulus, e.g. positive phototropism – growth towards light.

PHOTOTROPISM

This is a growth movement produced in response to light by most shoots (stems and coleoptiles). The normal response is positive phototropism, i.e. bending towards the light stimulus.

EXPERIMENT TO INVESTIGATE THE EFFECT OF LIGHT ON GERMINATING OAT SEEDLINGS

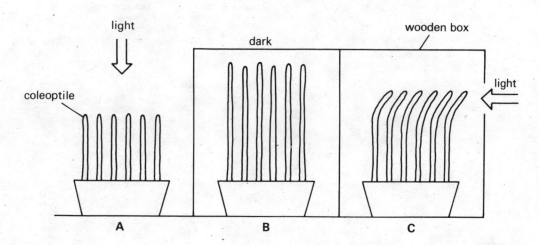

Fig 7.3

Apparatus
See Fig 7.3.

Method
Oat seedlings are planted in moist compost in three pots and set up in the apparatus and under the light conditions shown in Fig 7.3.

Results
After 10 days the coleoptiles grow as shown.

Conclusions
Normal upward growth occurs in pot **A** due to equal illumination from above. Excessive growth occurs in pot **B** due to lack of light. Bending of the coleoptiles towards light occurs in pot **C** when illuminated from one side only.

Light either destroys auxins or causes them to accumulate on the dark side of the shoot. The above results can be explained by Fig 7.4.

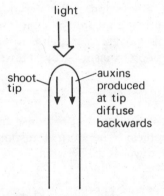

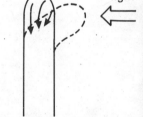

1 equal illumination on all sides
2 even distribution of auxins
3 shoot green and sturdy
4 normal growth upwards

1 total darkness
2 no inhibition of auxin activity
3 increased growth upwards
4 stem yellow and spindly
5 long internodes
6 this is **etiolation**

1 unilateral light stimulus
2 accumulation of auxin on dark side
3 unequal growth
4 bending towards light

Fig 7.4 Explanation of phototropism

EXPERIMENT TO INVESTIGATE THE RESPONSES OF INTACT AND DECAPITATED COLEOPTILES TO UNI-DIRECTIONAL LIGHT

Apparatus
See Fig 7.5.

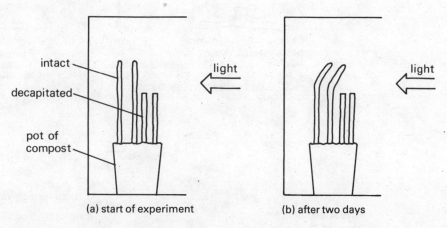

(a) start of experiment   (b) after two days

Fig 7.5 (a) At the start of the experiment. (b) After 2 days

Method
Twenty-four coleoptiles are grown from the same batch of seed. Twelve of the coleoptiles have the top 0.5 cm removed when they are 2.5 cm long. The intact and decapitated coleoptiles are placed in a light-proof box illuminated by light from one direction only and grown for a further two days, as shown in Fig 7.5.

Results
All the intact coleoptiles grow in the direction of the light source. The decapitated coleoptiles continue to grow upwards.

Conclusion
Decapitated coleoptiles are unable to respond to uni-directional light by growing towards it.

GEOTROPISM

This is a growth movement produced in response to gravity by shoots and roots. Shoots are negatively geotropic and roots are positively geotropic.

These opposite growth effects may be explained in terms of the different responses shown by shoots and roots to auxins, as shown in Fig 7.7.

A **clinostat**, by eliminating the effects of gravity, may be used to demonstrate that tropisms result from unilateral stimuli. Germinating seedlings are rotated slowly so that gravity exerts its effects on all

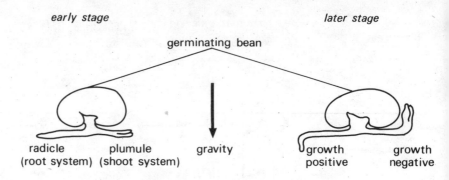

Fig 7.6 Demonstration of geotropism

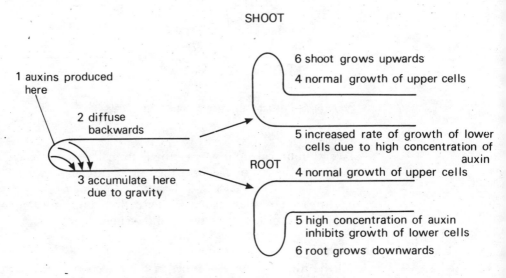

Fig 7.7 Explanation of geotropism

sides of the root in turn. Their radicles grow horizontally. The radicles of seedlings grown in a control clinostat, which is not rotating, grow downwards. This shows that these growth movements are made in response to gravity.

THE ANIMAL NERVOUS SYSTEM

In most animals the nervous system is composed of the central nervous system (**CNS** – brain and spinal cord) and the nerves connecting it to receptors (sense cells) and effectors (muscles and glands). This system allows coordination between stimulus and response.

The basic unit of the nervous system is the **neurone** (nerve cell).

There are three types of neurones, **sensory**, **intermediate** and **motor**, sharing the same basic function of transmitting electrical impulses. They vary in structure and are found in different regions of the nervous system (see Figs 7.8 and 7.9).

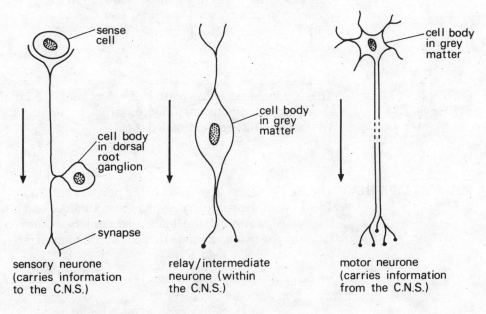

Fig 7.8 Types of neurones

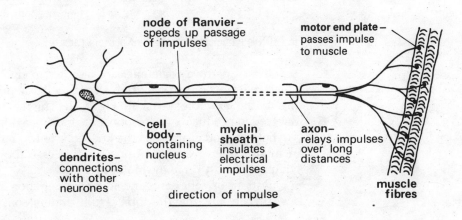

Fig 7.9 Motor neurone

NERVE IMPULSE AND SYNAPSE

Information passes from receptor to effector along nerves. A **nerve** is a collection of **nerve fibres**. Information is transmitted as a nerve impulse. A nerve impulse passes along an axon at a very high speed as a weak electric current. At the ending of each neurone there is a gap, called a **synapse**, between it and the next neurone or an effector. When a nerve impulse reaches a synapse it causes the release of small amounts of a chemical substance called a **transmitter substance.** This either sets up a nerve impulse in the connecting neurone, causes contraction of a muscle effector or secretion by a gland. Some transmitter substances act as hormones, e.g. adrenaline.

CENTRAL NERVOUS SYSTEM

This is composed of the brain and spinal cord. All information from the external and internal environments passes through the CNS, where reactions are coordinated.

REFLEX ARC AND REFLEX ACTION

The simplest form of reaction in the nervous system is a reflex action. This is a rapid involuntary response to a stimulus and is not under the conscious control of the brain (involuntary action). The pathway taken by the nerve impulses in reflex action forms a reflex arc.

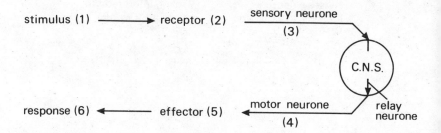

Fig 7.10 Diagrammatic representation of a reflex arc

The basic pathway of a reflex arc is shown in Fig 7.10 in the order in which reflex action is produced. Learn the basic principle and relate this to the example given in Fig 7.11. This shows the reflex arc involved in producing the response to pricking a finger on a pin.

Another good example is the knee jerk reflex, but it does not have an intermediate (relay) neurone. In this case the sensory neurone synapses directly on to the motor neurone.

Questions on reflex arcs and action are common in examinations. It is worth checking that this topic is fully understood.

Specimen question

(a)   What is a reflex action?   (3 marks)
(b)   Draw a large, clearly annotated diagram to show how reflex action is brought about in response to a painful stimulus.   (14 marks)

[*ULSEB*]

An answer to each of these questions should include the information given above.

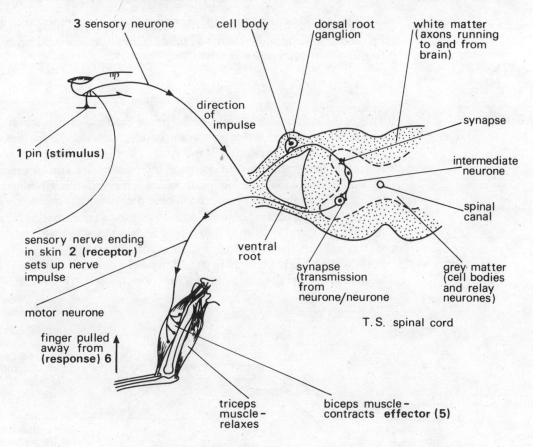

Fig 7.11 Reflex arc and reflex action

Simple reflex arcs allow the body to make automatic adjustments (involuntary) to changes in:

1 the external environment, e.g. iris–pupil reflex, balance during loco-motion;
2 the internal environment, e.g. breathing rate, blood pressure, and to prevent damage to the body, e.g. cuts, burns.

CONDITIONED REFLEXES

These are reflex actions where the type of response is modified by past experience. **Learning** forms the basis of conditioned reflexes, e.g. toilet training, awareness of danger, conscience, salivation on sight and smell of food.

In animals with a well-developed central nervous system, neurones send impulses from the sensory/intermediate synapse to the brain. Information stored here from past experiences allows a decision to be made concerning the nature of the response. Excitatory neurones carry impulses back to the motor neurone cell body of that reflex arc and a positive response is made. Inhibitory neurones prevent the automatic response from being made, e.g. a hot metal plate if picked up would be dropped whereas a boiling hot casserole would probably be put down quickly but gently.

BRAIN

This is the enlarged front end of the nerve cord in vertebrates. It acts as a reflex centre for reflex arcs in the head, involving the main sense organs – the eyes, ears, mouth and nose. The increased importance of these has led, during evolution, to an increase in size and complexity of the brain. Most of the information entering the CNS passes through the brain and it has control over most of the responses made by the body (voluntary action). It is an organ of coordination, memory, learning and reasoning and is highly developed in man.

It is unlikely that questions will be asked requiring a drawing of the brain – more likely you will be asked to label a diagram provided. The human brain has the structure and functions shown in Fig 7.12.

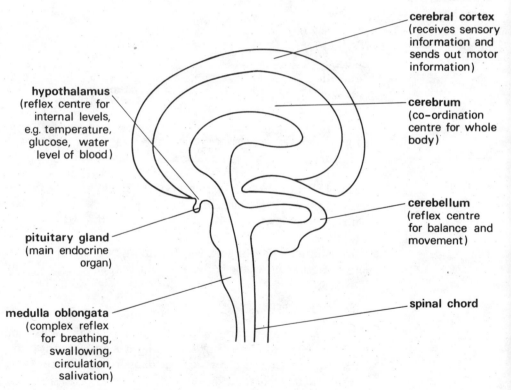

cerebral cortex (receives sensory information and sends out motor information)

hypothalamus (reflex centre for internal levels, e.g. temperature, glucose, water level of blood)

cerebrum (co-ordination centre for whole body)

cerebellum (reflex centre for balance and movement)

pituitary gland (main endocrine organ)

medulla oblongata (complex reflex for breathing, swallowing, circulation, salivation)

spinal chord

Fig 7.12 Section through the human brain

The largest part of the brain is the **cerebrum** (consisting of the two cerebral hemispheres), which spreads out and covers most of the brain. It is concerned with collecting information from sense organs and storing it for later use (learning and behaviour). Reasoning, conscience, learning and personality are controlled by the **cerebrum.** The outer covering of the cerebrum is the **cerebral cortex** and various regions of it are concerned with specific senses, e.g. sight, hearing, touch, and the control of specific parts of the body, e.g. fingers, tongue, neck, and functions, e.g. speech. Information from many sense organs is collected together in certain parts of the cerebrum called association centres. Here sensory information is compared with similar past experiences and impulses are sent to effectors to produce the appropriate response.

DRUGS

Drugs are chemical substances taken to relieve the body of disease or symptoms of disease. Increasingly the word 'drug' is associated with those chemical substances which change the natural processes of the body. Many of these latter substances affect the brain and influence mood and behaviour. They are often associated with 'abuse' of the body and are frowned on socially and medically. Over-use of some of these drugs leads to **addiction.**

There are three main categories of drugs which fit the description given above.

1 **Painkillers** – they relieve pain and are called **analgesics. Morphine** and **heroin** are powerful painkillers but their use can become addictive.

2 **Sedatives** – they reduce mental and physical activity. **Alcohol** is the commonest sedative and has an initial effect in reducing anxiety. **Barbiturates**, too, have similar effects including relaxation. They used to be used as sleeping tablets. Barbiturates are rarely prescribed by doctors now but are sought after by addicts. Alcohol and barbiturates taken together can have a dangerous effect on breathing and heart beat.

3 **Stimulants** – they increase mental and physical activity. **Caffeine** and **amphetamines** are the commonest stimulants. Addiction to caffeine is not too dangerous but addiction to amphetamines can severely affect the heart beat and blood pressure.

Addiction to drugs of any type can be dangerous because of side effects. Drugs taken under medical supervision are generally safe but drugs taken for any other reason can lead to addiction. Illegal drugs are both dangerous to use and very expensive. Addiction can lead to serious personal and social problems. Loss of job, crime, breakdown of marriage, suicide and death from infection or side effects are associated with untreated addiction to drugs.

Pregnant women should avoid *all* drugs because of the possible harmful effects that these may have on the foetus.

RECEPTORS (SENSE CELLS AND ORGANS)

All receptors have the same basic function of converting stimuli into electrical energy of the nerve impulse.

Receptors may be isolated single cells, e.g. pressure receptors in the skin, or collected together to form a highly efficient sense organ, e.g. the eye.

The strength of the stimulus determines the number of receptors sending impulses to the CNS.

SKIN RECEPTORS

The skin contains sense cells detecting heat, cold, touch, pressure and pain (see p.151). Each of these types of cell is capable of responding to a range of strengths of stimuli, so that the brain can register degrees of stimulation. Certain parts of the body are more sensitive to stimuli than others, e.g. tip of tongue and fingers and lips. In these areas each sense cell has its own nerve fibre running to the CNS. The skin may react as a receptor and effector in temperature regulation (see p.153).

SMELL AND TASTE

Certain receptors detect chemical substances which dissolve in the film of moisture covering them. Taste receptors on the tongue are situated in taste buds and are sensitive to bitterness, saltiness, sourness and sweetness.

EYE

The structure of the human eye enables it to convert light rays of various wavelengths coming from varying distances into electrical impulses which nerves carry to the brain, where an image of remarkable precision is produced.

When learning a diagram of the structure of the eye (see Fig 7.13) notice that: the conjunctiva is joined to the eyelids; the cornea and sclerotic layer form a continuous ring; the choroid, iris, ciliary body and lens form another ring; with the retina forming the inner lining.

▶ **Sclerotic layer** (sclera) External covering of the eye; very tough, maintains shape of eyeball.
▶ **Choroid** Contains blood vessels; supplies nutrients to rest of eye; black pigment prevents reflection within eye.
▶ **Retina** Contains sensory rods and cones.
▶ **Yellow spot** Most sensitive part of eye; cones only; most light rays are focused here.
▶ **Vitreous humour** Clear semi-solid substance supports eyeball.
▶ **Blind spot** Point where optic nerve leaves eye; no rods or cones here, therefore not light-sensitive.
▶ **Optic nerve** Bundle of nerve fibres carrying impulses to brain.

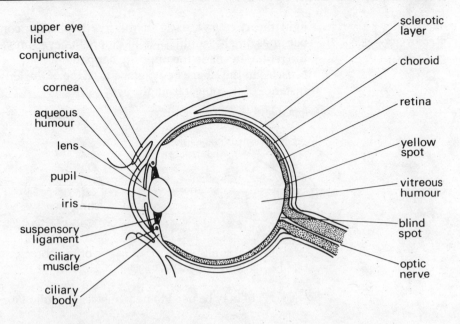

Fig 7.13 The human eye

▶ **Eyelid** Protects eye from damage by reflex action.
▶ **Conjunctiva** Thin layer of transparent cells protecting cornea.
▶ **Cornea** Transparent front part of sclerotic; curved surface with aqueous humour beneath acts as main structure refracting (bending) light towards retina.
▶ **Pupil** Opening in iris; all light enters eye through here.
▶ **Iris** Coloured muscular diaphragm; adjusts amount of light entering eye.
▶ **Aqueous humour** Clear watery fluid supports lens (see cornea).
▶ **Lens** Transparent and elastic; gives final adjustment of focus to light rays.
▶ **Suspensory ligament** Attaches lens to ciliary body.
▶ **Ciliary body** Edge of choroid; contains the ciliary muscles.
▶ **Ciliary muscles** Circular muscles; alter shape of lens during accommodation.

Light entering the eye takes the following path:

conjunctiva → cornea (where light rays are refracted for focusing on to retina) → aqueous humour → pupil → lens (precise focusing on to retina) → vitreous humour → sense cells in retina

A comes before *V* in the alphabet, helping you to remember the order of the humours.

Accommodation

This is the mechanism by which light rays from an object are focused on to the retina so as to produce an image. It involves two processes.

1 Reflex adjustment of pupil size according to light intensity. In bright

light the circular muscle of the iris diaphragm contracts, the pupil becomes smaller and less light enters the eye, preventing damage to the retina. In shade the opposite happens.

2   Muscles in the ciliary body alter the shape of the lens according to the distance of the object from the eye.

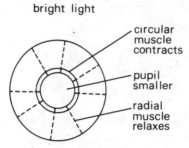

Fig 7.14 The iris/pupil response to light

Fig. 7.14 may be used to help answer the following question.

Specimen question Explain how the amount of light reaching the retina is regulated.   (3 marks)   [JMB]

light from distant object   light from near object

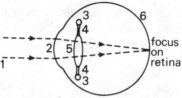

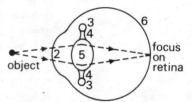

1 parallel light rays each eye
2 cornea refracts (bends) light rays
3 circular ciliary muscle relaxed
4 suspensory ligament taut
5 lens pulled out thin
6 light focused on retina

1 diverging light rays reach eye
2 cornea refracts (bends) light rays
3 circular ciliary muscle contracted
4 suspensory ligament slack
5 elastic lens more convex
6 light focused on retina

Fig 7.15 Mechanisms of accommodation

Fig 7.15 would be useful in answering questions of the following type.

Specimen question Give labelled diagrams and explain the functions of ciliary muscles and suspensory ligaments of the eye in focusing.

                                        [ULSEB]

Colour vision

There are two types of sense cells in the retina: **rods**, which are sensitive to low-light intensities; and **cones**, which respond only to bright light. Cones detect colour and there are thought to be three types of cone cell in mammals, each responding to one of the primary colours, red, green and blue. Light of other colours and shades stimulates varying proportions of these cones. Impulses from these pass to the brain where the sensation of colour is produced. Nocturnal animals have many rods and few cones, giving them better night vision but poor colour discrimination, e.g. owls.

Stereo-vision (binocular vision)

This occurs when both eyes focus on the same object simultaneously. It enables distance and depth to be judged accurately. Man and predatory animals, particularly birds of prey, have well-developed stereo-vision since their eyes are placed in the front of the head.

EFFECTORS (MUSCLES AND GLANDS)

These are cells or organs which produce a particular response when stimulated by motor neurones.

MUSCLES

An example of a muscle effector system may be demonstrated by the bending of the forearm at the elbow (see diagrams on p.199 and p.200). Other examples are swallowing (see p.69), accommodation (see p.183) and peristalsis (see p.69). Coordinated muscle effector systems are involved in movement of the whole organism in response to stimuli (see p.189, taxes).

GLANDS

Some motor neurones supply glands which respond by secreting substances such as enzymes, e.g. salivary glands, tears or mucus, whilst those supplying endocrine glands cause the secretion of hormones, e.g. pituitary gland.

ENDOCRINE SYSTEM

This works either separately or in conjunction with the nervous system to coordinate growth, development and activity within an organism. Hormones are released by glands (see definitions, p.171).

There are two types of glands, called **exocrine** and **endocrine** (see Fig 7.16). Questions testing understanding of the important terms given above are quite common.

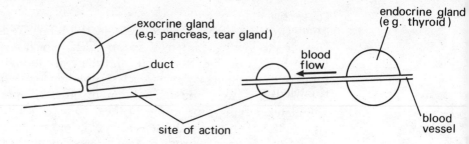

Fig 7.16 (a) Exocrine (ducted) and (b) endocrine (ductless) glands

Specimen question Explain what is meant by the terms hormone and endocrine organ.   [*UCLES*]

Always be sure that terms such as these are well known.
  The main endocrine glands in the body are the:
1 pituitary;
2 thyroid;
3 pancreas;
4 adrenals; and
5 reproductive glands
  The **pituitary gland** coordinates and controls the activity of the other glands by the release of hormones which stimulate them to produce or release their own hormones.
  The level of circulating hormone is controlled by a process called **feedback.** In this, the level of hormone in the blood is monitored as it

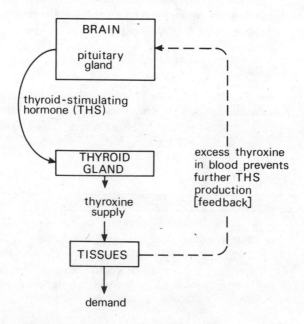

Fig 7.17 Feedback control of thyroxine output

passes through the brain (see Fig 7.17). If too much is present the pituitary is prevented from releasing a stimulating hormone; if too little is present it releases even more. In this way a very precise control of hormone levels can be achieved to suit the varying needs of the organism. Table 7.1 is a summary for the topic of hormones. Knowledge of these glands, their hormones and their effects is frequently demanded on objective test papers. Learn the table.

Table 7.1 Summary of hormones

Gland/position	Hormone produced	Stimulus	Function
Pituitary (base of brain)	Anti-diuretic hormone (ADH)	Dehydration	Reabsorption of water into blood from kidney tubule (p.160)
	Oxytocin	Mature foetus	See p.227
	Thyroid stimulating hormone (TSH)	Feedback	Release of thyroxine by thyroid gland
	FSH	Lack of progesterone	See p.226
	LH	Oestrogen	See p.226
Thyroid (neck on each side of larynx)	Thyroxine	TSH	Regulation of metabolic rate
Islets of Langerhans of pancreas (below stomach)	Insulin	Increased blood sugar level	Lowers blood sugar level, stimulates glucose uptake by cells
Adrenal medulla (above kidney)	Adrenaline	Danger, fright, stress	Increases heart and breathing rate, and blood flow to brain and muscles, raises blood sugar level, stops peristalsis
Ovary, uterus, testis	See p.226		

In some important metabolic activities, hormones from several glands may be required to produce precise chemical coordination, e.g. the control of blood sugar level. Adrenaline and thyroxine raise the blood sugar level. Insulin lowers it. The control of glucose metabolism is shown in Fig 7.18.

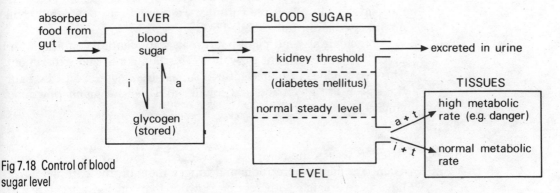

Fig 7.18 Control of blood sugar level

This is a good example of a topic which requires details from various parts of the syllabus. List the processes shown in Fig 7.18 and look them up in detail in other sections of this book.

NERVOUS AND CHEMICAL COORDINATION

Table 7.2 Differences
between nervous and
chemical coordination

Nervous	Chemical
1 Information passes as electrical impulses along axons, (chemical across synapses)	Information passes as a chemical substance through bloodstream
2 Rapid transmission	Slow transmission
3 Response immediate	Response usually slow, e.g. growth
4 Response short-lived	Response long lasting
5 Response very exact	Response usually widespread

PLANT HORMONES

Substances have been isolated from plants which influence chemical control over growth and other plant activities. These are plant growth regulator substances. Some can hasten the time for flowering or ensure the development of large fruit. Some of these substances cause such rapid growth that they lead to the death of the plant. Several weedkillers work in this way.

One of the best known uses of plant hormones is to encourage root development in stem cuttings.

EXPERIMENT TO INVESTIGATE THE EFFECT OF ROOTING POWDER ON THE DEVELOPMENT OF ROOTS IN STEM CUTTINGS

Method
Ten plant pots containing compost are labelled **A–J.** Ten cuttings are taken from a well-developed geranium plant. The lower leaves are removed from each cutting and an oblique cut made in the stem, just below the lowest node. The cut ends of five cuttings are dipped into hormone rooting powder and planted in the pots labelled **A–E.** The cut ends of the other five cuttings are dipped into powdered chalk and planted in the pots labelled **F–J.**

All the cuttings and plant pots are kept in identical conditions and given the same amount of water. (This is a controlled experiment. The two batches of plants receive similar treatment except that cuttings **A–E** are given rooting powder and **F–J** are given powdered chalk.)

Results
After 10 weeks the compost is removed from all the stem cuttings. There are many more roots and longer roots on the cuttings which have been treated with rooting powder than on those treated with chalk powder.

Conclusion

Rooting powder encourages the growth and development of roots in stem cuttings.

PLANT AND ANIMAL RESPONSES

Table 7.3 Differences between plant and animal responses

Plants	Animals
1 Lack a nervous system	Possess a nervous system
2 Coordination by hormones only	Coordination by nerves and hormones
3 A prolonged stimulus usually required	A short stimulus usually required
4 Responses usually slow	Responses usually rapid
5 Responses usually involve growth	Responses usually involve movement
6 Effect usually permanent	Effect usually temporary

BEHAVIOUR

This describes the variety of ways animals respond to stimuli. In lower animals, e.g. earthworms and woodlice, behaviour is usually predictable, whilst in mammals, particularly Man, responses may be extremely variable. In all cases the central nervous system controls the response.

The simplest form of behavioural response is a **taxis**. This is the movement of the whole organism in response to a directional stimulus. Tactic movements may be *towards* the stimulus (positive) or *away from* the stimulus (negative). Taxes can be demonstrated in small invertebrates by the use of a choice-chamber.

EXPERIMENT TO INVESTIGATE THE RESPONSE OF WOODLICE TO A CHOICE OF DAMP AND DRY ENVIRONMENTS

Apparatus
See Fig 7.19.

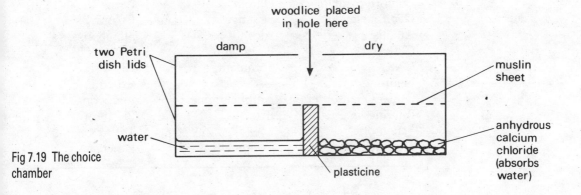

Fig 7.19 The choice chamber

Method

The apparatus is set up as in Fig 7.19 and 10 woodlice are placed in the centre of the upper dish. The atmosphere in one half of the chamber is kept drier than the other half by the use of anhydrous calcium chloride. All other factors, e.g. light and temperature, are kept constant. Recordings are taken of the activity of the woodlice every 2 minutes for 20 minutes.

Results

Typical data reveal that for most of the time the woodlice on the dry side are moving, whereas those on the damp side are stationary. After 20 minutes most of the woodlice are found to be on the damp side and are stationary.

Conclusions

Woodlice move towards and tend to settle in a damp atmosphere in preference to a dry atmosphere – this is a positive hydrotactic response.

Check that this topic is on your syllabus before revising it.

Specimen question Describe with experimental detail how you could demonstrate one tactic response. (8 marks)   [O & C]

Questions of the type given could include the detail given in the experiment.

KEY WORDS ▶		
Irritability	Conditioned reflex	Lens
Stimulus	Learning	Yellow spot
Receptors	Brain	Aqueous humour
Impulse	Cerebrum	Vitreous humour
Effector	Cerebral cortex	Blind spot
Response	Drug	Optic nerve
Coordination	Addiction	Pupil
Homeostatic	Painkiller	Suspensory ligament
Hormones	Analgesic	Accommodation
Tropism	Morphine	Rods
Phototropism	Heroin	Cones
Geotropism	Sedative	Colour vision
Auxins	Alcohol	Stereo-vision
Clinostat	Barbiturate	Muscles
CNS	Stimulant	Glands
Neurone	Caffeine	Exocrine
Sensory neurone	Amphetamine	Endocrine
Intermediate	Eye	Pituitary
neurone	Eyelid	Thyroid
Motor neurone	Conjunctiva	Pancreas

Nerve	Cornea	Adrenals
Nerve fibre	Sclerotic	Reproductive glands
Synapse	Choroid	Feedback
Transmitter	Iris	Behaviour
substance	Ciliary body	Taxis
Reflex arc	Ciliary muscle	Choice-chamber
Reflex action		

SPECIMEN EXAMINATION QUESTIONS

1   An experiment was performed to investigate the effect of light on the
growth of the coleoptiles (shoot tips) of oat seedlings. In Fig 7.20 row
A shows three seedlings at the beginning of the experiment. The
seedlings were exposed to light from one side for three hours. Row B
shows the results.

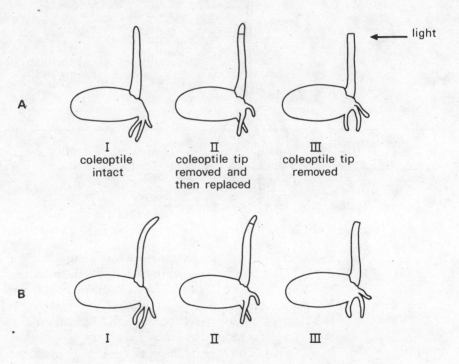

Fig 7.20

(a)   What is the name given to the response shown by seedlings I
        and II?   (1 mark)

(b)   How does this experiment support the idea that the response
        is produced by auxins (plant hormones)?   (2 marks)

(c)   State TWO properties possessed by auxins.   (2 marks) (d)　A similar response is shown by leafy shoots to light from one side. What is the importance of this response? (2 marks)

(e)　What stimulus causes roots to respond to auxins if the roots are placed horizontally? (1 mark) [MEG]

2　Fig 7.21 shows a young plant growing towards the light, which came from one side only.

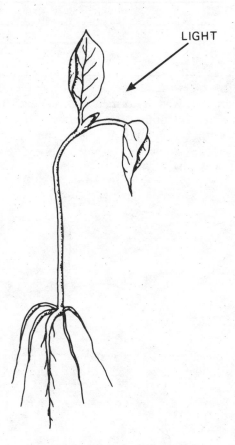

LIGHT

Fig 7.21

(a)　(i) In this example what was the stimulus? (1 mark)
(ii) In this example what was the response? (1 mark)

(b)　Give ONE advantage to the plant of this response. (1 mark)
[LEAG]

3　Fig 7.22 shows a section through a human eye.

(a)　On the diagram:
(i) Where is the optic nerve? (1 mark)
(ii) Where is the retina? (1 mark)

(b)　(i) What happens to the pupil when you enter a dark room? (1 mark)
(ii) What happens to the shape of the lens when you look down to read this book? (1 mark) [NEA]

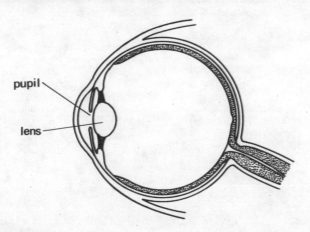

pupil

lens

Fig 7.22

4   Fig 7.23 is a diagram of a horizontal section through the eye. Suppose that a girl is looking at a fly on a book that she is reading.

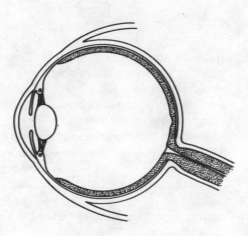

Fig 7.23

(a)   In Fig 7.23, what part of the eye contains muscles that focus light from the fly?   (1 mark)

(b)   Where on Fig 7.23 would the image of the fly appear? (1 mark)

(c)   Assume that the fly now flew off and landed on a wall and that the girl continued to watch it.
(i) Draw the shape of the lens when focused on the fly on the wall.   (1 mark)
(ii) What brings about the change in shape of the lens in (i)? (2 marks)

(d)   (i) Where is the iris in Fig 7.23? (1 mark)
(ii) Explain the effect of bright light on the iris of the eye.
(2 marks)   [MEG]

5   (a)   Complete Fig 7.24 by drawing the pathway of the reflex arc in the following stages.
(i) Draw single lines to show the following nerve fibres:
sensory (afferent); relay (intermediate); motor (efferent).

Fig 7.24

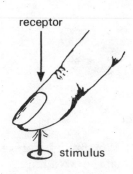

receptor

stimulus

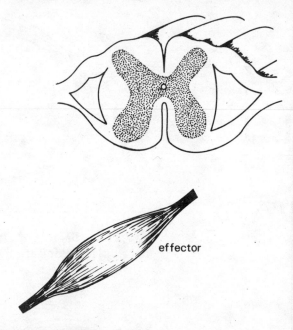

effector

(ii) LABEL the nerve fibres clearly.

(iii) Draw arrows on the nerve fibres to show the direction of a nerve impulse.

(b)   List THREE differences between a reflex action and an action brought about by hormones.

(c)   When the impulse reaches the effector, it causes it to contract.

(i) Name TWO substances required to provide energy for contraction.

(ii) State how these substances are carried to the effector.   (11 marks)   [WJEC]

6   Which of your sense organs would be sensitive to each of the following?

(a)   Music on radio.   (1 mark)

(b)   A red traffic light.   (1 mark)

(c)   Salt solution.   (1 mark)   [LEAG]

7   (a)   In an experiment on social behaviour in robins, a stuffed robin was fixed to a branch inside the territory of a male robin. The stuffed robin was attacked by the male robin. When red breast feathers were removed from the stuffed bird, it was not attacked again.

(i) In this example of social behaviour, identify:

the stimulus;

the response.

(ii) Describe briefly another example of social behaviour shown by an animal.

(b)   Which of the following regions of the central nervous system are you using in thinking about this question?

cerebrum   spinal cord   cerebellum   medulla

(c)   What is meant by the term 'reflex action'? Give an example of a reflex action.   [SEG]

SKELETON AND LOCOMOTION

CONTENTS

Movement Change in position of one structure relative to another.
Locomotion Movement of an organism from one place to another.
Endoskeleton A skeleton inside an organism.
Exoskeleton A skeleton outside the body of an organism.
Voluntary muscle A muscle under the conscious control of the brain.
Contraction Shortening and thickening of muscle fibres.

SUPPORT IN ANIMALS

The medium of air provides little support for terrestrial organisms. Therefore plants and animals must rely on a skeleton of some sort as a means of providing support and, where appropriate, propulsion.

In tetrapods, support is achieved by the limbs acting as the struts and the backbone as the span of a cantilever bridge (see Fig 8.1).

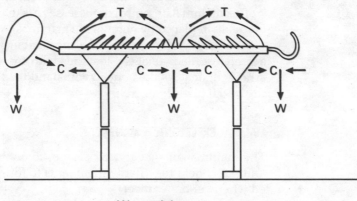

W - weight
T - tension
C - compression

Fig 8.1 Skeleton of a tetrapod acting as the strut and span of a cantilever bridge

SKELETONS

All skeletons are resistant to compression and provide a rigid framework for the body. They perform the functions of:

1   **Support** – involves raising the body off the ground to allow efficient

movement, suspension of soft parts of the body and maintenance of body shape;

2   **protection** – of internal organs; and

3   **movement** – provides attachment for muscles, and forms levers on which muscles can act.

    Two major types of skeleton are seen in the Animal kingdom.

1   **Exoskeleton** in arthropods. This is a hard outer covering, called the cuticle, and is composed of chitin. At the joints it is soft and flexible. Limbs are jointed and hollow and possess inward extensions for muscle attachment.

2   **Endoskeleton** in vertebrates. It is composed of cartilage or bone. Bone consists of inorganic calcium phosphate, organic protein, bone cells and blood vessels. Limbs are jointed, and bones are internal to muscles.

    The presence of an exoskeleton limits arthropods from becoming too large. As the exoskeleton becomes larger it becomes increasingly heavy to carry around. Above a certain size it becomes too heavy and cumbersome for the muscles to move the limbs.

CARTILAGE AND BONE

Cartilage and bone are living tissues with common functions of support, protection and locomotion.

    Cartilage is compressible and elastic and commonly found at the ends of bones where joints occur. It can withstand the strains and sudden mechanical shocks that often occur at joints.

    The mammalian embryo possesses a skeleton of cartilage. This is gradually replaced by bone as the mammal grows.

    Bone is a hard, tough tissue. The combination of calcium salts and a protein called collagen, together with the way these materials are arranged, enables the bone to withstand the forces acting upon it and the load it carries.

MAMMAL SKELETON, e.g. MAN

The mammalian skeleton consists of many bones of various shapes and sizes, held together by **ligaments** to form **joints.** Joints are formed wherever bones meet.

    The commonest type of joint is the movable **synovial joint**, e.g. shoulder and elbow (see Fig 8.2). There are two main types of synovial joint.

1   **Ball and socket** – allows for movement in all planes, e.g. at the shoulder between scapula and humerus.

2   **Hinge** – movement in one plane only, e.g. at the elbow between humerus and ulna.

Specimen question By means of a large labelled diagram, describe the structure of a movable joint in the mammalian skeleton.   (5 marks)

[O & C]

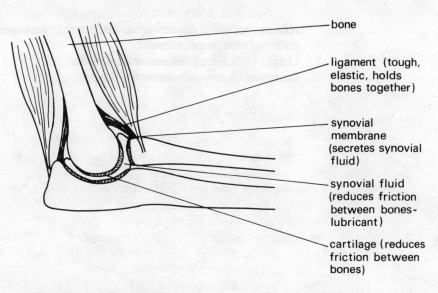

Fig 8.2 Structure of a synovial joint

MUSCLE TISSUE

This is made up of elongated fibres which have the ability to contract and relax. A **muscle**, e.g. biceps, is a collection of muscle fibres. When a muscle contracts it shortens and thickens. This brings its two ends closer together. It may shorten to two thirds of its original length and relax back to its original length.

Muscles are well supplied with blood, which brings the food and oxygen required to produce energy for the work they perform (contraction). The blood flow can be adjusted according to muscle need.

Each muscle has its own nerve supply consisting of:

1 motor neurones, which activate (stimulate) the muscle fibres to contract;
2 sensory neurones (from proprioceptors) which indicate the relative position of the muscle.

Muscle contraction occurs as shown in Fig 8.3.

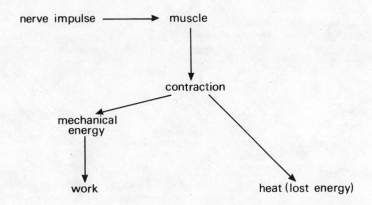

Fig 8.3 Muscle contraction

Muscles are attached to bone by **tendons** which are inelastic and able to withstand sudden stress. Each muscle possesses at least two points of attachment to bone.

1 **Origin** – to a firm, fixed part of the skeleton.
2 **Insertion** – to a mobile part of the skeleton.

MUSCLE ACTION

Skeletal muscles usually act in pairs, the two muscles of a pair having an opposing action. When one of the pair contracts, the other must relax for movement to take place. These pairs are called **antagonistic** muscles, and are classified according to the type of movement they produce in the limbs.

▶ **Flexors** bend a limb at a joint.
▶ **Extensors** straighten a limb at a joint.

Some muscles work together to rotate a limb or other part of the body to produce precise movement.

Movement is produced by the contraction and relaxation of antagonistic muscles which are attached to bones acting as levers. The joint acts as the fulcrum (see Figs 8.4 and 8.5).

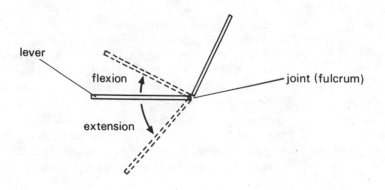

Fig 8.4 Movement at a joint

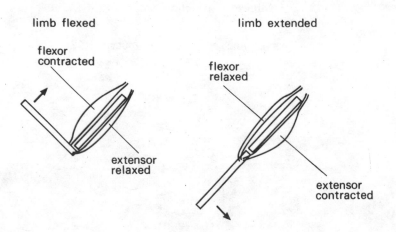

Fig 8.5 Movement at the elbow joint

Specimen questions

1   The diagrams in Fig 8.6 show the three positions of a toad as it 'takes off' into a jump. What part is played in 'take off' by the (a) extensor muscles of the hind limb, (b) flexor muscles of the hind limb, (c) skeleton of the hind limb, (d) joints of the hind limb, (e) firm ground below the feet?   [AEB]

2   With the aid of a diagram show how a pair of antagonistic muscles brings about movement in a mammalian limb.   (5 marks)
                                                                [JMB]

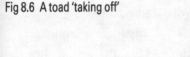

Fig 8.6 A toad 'taking off'

EXPERIMENT TO INVESTIGATE THE PARTS PLAYED BY CALCIUM SALTS AND PROTEIN IN PRODUCING BONE STRENGTH

Method
Weigh a limb bone such as a femur. Place the bone in dilute hydro-chloric acid and leave for several days. This dissolves out the calcium salts. Wash thoroughly in water and dry. Test for the strength of the bone by bending it. Note how far it bends before breaking. Reweigh the bone.

Results
Bone retains its original external shape but is very pliable. It does not break on bending. There is a 65% decrease in mass.

Method
Weigh another femur. Remove the organic material (primarily pro-tein) by burning to a constant mass. Allow to cool. Reweigh. Test for strength as described in method above.

Results
Bone retains its original external shape but is very brittle. It easily breaks on bending. There is a 35% decrease in mass.

Conclusions

Bone is composed of 65% calcium salts and 35% protein. The pliable and brittle nature of bone combine to give a tough resilient structure.

SUPPORT IN PLANTS

The tissues which contribute towards the support of plants are:

1 **parenchyma** – by turgor;
2 **collenchyma** – cell walls unevenly thickened with cellulose,
3 **sclerenchyma** }
  xylem } – cell walls thickened with **lignin.**

All plant cell walls are composed of cellulose. Cellulose is a molecule which can withstand stretching. This property makes cell walls resistant to expansion as the cell vacuole absorbs water and swells. The increasing pressure of the cytoplasm against the cell wall makes the cell turgid. This means that the cell becomes firm, just like a fully inflated balloon (see Fig 8.7).

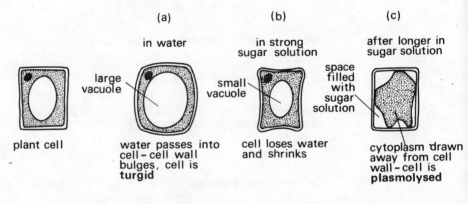

Fig 8.7 Osmotic effects on plant cells

Parenchyma cells, which form the general packing tissue of stems and roots, also develop turgor. When turgid, they become tightly pressed against each other and provide support. This is the chief means of support in stems.

The distribution of other supporting tissues in dicotyledonous plants relates to the stresses and strains encountered by the plants.

ROOT

Xylem tissue is located centrally (see Fig 8.8). This helps resist the pulling strains of the aerial parts of the plant as they sway to and fro. The mechanical strength of the xylem is further increased by the presence of lignin in the cell walls. This forms a very hard rigid structure surrounding these walls, which provides extra strength.

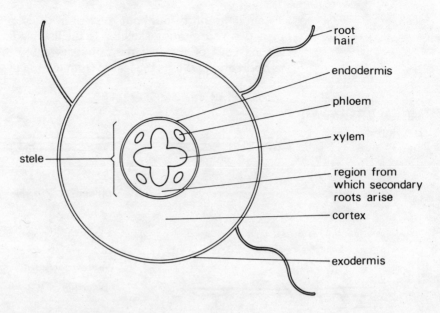

Fig 8.8 TS primary root of bean

STEM

The arrangement of xylem tissue on the outside of the stem provides maximum support for the stem (see Fig. 8.9). The presence of lignin in the xylem fibres provides additional strength and support. Collenchyma cells, arranged close to the outside of the stem, and possessing unevenly thickened cellulose walls, provide further mechanical strength to the outer layers of the stem. This is particularly important in young plants which have not yet developed xylem tissue.

Fig 8.9 TS young stem of sunflower

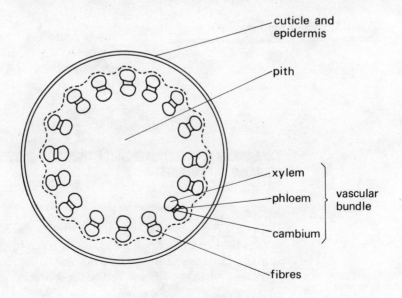

LEAF

Xylem is found throughout the leaf in the supporting veins. Here it provides a supporting skeleton to the leaf blade. Turgor in the parenchyma cells of the leaf mesophyll (see Fig 8.10) provides further support and prevents the leaves from tearing in windy weather.

Fig 8.10 (a) TS through leaf blade. (b)TS through privet leaf

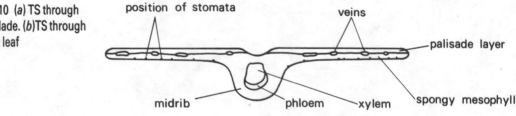

(a)

(b)

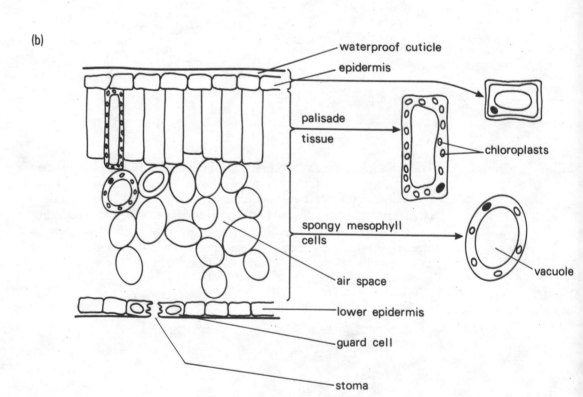

EXPERIMENT TO INVESTIGATE THE DISTRIBUTION OF SUPPORTING TISSUES IN SECTIONS OF PLANT STEMS

Method

Using Fig 8.9, examine prepared slides under a microscope. Find out which tissues the dyes have stained. Note in particular the distribution of xylem tissue, sclerenchyma and collenchyma.

Place a bean seedling in red eosin solution. When the dye becomes visible in the leaf stalks, make thin horizontal sections of the shoot and examine under a microscope.

Results
Xylem tissue contains the red stain. Eosin does not stain cellulose.

Method
Make thin sections from another bean shoot and stain with phloroglucinol and dilute hydrochloric acid.

Results
Xylem tissue is stained red.

Conclusions
Xylem is the inner component of vascular bundles, distributed peripherally. Sclerenchyma is seen as 'caps' on the outer side of the vascular bundles. Collenchyma is located just below the epidermis.

EXPERIMENT TO INVESTIGATE THE DISTRIBUTION OF SUPPORTING TISSUES IN SECTIONS OF LIMB BONES

Method
Examine a longitudinal section of an actual limb bone, e.g. femur. Using Fig 8.11, identify the various types of bone and record their distribution.

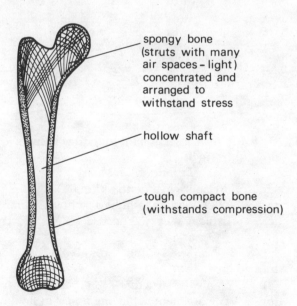

spongy bone
(struts with many
air spaces – light)
concentrated and
arranged to
withstand stress

hollow shaft

tough compact bone
(withstands compression)

Fig 8.11 LS of a femur

Conclusion

Distribution of spongy bone is in regions where stress and shock must be absorbed. Compact bone is arranged around the outside (compare distribution of xylem in plants); it can withstand compression.

KEY WORDS ▶

Skeletons	Synovial joint	Extensors
Exoskeleton	Ball and socket	Biceps
Endoskeleton	Hinge	Triceps
Cartilage	Tendons	Parenchyma
Bone	Antagonistic	Collenchyma
Ligaments	Muscle	Sclerenchyma
Joint	Flexors	Xylem

SPECIMEN EXAMINATION QUESTIONS

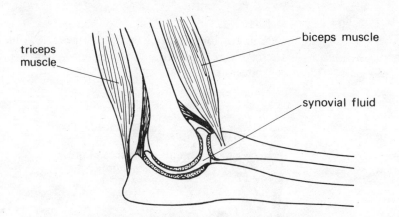

Fig 8.12

1   Fig 8.12 shows a section through the elbow.
    (*a*)   In Fig 8.12:
        (i) label a tendon;   (1 mark)
        (ii) label a ligament.   (1 mark)
    (*b*)   Why does the joint have synovial fluid?   (1 mark)
    (*c*)   Explain why we need a triceps muscle as well as a biceps muscle.   (3 marks)   [*NEA*]
2   Fig 8.13 shows a section through the ball and socket joint in the human hip.
    (*a*)   Name the structure X.   (1 mark)
    (*b*)   The ligament is playing a part in holding the bones together. As well as being strong, suggest another important property of the ligament.   (1 mark)

(c)   What is the function of the synovial fluid in the joint?
(1 mark)

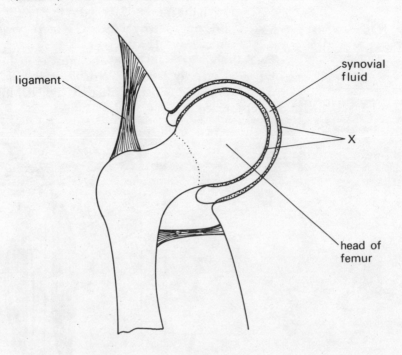

Fig 8.13

(d)   Fig 8.14 shows the positions of the bones and main muscles of the legs of a human when running. (*For clarity, each muscle is shown on one leg only.*)

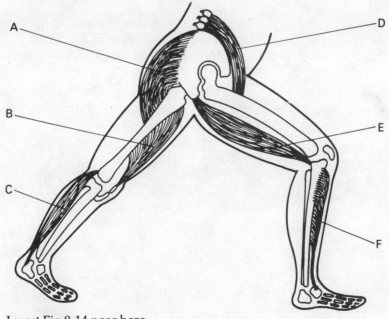

Fig 8.14   Insert Fig 8.14 near here

(i) Explain the term 'antagonistic muscles', illustrating your answer by reference to TWO sets of antagonistic muscles from the muscles labelled A to F on the diagram.   (4 marks)

(ii) Suggest why muscle C is more powerfully developed than muscle F.   (1 mark)   [NEA]

3   Fig 8.15 shows certain bones and muscles in the arm.

(a)   Correctly label the structures shown, using names chosen from the following list. Write only the NUMBER of the name in the box provided.

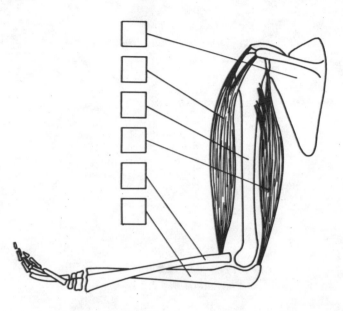

Fig 8.15

1 Ligament 2 Shoulder blade 3 Biceps 4 Tendon 5 Ulna 6 Triceps 7 Humerus 8 Radius   (3 marks)

(b)   Which of the muscles shown would raise the lower arm by contraction?   (1 mark)

(c)   Name the structure which attaches muscle to bone.   (1 mark)

[WJEC]

REPRODUCTION, GROWTH AND DEVELOPMENT

CONTENTS

Reproduction The production of a new generation of individuals of the same species.

Gamete A specialized haploid cell produced for sexual reproduction.

Haploid A single set of chromosomes (n) consisting of one chromosome from each pair of homologous chromosomes.

Fertilization The fusion of the haploid nucleus of the male gamete with the haploid nucleus of the female gamete to form a diploid zygote.

Zygote The diploid product of fusion of two gametes.

Diploid The number of chromosomes ($2n$) found in body cells, made up of homologous pairs.

Spore An asexually produced body, produced in large numbers, which may develop directly into a new organism.

Clone A population of cells or individuals with identical genotypes derived from a single cell by mitosis.

Perennation The method of survival of some plants from year to year by vegetative means.

Pollination The transfer of pollen from the ripe anther of one flower to the stigma of the same flower, or a different flower of the same species.

Seed A ripened fertilized ovule, containing an embryo which may grow into a new plant.

Fruit The ripened ovary of a flower containing seeds.

Germination The development of a seed into a photosynthesizing plant.

Growth An irreversible increase in dry mass of an organism.

Development A progressive change in structure of an organism (differentiation) during its life cycle.

REPRODUCTION

Reproduction is a characteristic of living organisms. It is essentially a cyclical process which ensures the continuity of life. It involves a sequence of development, maturity, reproduction and death. There are two forms of reproduction, **asexual** and **sexual.**

ASEXUAL REPRODUCTION

MAIN FEATURES

1   Offspring formed from one parent. There is no fertilization.
2   All offspring are genetically identical to each other and their parent. There is no variation.
3   Rapid multiplication in numbers in favourable conditions.

MITOSIS

Asexual reproduction occurs by a type of cell division called **mitosis** in which:

1 exact duplication of genetic material (**chromosomes**) occurs within the nucleus of the parent cell;
2 the nucleus divides and each daughter nucleus receives identical genetic material;
3 cytoplasm divides to produce two daughter cells.

Mitosis is a component of growth in all multicellular organisms and a means of producing a new generation in a variety of simpler organisms.

Some of the most common methods of asexual reproduction are:

1 **binary fission;**
2 **spores;**
3 **vegetative propagation;**
4 **artificial propagation;**
5 **tissue culture.**

Binary fission

Division of an acellular organism into two identical individuals which then separate. Examples include the following.

1 *Amoeba* – see Fig 9.1
2 Bacteria – on reaching a certain size bacteria divide by binary fission. This is preceded by replication of the nuclear material, which is shared equally between the two daughter bacteria.

Fig 9.1 Binary fission in *Amoeba*

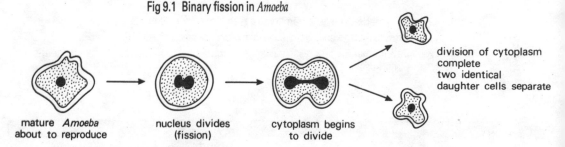

mature *Amoeba* about to reproduce

nucleus divides (fission)

cytoplasm begins to divide

division of cytoplasm complete two identical daughter cells separate

Spores

Cells divide by mitosis to produce a great many spores which are dispersed into the air. Each spore is capable of developing into a new individual, e.g. *Mucor*, a fungus (see Fig 9.2).

Vegetative propagation

This is a feature of some flowering plants. It involves the separation of a developed structure from its parent, which then develops into a new plant.

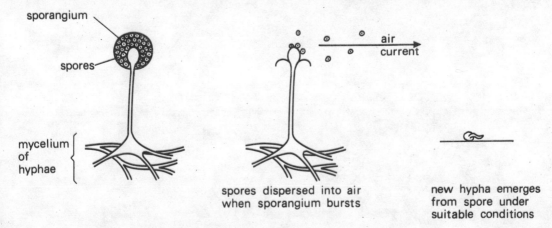

Fig 9.2 Spore production in *Mucor*

Stem tuber – potato Food made in the leaves of the plant is passed to the tips of underground lateral stems. These swell to become stem tubers (the potatoes). The tubers possess **axillary buds**, each of which develops into a new shoot. As the shoot grows it uses up the food stored in the tuber. **Adventitious roots** develop from the region of the bud and they become the root system of the new plant (see Fig 9.3).

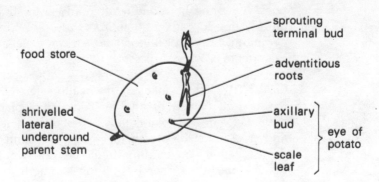

Fig 9.3 Potato stem tuber

Runner – strawberry Some of the buds on the short strawberry stem develop into shoots which grow horizontally over the ground. These are called **runners**. At a distance from the parent plant the end of a runner develops adventitious roots, followed by the foliage of a new daughter plant (see Fig 9.4). The runner permits food to be transported to the growing plant. Eventually, however, it dies away when the new plant is well established.

Artificial propagation
Horticulturalists use this method to maintain desirable characters in their stock.

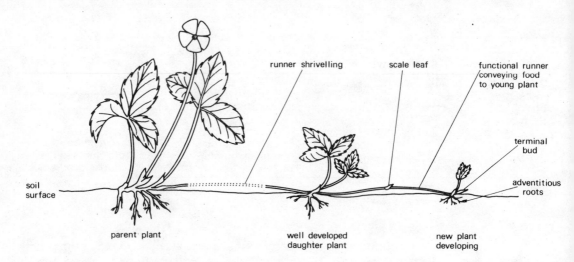

Fig 9.4 Strawberry runners

Cuttings Short shoot lengths bearing leaves are planted in moist compost. A rooting hormone is often added to stimulate rooting. They quickly develop adventitious roots and grow into new plants, e.g. geranium. Leaves of *Begonia* and African violet can also be treated in this way to provide successful cuttings.

Grafting This is the transplant of a healthy stem (**scion**) of one plant on to the root (**stock**) of another compatible plant. In this way the advantages of both plants may be obtained. The tissues of the scion and stock must be placed together and bound tightly so that they grow together. The binding should be waterproof to minimize drying up and infection. Generally grafting is undertaken during the autumn when transpiration rates are low. Grafting is commercially important for fruit tree and rose bush growers.

Tissue culture

This is a method of producing many identical organisms (**clones**) from one piece of tissue. For example, individual carrot cells when grow in a medium containing suitable nutrients and hormones can be induced to begin dividing again to produce new plants (clones).

Tissue culture is used commercially for many plant types, e.g. strawberries, palm trees and house plants.

ADVANTAGES AND DISADVANTAGES OF VEGETATIVE PROPAGATION

Advantages of vegetative propagation (reproduction)

1. Offspring are genetically identical, therefore able to survive in conditions which are favourable to parents.
2. Can withstand unfavourable conditions using stored food.
3. Localized spreading may prevent competition from other species.
4. It is the only way that specialized varieties can be grown (propagated) without change.

Disadvantages of vegetative propagation

1. Overcrowding may occur.
2. New varieties cannot be produced vegetatively.
3. Disease may spread rapidly since, being genetically alike, they may all be affected by the same disease.

PERENNATION

Some organs of vegetative propagation are also organs of perennation. There are two types of perennial plants.

1. **Herbaceous perennials.** Aerial parts die down. Underground parts persist, containing food stores which are utilized for rapid growth in the following spring, e.g. iris (rhizome), daffodil (bulb).
2. **Woody perennials.** Aerial parts persist, bearing buds. These are supplied with food stored in the stems and roots. They develop in spring into new branches, e.g. oak (deciduous perennial), holly (evergreen perennial).

Specimen question Give TWO advantages of perennation and TWO advantages of variability among offspring. (4 marks) [O&C]

SEXUAL REPRODUCTION

MAIN FEATURES

1. Involves the fusion of two **gametes**, usually from two different individuals of the same species, to form a zygote. This process is called fertilization.
2. The zygote is often adapted for survival in adverse conditions, e.g. eggs of birds.
3. The offspring are genetically different from either parent. This produces variation within the species.

Specimen questions

1. Distinguish between asexual and sexual reproduction.
2. What is the biological significance of sexual reproduction?

GAMETE PRODUCTION

The nucleus of every cell in the body of an organism contains a fixed number of chromosomes. This number is made up of pairs of homologous chromosomes.

When male and female gametes fuse to form a **zygote** each contributes an equal number of chromosomes. Therefore each gamete contains only half the number of chromosomes of the zygote (**haploid number** or n).

MEIOSIS

Haploid gametes are produced by a special type of cell division called meiosis (reduction division) shown in Fig 9.5.

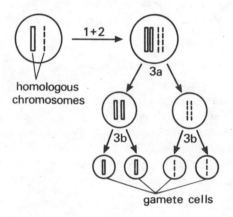

Fig 9.5 Meiosis

The main points of meiosis are as follows.
1 Exact duplication of genetic material.
2 Pairing of homologous chromosomes.
3 (a)   Halving of chromosome content to produce haploid condition by separation of homologous chromosomes, so that:
   (b)   one chromosome from each pair goes into each gamete.

FERTILIZATION

Fusion of male and female gametes restores the **diploid** chromosome number and produces the zygote (see Fig 9.6). The zygote contains hereditary material which is different from that of either parent, and this difference is a source of variety in that species.

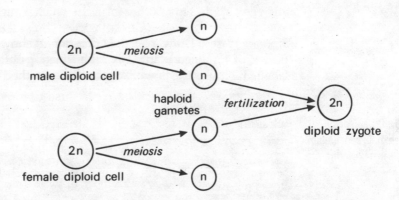

Fig 9.6 Gamete formation
and fertilization

SEXUAL REPRODUCTION IN A FLOWERING PLANT

It is essential that you know the structure of a named flower and the functions of its parts. The structure of the buttercup is shown in Fig 9.7. The following question is typical and the knowledge required to

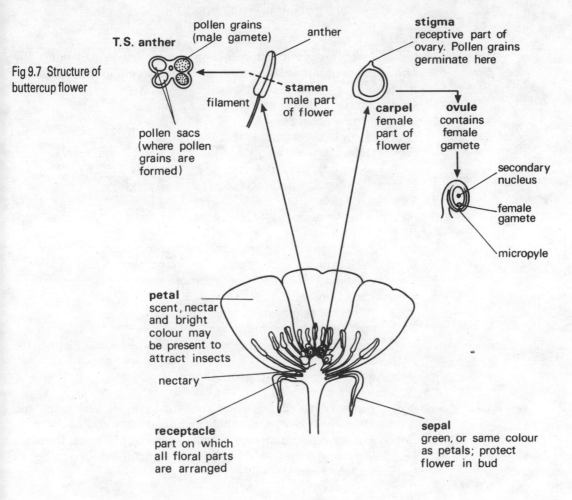

Fig 9.7 Structure of buttercup flower

answer it applies to all other forms in which it might be asked.

Specimen question Draw a labelled diagram to show the structure of the flower of a named plant. Give the functions of each part you have labelled. How is the flower adapted to its method of pollination?

[ULSEB]

Table 9.1 Differences between male and female gametes in a flowering plant

Male gamete	Female gamete (ovule)
Very small nucleus in pollen grain	Large egg cell in ovule
No food reserves	Cytoplasm may contain food reserves
Transported from plant by the external agencies of wind, animals and water	Usually immobile and remains within parent plant
Vast numbers produced to offset high mortality rate	Relatively few produced; well protected

EXPERIMENT TO INVESTIGATE THE STRUCTURE OF A FLOWER USING A HAND LENS

This is an exercise you can perform at home using any reasonably sized flowers, e.g. daffodil, wallflower.

Method

1 If the flowers are grouped together on a single flower stalk notice the arrangement of this inflorescence, and that the younger flowers are at the top.
2 Examine a single flower using Fig 9.7 as a guide.
3 Observe the sepals.
    (a)   How many sepals are there?
    (b)   How are they arranged?
    (c)   Note how the sepals enclose and protect a flower bud.
4 Remove the sepals with a forceps to expose the petals.
5 Observe the petals.
    (a)   How many petals are there?
    (b)   How are they arranged?
    (c)   Are they opposite or alternate with the sepals?
    (d)   Relate their structure and position to their function.
6 Remove the petals with a forceps to expose the stamens.
7 Observe the stamens.
    (a)   Note the arrangement of the stamens.
    (b)   Are they all the same length?
    (c)   Examine a single stamen under a hand lens and identify the anther and filament.
8 Remove the stamens to expose the ovary (carpel).
9 Observe the ovary (carpel).
    (a)   Identify the stigma, style and ovary (carpel). The shape and number of carpels vary considerably in different flowers.
    (b)   Take two separate ovaries, cut one horizontally and the other lengthways and examine the position, structure and number of ovules under a hand lens.

POLLINATION

Pollination must take place in flowering plants before fertilization can occur. There are two types of pollination.

1 **Self pollination.**
2 **Cross pollination.**

Self pollination

Pollen from the **anther** of the flower is transferred to the **stigma** of the same flower, or a flower on the same plant. It is prevented when the **stamens** and **carpels**:

1 ripen at different times; or
2 are situated in different regions of the same flower; or
3 have incompatible gametes.

In some species there are separate male and female flowers and plants.

Specimen question State **two** ways in which flowering plants may avoid self-fertilization.

Cross pollination

Pollen is transferred from the anther of one flower to the stigma of another flower of the same species on a different plant. This may be aided by wind or insects.

Table 9.2 A comparison of the characteristics of wind and insect pollinated flowers

Wind pollinated	Insect pollinated
1 No nectar	May possess nectar
2 No scent	Often scented
3 Small petals, not brightly coloured	Large, coloured petals
4 Feathery stigma with large surface area to trap pollen, often hangs outside flower	Stigma sticky to hold pollen, enclosed within flower
5 Pendulous stamens, hanging outside flower to aid pollen release	Stamens remain within flower
6 Vast quantities of small, light, smooth pollen	Smaller quantities of heavy pollen which is often spiny and sticky to adhere to insect bodies
7 Flowers often open before leaves which might hinder pollen reception	Flower structure adapted to pollination by one type of insect

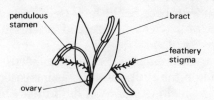

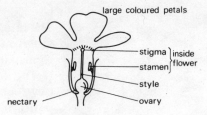

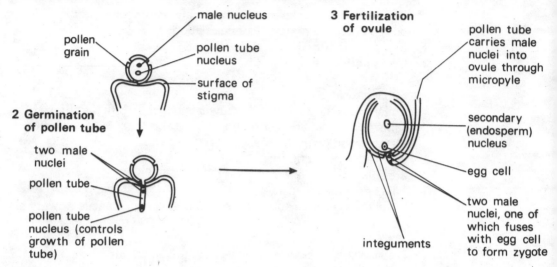

Fig 9.8 Events leading up to fertilization of a flowering plant

FERTILIZATION

See Fig 9.8 for events leading up to fertilization.

Specimen questions

1 Explain why it is important for a wind pollinated flower to produce a large amount of pollen.
2 Distinguish between pollination and fertilization.   [UCLES]
3 The ovule contains a female gamete (nucleus) which will be fertilized by a male gamete (nucleus). Explain briefly how the male gamete(s) reach the **ovule**, so that fertilization can occur.

FORMATION OF SEED AND FRUIT, e.g. BROAD BEAN

1 The floral parts gradually wither away.
2 The zygote divides mitotically and differentiates into:
   (a)   a **radicle** (embryonic root);
   (b)   a **plumule** (embryonic shoot); and
   (c)   two **cotyledons**.
3 The **integuments** become the **testa** (seed coat) which is often lignified, tough and protective. At the end of this development a **seed** is formed (see Fig. 9.9).

    The **ovary** containing the seed or seeds has in the meantime developed into the **fruit**. Its wall has increased in size to become the **pericarp**. The main functions of the fruit are to protect the seeds and to aid their dispersal. Fruits are variable in form and size.

Fig 9.9 Structure of a broad bean seed

FRUIT AND SEED DISPERSAL

As plants are generally fixed, they need to disperse their offspring. Dispersal allows colonization of new habitats and diminishes competition with the parent plant for space, light and water. Most fruits and seeds are dispersed by **wind** and **animals**.

Adaptations for wind dispersal

The fruit or seed develops a large surface area with respect to its volume. This delays the descent of the structure to the ground by offering greater resistance to the air as it falls: e.g. seed parachutes with hairy outgrowths of seed (willowherb Fig 9.10); winged fruit with an outgrowth of the pericarp (sycamore, Fig 9.11).

Fig 9.10 Willowherb seed

Fig 9.11 Sycamore fruit

Adaptations for animal dispersal

1   Development of hooks/spines on fruit or seed which may catch in fur

Fig 9.12 Goose grass fruit

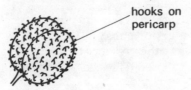

of passing animals and be carried some distance, e.g. pericarp develops hooks as with goose grass (Fig 9.12).

2   Fruits may be succulent, brightly coloured and edible.

(*a*)   They may be eaten by birds. The seeds resist digestion and are egested in the bird's faeces at some distance from the parent plant.

(*b*)   The fruit may be eaten and the seeds discarded by the animal, e.g. cherry (Fig 9.13).

Fig 9.13 Cherry

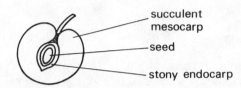

Specimen question (*a*) Why is it important to plants that their seeds should be dispersed? (*b*) With reference to a named example, explain how insect pollination may occur. (*c*) With reference to a named example, explain how seed dispersal may be brought about when the seeds or fruits of a flowering plant become attached to the outside of an animal's body.   [*UCLES*]

EXPERIMENT TO INVESTIGATE SELF POLLINATION USING FLOWERS ENCLOSED WITHIN BAGS

Method

Select a number of flowers from a pea plant. Enclose three flowers (**A**) in separate plastic bags before the flowers are mature.

Remove the stamens from three other young flowers (**B**) and enclose the flowers in separate plastic bags.

Remove the carpels from three further young flowers (**C**) and enclose the flowers in separate plastic bags.

The plastic bags prevent pollen from other flowers pollinating the flowers being used for the experiment.

Observe the flowers regularly, especially the size of the ovaries.

Allow the flowers to grow for several weeks.

Results

Ovaries of flowers (**A**) possessing carpels and stamens have swollen. Ovaries of flowers with stamens removed (**B**) or carpels removed (**C**) remain at their original sizes.

Conclusions

Self pollination occurs in flowers possessing stamens and carpels (**A**). Self pollination is prevented in the other two sets of conditions (**B**) and (**C**). Therefore the presence of stamens and carpels is essential for pollination and subsequent seed/fruit formation.

SEXUAL REPRODUCTION IN THE TROUT

The female selects a spot in the gravel bed of a river and scrapes out a hollow **redd** (nest). Her activity attracts a male trout, and together they drive away any other males to prevent them from eating the eggs.

The female spawns during winter. She produces about 100 eggs at a time. The male sheds his many sperms (called **milt**) over the eggs. External fertilization occurs.

The zygotes produced are protected by gravel placed over them by the fanning of the tail of the female. The male then leaves, followed by the female a few hours later.

As there is no parental care of the zygotes, of the embryos and of the young trout, the mortality rate is very high.

The young hatch after four months. They feed on small animals in the water and grow to maturity over two to three years.

SEXUAL REPRODUCTION IN HUMANS

Female humans produce fewer ova than fish since their higher success rate of fertilization, their method of protection and nourishment provided during development, their birth at an advanced stage (viviparity) and their extended period of parental care ensure that more offspring reach maturity.

Fig 9.14 Male reproductive organs

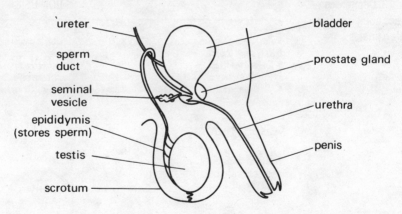

Fig 9.15 Female reproductive organs

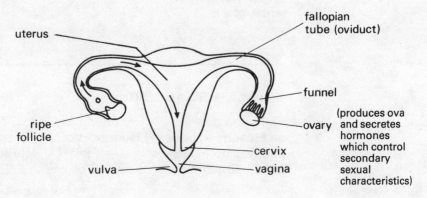

SPERM PRODUCTION

Spermatozoa are produced in the **seminiferous tubules** of the **testes**. The testes are held in the **scrotal sac** just outside the body cavity because sperm need a lower temperature for development. Sperms pass from the testes as follows.

tubules → epididymis → sperm ducts → urethra
(produced)   (stored)   (during **ejaculation**)   (penis)

Secretions from the **seminal vesicle** and **prostate gland** containing nutrients and enzymes are added to sperm to activate them into swimming.

EGG PRODUCTION

Every 28 days one of the **ovaries** releases an **ovum**. It passes through the reproductive system as shown by arrows in Fig 9.15. The development of the ovum, its release (**ovulation**) and subsequent events occur in a cyclical process controlled by hormones. This is called the **menstrual (oestrous) cycle** (see Fig 9.16) and is modified if pregnancy occurs. Each month the **uterus** is prepared to receive the developing embryo in case fertilization occurs. When no embryo is present the uterus lining is shed and the ovary produces another ovum.

Table 9.3 Differences between human male and female gametes

Sperm	Egg (ovum)
1 Are able to propel themselves	Unable to propel themselves
2 Very small (2.5 μm across widest part)	Much larger than sperms (120 μm in diameter)
3 No food reserves	Cytoplasm with yolky droplets provides a source of food for embryo during initial stages of development
4 Vast numbers expelled during each ejaculation	Usually produced singly at monthly intervals

nucleus + DNA

head

middle piece + mitochondria – energy liberation

tail – organelle of locomotion

nucleus + DNA

vitelline membrane

plasma membrane

cytoplasm

PHYSICAL CHANGES AT PUBERTY

The sex organs are inactive during childhood. They begin to change and mature at **puberty**. Hormones control the development of male and female characteristics (see Table 9.4). Full sexual maturity in the female is indicated by the onset of **menstruation**. The visible body changes that occur during puberty are called **secondary sexual characteristics.**

Table 9.4 Changes which take place during puberty

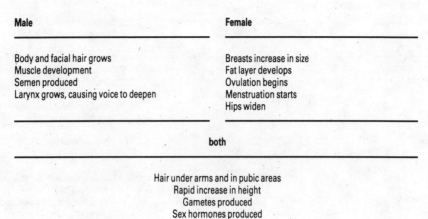

Male	Female
Body and facial hair grows	Breasts increase in size
Muscle development	Fat layer develops
Semen produced	Ovulation begins
Larynx grows, causing voice to deepen	Menstruation starts
	Hips widen

both

Hair under arms and in pubic areas
Rapid increase in height
Gametes produced
Sex hormones produced
Sex organs enlarge

MENSTRUAL CYCLE

This is controlled by hormones as described on p.226.

Fig 9.16 gives a diagrammatic representation of the menstrual cycle.

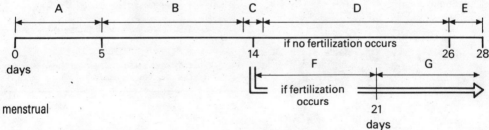

Fig 9.16 The menstrual cycle

(*a*)   Uterine lining expelled from body – **menstruation.**
(*b*)   Graafian follicle in ovary develops; egg ripens and follicle produces **oestrogen**; uterus lining thickens.
(*c*)   Follicle releases egg (**ovulation**) and develops into **corpus luteum.**
(*d*)   Corpus luteum secretes **progesterone** – maintains uterus lining.
(*e*)   Corpus luteum breaks down; progesterone level falls; cycle begins at **1** again.
    If **fertilization** occurs:
(*f*)   Embryo implants in uterus wall by day 21.
(*g*)   Corpus luteum persists and secretes progesterone which maintains uterus lining – no menstruation and normal cycle stops while embryo develops.

Table 9.5 Functions of hormones in female mammal (grouped under site of origin)

Hormone	Function
Pituitary gland	
Follicle stimulating hormone (FSH)	1 Stimulates Graafian follicle development in ovary 2 Stimulates ovary to secrete oestrogen
Luteinizing hormone (LH)	1 Causes ovulation 2 Conversion of Graafian follicle into corpus luteum 3 Stimulates secretion of progesterone
Oxytocin	1 Stimulates uterine muscle contraction in labour 2 Stimulates flow of milk
Prolactin	1 Promotes secretion of milk
Ovary	
Oestrogen	1 Causes onset and maintenance of secondary sexual characteristics (see Table 9.4) 2 Aids healing/repair of uterus wall after menstruation 3 Increases thickness of uterus wall
Corpus luteum	
Progesterone	1 Prepares uterine wall for implantation 2 Maintains uterus lining in early pregnancy 3 Inhibits oxytocin

Table 9.6 Functions of hormones in male mammal (grouped under site of origin)

Hormone	Function
Pituitary gland	
FSH	1 Stimulates sperm production
LH	1 Stimulates testes to secrete male hormones
Testis	
Testosterone	1 Causes onset and maintenance of male secondary sexual characteristics (see Table 9.4)

COPULATION AND FERTILIZATION

The erect **penis** is inserted into the **vagina** of the female during mating (pairing), and sperms are discharged at ejaculation. The sperms swim towards the **oviduct** where fertilization may occur.

The fertilized egg begins to divide mitotically, forming a small ball of cells which becomes **implanted** in the wall of the uterus. The **placenta** develops from tissue derived partly from the uterine wall and partly from that of the embryo (see Fig 9.17).

The umbilical cord connects the embryo to the placenta. The blood vessels of the placenta form an intimate association with the uterine blood vessels (see Fig 9.17). No mixing of the mother's blood and foetal blood takes place. Diffusion of oxygen and dissolved food materials from mother to **foetus**, and carbon dioxide and soluble excretory products, e.g. urea, from foetus to mother takes place. The

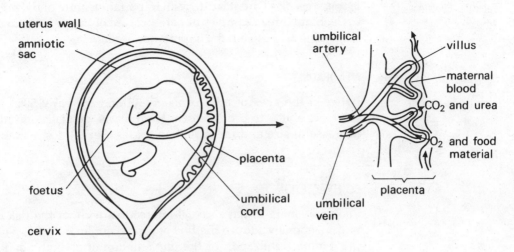

Fig 9.17 Foetus, placenta and uterus

placenta also produces oestrogen and progesterone throughout pregnancy.

The foetus is contained in the **amniotic sac** which is filled with **amniotic fluid.** This serves to protect the foetus from buffeting and sudden temperature changes, and enables the foetus to move about freely.

Specimen question Briefly outline the menstrual cycle of a woman and describe what changes occur in her between fertilization of the egg and giving birth.   (10 marks)   [O&C]

BIRTH

Full development normally takes 280 days – the **gestation** period. Prior to normal birth the foetus has its head placed downwards in the uterus. Oxytocin produces periodic gently rhythmic contractions of the uterine wall. They increase in intensity and number. The amniotic sac bursts, liberating the amniotic fluid, and the foetus is expelled from the body. The placenta follows as the 'after-birth', and the umbilical cord is tied and cut.

The baby is fully dependent on its mother for food in the form of milk. Breast milk contains virtually all the materials the baby requires, except iron. The mother's milk production increases to match the needs of the growing baby. Later on the young baby takes solid food and becomes increasingly independent of its mother's milk.

Parental care continues for a long time. It is carefully organized and includes feeding, a home to live in, education and general moral well-being.

Specimen question Parental care is an important feature of the human life cycle. State **three** examples of parental care of the child during its first year of life and explain the importance of each.

MENOPAUSE

Between the ages of approximately 43 and the early 50s a woman loses her ability to produce ova. Her breasts, genitalia and uterus all decrease in size and menstruation ceases. Sexual desire may also be reduced.

CONTRACEPTION

People wishing to have sexual intercourse without the risk of pregnancy generally adopt a method of contraception, which is a means of preventing fertilization or the implantation of an embryo. Table 9.7 shows the common methods of **birth control** used today.

Birth control is used widely by parents who wish to limit the size of their family. This is called **family planning.**

Table 9.7 Common methods of birth control

Type	Method	Notes	Reliability (average no. of pregnancies in every 100 women who use the method for a year)
Surgical	**Sterilization** Female: cut and tie oviduct Male: cut and tie sperm ducts	Reliable, safe; not reversible	0
Chemical	**Spermicides** Creams, aerosols, foams that kill sperms	Easily available, but should only be used with a barrier method	4
Barrier (should be used with spermicides)	**Sheath** Fits erect penis	Easily available: helps prevent disease	4
	Diaphragm (cap)	Fits inside vagina; closes entry to uterus	Must be supplied by a doctor
Hormonal	**Pill** Prescribed by doctor; instructions must be followed exactly	Some side effects possible; medical supervision essential	0
Intrauterine device (IUD)	**Coil** or **loop** Plastic device placed inside the womb	Once inserted can remain in place for 2 years	2
'Safe' period	Depends on knowing the menstrual cycle, which can change from month to month	Very unreliable	30

(Source: Cadogan and Green, Biology. Heinemann)

SEXUALLY TRANSMITTED DISEASES

These are spread by direct contact with an infected person during intercourse, or by touching the genital organs (see Table 9.8).

Disease	Bacterium	Early symptoms		If left untreated	Treatment
		Male	Female		
Gonorrhoea	Gonococcus	Burning pain in penis Yellow discharge of pus	Generally none If they occur: pain in passing urine; discharge from urethra	Infertility	Antibiotics
Syphilis	Spiral bacterium	Hard sore on penis or the point of sexual contact Skin rash, fever	Hard sore in vagina or other point of sexual contact Skin rash, fever	Heart disease Insanity Blindness	Antibiotics, e.g. penicillin
AIDS	HIV virus	Fatigue, fever, loss of appetite, sweats, weight loss, diarrhoea, dry cough, skin lesions		Dementia Death	No anti-viral drugs or vaccines at present

Table 9.8 Causes, signs, symptoms, effect and treatment of sexually transmitted diseases

ARTIFICIAL INSEMINATION

This occurs when an egg is fertilized within the woman's body by a sperm which has been introduced into the womb by means of a syringe. Artificial insemination may use sperm from the husband or from a donor.

Another form of artificial fertilization occurs when an egg is removed from a woman and fertilized by the father's sperm outside the body. Development is allowed to proceed under carefully controlled conditions. When an eight-celled stage (embryo) is reached, usually about 40 hours after fertilization, the developing embryo is returned to its mother's womb. The baby produced by this technique is commonly, but incorrectly, called a 'test tube' baby.

FERTILITY DRUGS

These are used to stimulate the ovaries to produce ova artificially.

1 A drug can be administered which causes the pituitary gland to make more of the hormone which stimulates the ovary to produce eggs.
2 Extra hormones can be injected if the woman is making insufficient of her own.

Such treatment can cause more than one egg to be produced at a time. If each egg is fertilized then this will give rise to twins or multiple pregnancies.

Table 9.9 Differences in sexual reproduction between mammals and flowering plants

Mammals	Flowering plants
Sexes separate	Usually hermaphrodite
Reproductive structures present throughout life	Reproductive structures temporary
Copulation; sperms swim to egg	Pollination usually by external agents; male nucleus reaches ovule via pollen tube
Offspring grows continually until maturity	Embryo often enters a dormant period as a seed before development proceeds
Offspring motile: no need for agents of dispersal	Dispersal effected by external factors
Relatively few offspring formed	Many offspring produced
Survival rate of offspring high	Survival rate low

GROWTH

Growth is a characteristic of all living organisms. Raw materials are assimilated and energy is used up in order to increase the dry mass of protoplasm. Growth in multicellular organisms is accompanied by an increase in cell number.

Growth is quantitative (can be measured) and may be represented graphically. Growth in cells, tissues, organs, organisms and populations is usually measured in terms of wet mass (fresh mass), dry mass, length or number, and plotted against time. For most purposes other than population growth, dry mass (wet mass with all water removed) is more significant, particularly in plants, as it measures the exact amount of biological material present and overcomes fluid-level fluctuations. Length is easy to measure but disregards growth in other directions, which may be significant.

GROWTH CURVES

There are a variety of characteristic growth curves, which show the effect of particular influences (see Figs 9.18, 9.19, 9.20 and 9.28).

DISCONTINUOUS GROWTH

Fig 9.18 shows an example of discontinuous growth. Growth eventually ceases and cell breakdown outstrips synthesis during senescence.

Examples include flowering plants, birds, mammals and colonies of unicellular organisms.

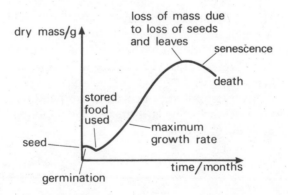

Fig 9.18 Growth curve for an annual flowering plant

CONTINUOUS GROWTH

Fig 9.19 shows an example of continuous growth, in which growth never entirely ceases. Examples include algae, fungi, woody perennial plants, fish and reptiles.

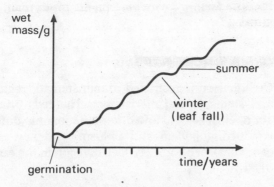

Fig 9.19 Growth curve for a perennial plant

GROWTH IN ARTHROPODS

Fig 9.20 shows the growth curve for a typical arthropod. Growth is achieved by shedding the exoskeleton, after which there is a rapid period of growth before the new exoskeleton hardens.

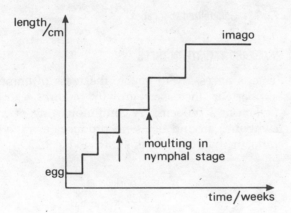

Fig 9.20 Growth curve for a locust

GROWTH IN PLANTS

FACTORS AFFECTING PLANT GROWTH

1 **Nutrition** – carbon dioxide, water, light and mineral salts must all be freely available.

2 **Auxins** – growth hormones produced at the apices of roots and shoots. Specific quantities stimulate cell division and elongation (see p.172).

3 **Light** – slows growth by inactivating/destroying auxins. Result of growth in complete darkness is an etiolated shoot.

4 **Temperature** – if all other conditions are constant the rate of growth varies, within certain limits, according to the temperature.

5   **Genetic factors** – provide potential for growth if all other factors are optimal.

GROWTH IN FLOWERING PLANTS

Cell division is restricted to meristematic regions in the tips of roots and stems (**apical meristems**). The cells produced undergo elongation, enlargement and differentiation into different tissue-types, e.g. conducting (xylem and phloem) and non-conducting (cortex and cambium) (see Fig 9.21). Cell division in the **cambium** allows increase in girth.

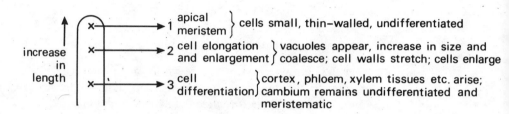

Fig 9.21 Generalized shoot apex

INCREASE IN GIRTH IN TREES

This is necessary to enable the mass of branches and leaves to be supported. Increased growth requires extra conducting tissues (xylem and phloem). A continuous ring of meristematic cells (the cambium) around the stem produces extra xylem on its inside and phloem on its outside, as shown in Fig 9.22.

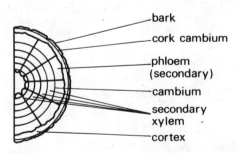

Fig 9.22 Increase in girth of a tree

    The additional xylem forms growth rings, each of which corresponds to a year's growth. A cork cambium below the epidermis gives rise to a layer of cork which is impermeable to water.

DORMANCY

Dispersed seeds rarely germinate immediately, even if conditions are favourable. Seeds may be regarded as a resistant stage, able to survive conditions of cold and desiccation. This period of inactivity prior to germination is called dormancy.

GERMINATION

External conditions necessary for dormancy to be broken and germination to begin are as follows.

1 **Water** – to activate enzymes and aid hydrolysis of stored food into soluble material for transport to growing regions.
2 Optimum **temperature** – for optimum enzyme activity.
3 **Oxygen** – for aerobic respiration to liberate the necessary energy needed for germination.

EXPERIMENT TO INVESTIGATE THE EFFECTS OF VARIOUS ENVIRONMENTAL FACTORS ON GERMINATION

Method
Set up four boiling tubes as shown in Fig 9.23 with cress seeds.

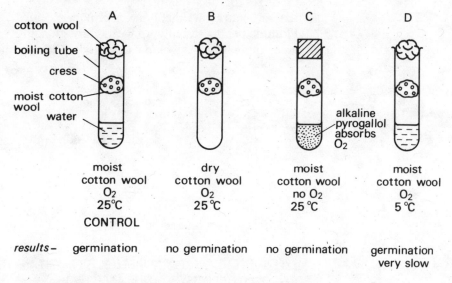

Fig 9.23 To investigate the conditions necessary for germination

Conclusion
Oxygen, an optimum temperature and water are necessary for germination.

Specimen question Describe investigations which you could carry out in the laboratory to demonstrate the conditions essential for germination of seeds.   (10 marks)   [O & C]

GERMINATION OF BROAD BEAN

1 Water is absorbed by the bean.
2 Cotyledons swell and split the testa.
3 Enzymes begin to convert insoluble food stores of cotyledons (starch/protein) into soluble components. These are passed to growing points of the plant where they are utilized (see Fig 9.24).

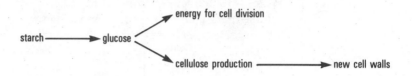

Fig 9.24

4 Presence of glucose also increases osmotic pressure of tissues of seed; this promotes entry of water into embryo and aids extension of newly formed cells.
5 Radicle grows down into soil; root hairs appear behind meristematic region (see Fig 9.25). These absorb water and salts which are passed to the rest of the seedling.
6 Lateral roots grow; anchorage is provided.
7 Plumule begins to grow upwards through soil. At surface it straightens, young leaves develop chlorophyll, photosynthesis begins.

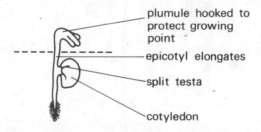

Fig 9.25 Broad bean germination

EXPERIMENT TO INVESTIGATE THE EFFECTS OF LIGHT AND TEMPERATURE ON THE RATE OF CONTINUOUS GROWTH IN A SEEDLING

Method
This involves the use of an **auxanometer** which records the growth of the shoot. The auxanometer is attached to the shoot apex of a plant (see Fig 9.26).

As the disc of the auxanometer rotates, the pointer makes a trace on its surface. The distance between adjacent lines on the disc is proportional to the amount of growth that occurs.
▶ Lines close together – little growth.
▶ Lines further apart – more growth.

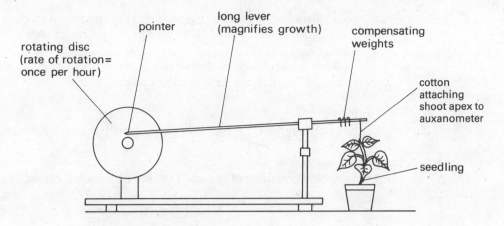

Fig 9.26 The auxanometer

The disc is replaced every 24 hours. To investigate the effect of light the apparatus is kept in light conditions for 48 hours, then in darkness for 48 hours. Throughout this time the temperature is kept constant.

To investigate the effect of temperature the apparatus is kept at 25°C for 48 hours, then at 10°C for 48 hours. Throughout this time the light intensity is kept constant.

Results

▶ In light – lines close together.
▶ In darkness – lines further apart.
▶ 25°C – lines far apart.
▶ 10°C – lines close together.

Conclusions

Growth is more rapid in darkness and warm conditions than in light and colder conditions.

EXPERIMENT TO INVESTIGATE THE EFFECTS OF AVAILABLE NUTRIENTS ON PLANT GROWTH

Principle

To observe the effects of excluding a single element or mineral salt from the plant's nutrient medium. Different experiments can omit different components.

Method

A flask is filled with complete plant nutrient medium (the control). Other flasks are filled with a medium lacking in one specific element or mineral salt. Each flask is covered with black paper to reduce algal growth. All flasks are labelled and dated.

Two holes are drilled into corks that fit into the flasks. A young seedling is placed into one of these holes and held in place with dry cotton wool. The roots of the seedling are immersed in the medium.

The medium is aerated daily via the second cork hole and the pH is maintained at 5–6.

After several weeks the seedlings grown in deficient media are compared with those grown in the control.

Results
Growth is reduced in those seedlings grown in the deficient medium.

Conclusions
Specific elements and mineral salts are necessary for healthy growth.

GROWTH IN ANIMALS

EXPERIMENT TO INVESTIGATE DISCONTINUOUS GROWTH IN LENGTH OF A STICK INSECT

Method
Using a pair of dividers the length of the body of a newly hatched nymph is measured. The measurements are taken from the most anterior part of the head to the posterior end of the abdomen.

The date on which each measurement is taken is recorded. Measurements are continued until six readings produce identical results. The results are plotted as a graph, plotting body length against time.

Results
A graph similar to that in Fig 9.20 is obtained.

Conclusions
Growth occurs in a series of spurts/steps. Size remains constant between each step. No further increase in size occurs once the imago stage is reached.

HUMAN GROWTH

Growth is independent of temperature, and it is limited – it ceases once adult size has been reached. It occurs throughout the body, but different parts of the body grow at different rates, and at different times during the growth period. These progressive changes in structure (differentiation) which occur during the life cycle are called development.

Fig 9.27 shows how the relative proportions of various structures in Man change during the course of development.

Specimen question State one way in which the growth of a plant differs from that of an animal.   (2 marks)   [*JMB*]

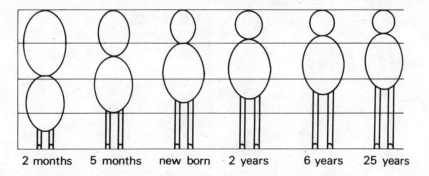

2 months 5 months new born 2 years 6 years 25 years

Fig 9.27 Relative rates of growth of limbs, trunk and head in Man

POPULATION SIZE

Many natural populations of organisms exhibit a growth curve similar to that shown in Fig 9.28 Ultimately the rate of reproduction cannot be maintained and a balance is reached between numbers reproduced and numbers dying.

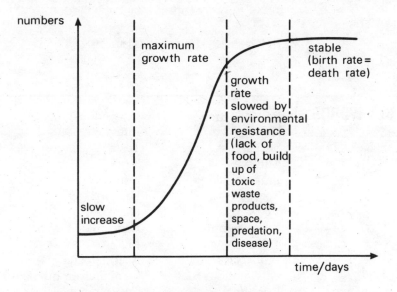

Fig 9.28 Population growth curve – water fleas in a pond

Human population differs from this (see Fig 9.29) for several reasons.

1 Increased expectation of life due to increased hygiene and sanitation.
2 More people are now surviving to old age due to improved medicine and care.
3 Better methods of food production.

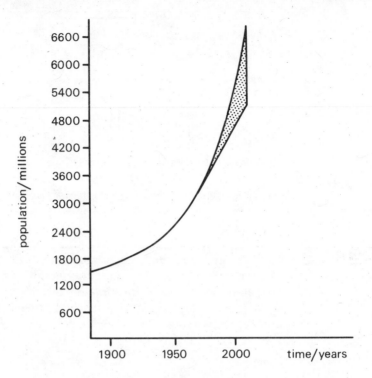

Fig 9.29 Projected world population in 2000 AD

KEY WORDS ▶		
Reproduction	Cotyledons	Oxytocin
Asexual	Integuments	Prolactin
Sexual	Testa	Testosterone
Mitosis	Seed	Copulation
Binary fission	Fruit	Penis
Spores	Pericarp	Vagina
Vegetative	Dispersal	Vulva
propagation	Redd	Oviduct
Tuber	Milt	Implanted
Axillary bud	Spermatozoa	Placenta
Adventitious root	Seminiferous tubules	Umbilical cord
Runner	Testes	Foetus
Artificial	Scrotal sac	Amnion
propagation	Epididymis	Amniotic fluid
Grafting	Sperm duct	Gestation
Scion	Ejaculation	Suckle
Stock	Urethra	Mammary glands
Tissue culture	Seminal vesicle	Menopause
Clone	Prostate gland	Contraception
Perennation	Ovaries	Birth control

Gametes	Ovum	Family planning
Zygote	Ovulation	Gonorrhoea
Haploid	Menstrual cycle	Syphilis
Meiosis	Pregnancy	Artificial
Fertilization	Uterus	insemination
Fusion	Embryo	Fertility drugs
Diploid	Graafian follicle	Growth
Anther	Puberty	Apical meristem
Stigma	Menstruation	Cambium
Stamens	Secondary sexual	Cell elongation
Carpels	characteristics	Differentiation
Inflorescence	Oestrogen	Dormancy
Pollination	Corpus luteum	Germination
Self pollination	Progesterone	Auxanometer
Cross pollination	Pituitary gland	Development
Radicle	FSH	Population size
Plumule	LH	

SPECIMEN EXAMINATION QUESTIONS

1   Fig 9.30 shows a half flower.

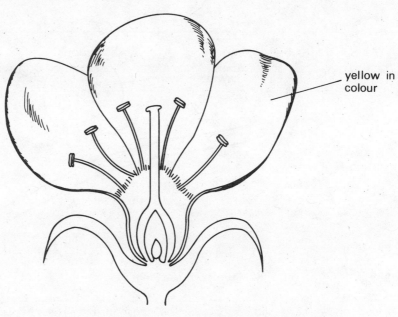

yellow in colour

Fig 9.30

(a)   How many stamens are there in this half flower?   (1 mark)
(b)   What is meant by the term *pollination*?   (2 marks)
(c)   (i) Name TWO features of this flower which suggest that it might be pollinated by insects.   (2 marks)

(ii) How does each of these features help in pollination? (2 marks)

(d)   How would the stigma be different in structure in a wind pollinated flower? (1 mark)

(e)   Suggest ONE other feature of the flower, not shown by the diagram, that might be important for attracting night-flying moths. (1 mark)   [MEG]

2 (a)   Give TWO examples each of wind and insect pollinated flowers. (4 marks)

(b)   Write a sentence to explain the following:

(i) The advantage of cross pollination. (2 marks)

(ii) Why some plants self pollinate (2 marks)

(c)   Draw one plant structure (NOT a seed) which stores food. Add two labels to your drawing.

Give the name of a food stored.

Give one reason why plants store food in this way. (6 marks)

(d)   Some plants grow in very dry habitats. Write down THREE modifications which plants growing in these habitats may have and explain how each modification helps the plant. (9 marks)

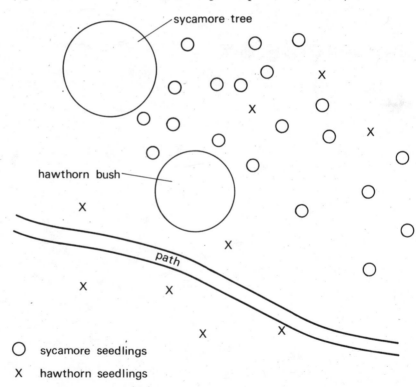

sycamore tree

hawthorn bush

path

O   sycamore seedlings

X   hawthorn seedlings

Fig 9.31

(e)   Study the map in Fig 9.31. Explain the distribution of: sycamore seedlings; hawthorn seedlings. (7 marks)   [SEG]

3 (a)   Fig 9.32 shows the human female reproductive organs. Read the following passage and with the help of the diagram answer the questions opposite.

A woman with blocked oviducts/Fallopian tubes cannot have a baby in the normal way but can now have a 'test-tube baby'. A doctor, using a fine tube through the body wall, sucks up several eggs from the ovary, puts them in a dish and mixes sperm with them. The eggs are then kept for a few days before they are put back into the woman's uterus via the cervix.

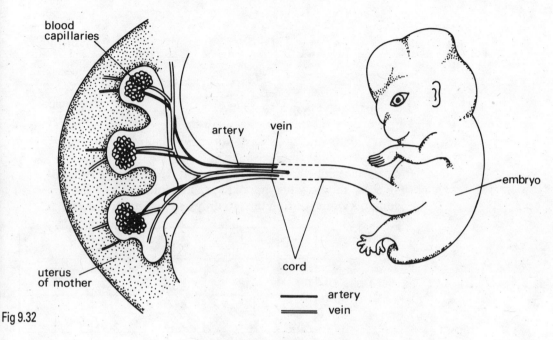

Fig 9.32

(i) Describe what can normally happen in the oviduct/Fallopian tube. (3 marks)

(ii) Why does the doctor get the eggs from the ovary through the body wall and not through the vagina and uterus? (1 mark)

(iii) Why must sperm be mixed with the eggs before they are put back into the woman? (1 mark)

(iv) Why do you think the eggs are kept for a few days before they are put back into the woman? (1 mark)

(v) Why are the eggs put into the uterus? (2 marks)

(vi) Why do you think they are called 'test tube babies'? (2 marks)

(b)   Fig 9.33 shows the circulation of blood to and from the embryo inside a pregnant woman.

(i) What is the name of the cord? (1 mark)

(ii) Name the part where the cord is attached to the uterus. (1 mark)

(iii) Draw an arrow on the diagram to show the direction in which the blood flows in the arteries in the cord. (1 mark)

(iv) How does the embryo get the food and oxygen it needs? (1 mark)

Fig 9.33

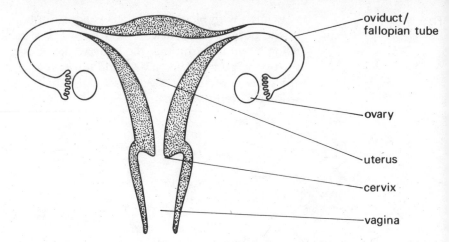

(v) Name ONE waste substance the embryo produces.
(1 mark)

(c)   Describe how the baby is born.   (5 marks)   [LEAG]

4   Fig 9.34 shows what happens to the thickness of the lining of a woman's womb during the monthly cycle (menstrual cycle).

Fig 9.34

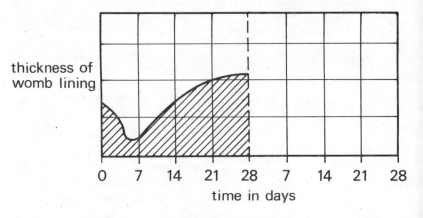

(i) Explain what is happening to the lining of the womb during the first five days.   (1 mark)

(ii) On the chart, when is an egg most likely to be released? (1 mark)

(iii) An egg is fertilized during the first month. Draw a line on the chart to show what would happen to the thickness of the lining of the womb during the second month.   (1 mark)

[NEA]

5   (a)   Describe the events which occur after the release of sperms into the vagina of a human female until implantation of the embryo. (2 marks)

(b)   Fig 9.35 shows how the thickness of the uterus lining and the levels of two hormones A and B, made in the ovaries, vary during the menstrual cycle. The first month is a normal menstrual cycle but fertilization occurs during the second month.

Fig 9.35

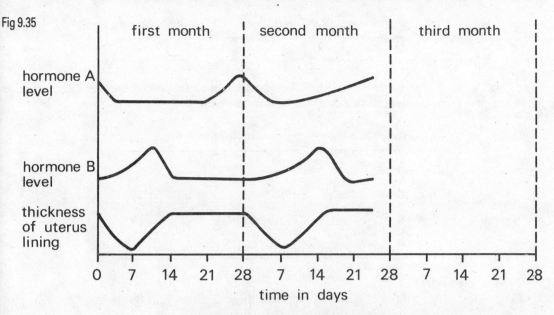

(i) On the chart mark the most likely time of ovulation in the first month. (1 mark)

(ii) During which period in the second month is fertilization likely to have occurred? (1 mark)

(c)   Complete the chart above to show what happens, following fertilization, to:

(i) the uterus lining in the third month;

(ii) the levels of hormones A and B in the third month.

(3 marks)

(d)   One type of contraceptive pill contains a mixture of hormones A and B.

(i) Explain briefly how this pill works as a contraceptive. (1 mark)

(ii) If she is using the contraceptive pill, it is usual for a woman to take a hormone pill each day for 21 days and then to take a pill without any hormones for the next 7 days. What is the advantage of taking the hormones for 21 days only?

[*NEA*]

6   (a)   When a mammal is a developing embryo, name the:

(i) liquid which cushions the embryo from blows;

(ii) part which will be severed after birth;

(iii) part which is normally the first to appear outside the mother at birth.

(b)   Name TWO soluble nutrients (foods) supplied to the embryo by the placenta.

(c)   Name TWO waste materials which pass from the embryo to the mother.

(d)   State PRECISELY what provides the pressure for the passage of these waste materials into the umbilical cord.

(e)   State what happens to the placenta after the mammal is born.

(f)   State ONE effect of EACH of the following on the developing embryo:

(i) rubella;

(ii) smoking.   (11 marks)   [WJEC]

7   Table 9.10 shows the approximate risk that women of different ages will have a baby with Down's syndrome.

Table 9.10

Mother's age (years)	Approximate risk per 10 000 births
17	4
22	6
27	8
32	11
37	34
42	100
47	217

(Source: Dr J. L. Hamerton)

(a)   Draw a graph of these figures. Join the points that you plot with straight lines.   (4 marks)

(b)   What is the risk that a baby born to a woman of 40 will have Down's syndrome?   (1 mark)

(c)   How many times greater is the risk that a woman will have a Down's syndrome baby if she is 42 than if she is 22?   (1 mark)

(d)   Suggest TWO reasons why babies with Down's syndrome are more often born to older mothers.   (2 marks)   [SEG]

8   Concern has been expressed at the number of children suffering from Down's Syndrome being born to families living along the east coast of Northern Ireland.

(i) What may have happened in the mother's body which could have been responsible for the condition appearing in the child?   (1 mark)

(ii) How would the chromosomes in a cell taken from a Down's syndrome baby differ from those taken from a baby who does not suffer from the condition?   (1 mark)

[NISEC]

9   (a)   Two technicians were asked to cut sections of onion roots to find out whether more cell division takes place in them in the morning or the afternoon. Their reports are shown below.

> **Technician X**
>
> Estimated percentage of cells dividing, viewed under the low power lens of a microscope.
>
>   At 10.00 am   10%
>   At 2.00 pm   7%
>
> **Answer:** the morning

Technican Y	Morning	Afternoon
No. of cells dividing in one high power field of microscope	6	10
No. of cells not dividing in one high power field of microscope	48	60

Answer: the afternoon

What advice would you give them to make this a fair test?

(b)   List the main steps which the technicians would have had to take in carrying out this investigation.   [SCE]

10   Fig 9.36 below shows the external appearance of a mung-bean seed.

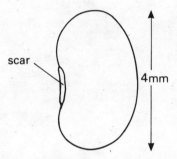

Fig 9.36

(a)   From what part of the flower has the seed developed? (1 mark)

(b)   You are asked to find the best temperature for sprouting (germinating) mung-bean seeds. You are given 100 seeds, 10 test tubes, cotton wool, 10 thermometers, a clock and a supply of water.

(i) Draw and label one of the test tubes you would set up for the experiment.

(ii) Explain how you would carry out this experiment. (7 marks)

(iii) Describe ONE difficulty you might have in carrying out this experiment.   (1 mark)   [LEAG]

11   Two batches of vegetable seeds were stored in two separate rooms A and B. The temperature in each room was kept constant at 10°C.

The humidity in room A was kept at 25% whereas the humidity in room B was kept at 75%.

At the time intervals given in Table 9.11, 200 seeds from each batch were removed from the rooms and placed in conditions ideal for germination. The percentage of seeds which germinated was recorded. The results are summarized in Table 9.11.

Table 9.11

Years of storage	Percentage germination of seeds stored in room A	Percentage germination of seeds stored in room B
0.5	56.0	52.0
1	52.0	45.0
2	49.0	34.0
3	47.0	23.0
4	46.0	15.0
5	45.5	9.0

(a)   Suggest why seeds survived better in room A than in room B.
(b)   What advice would you give to a seed merchant about storing and packaging the seeds?   (3 marks)   [NEA]

GENETICS AND EVOLUTION

CONTENTS

F_1 **generation** Offspring from a first cross between individuals.
F_2 **generation** Offspring from a cross between F_1 progeny.
Recessive A gene which, in the presence of its contrasting allele in the heterozygote, is not expressed in the phenotype.
Dominant The gene whose characteristic appears in the heterozygous phenotype.
Chromosome A thread-like structure in the nucleus, visible at cell division.
DNA A nucleic acid whose molecular form determines hereditary characteristics.
Gene The structures in the chromosome which determine hereditary characteristics.
Homologous Corresponding chromosomes inherited from male and female parents.
Alleles Alternative forms of a gene, occupying the same place on a chromosome and affecting the same character but in different ways.
Diploid The number of chromosomes ($2n$) found in body cells, made up of homologous pairs.
Haploid A single set of chromosomes (n) consisting of one chromosome from each pair of homologous chromosomes.
Homozygous The condition where a pair of identical alleles occurs in the same cell.
Heterozygous The condition where a pair of contrasting alleles occur in the same cell.
Genotype The genetic composition of an organism.
Phenotype The visible physical characteristics of an organism.
Linkage The effect of genes being on the same chromosome.
Carrier An apparently normal heterozygote which 'carries' a recessive abnormal gene.
Heredity The passing on of characteristics through successive generations.
Mutation A sudden (abrupt) structural change in a chromosome or gene which is inheritable.
Species The smallest unit of classification. Only organisms of the same species can interbreed and produce fertile offspring.
Natural selection The environmental selection of individuals best adapted to live and reproduce in that environment.

GENETICS

The science of genetics explains how similarities and differences in characteristics arise and are inherited.

THE NUCLEUS

The nucleus has two roles.
1 It carries instructions for the control of all of the cell's activities.
2 It ensures the accurate transmission of these instructions to the

daughter cells produced during mitosis and the gamete cells produced during meiosis.

Chromosomes inside the nucleus carry the instructions for all the cell's activities. Each chromosome contains a long molecule of **deoxyribonucleic acid** (DNA) covered by a protein coat. The chemical code carried in the DNA molecules determines the structure of protein molecules made by the cells. The code is copied in the nucleus and passes to the cytoplasm where proteins are manufactured. Most of the proteins produced directly act as enzymes allowing reactions to occur (cell metabolism). This process is summarized in Fig 10.1.

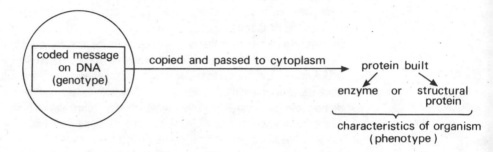

Fig 10.1 Protein synthesis

A **gene** is a region of the chromosome where DNA carries the code for a specific protein molecule. Each chromosome is made up of very many genes arranged in linear order along the chromosome length, as shown in Fig 10.2.

A   B   C   D   E   F   G   H   I   J   K

Fig 10.2 Position of genes on the chromosome

All body cells (somatic cells) have two sets of chromosomes. These cells are described as **diploid** (2n). They contain 23 pairs of chromosomes in humans, i.e.:

$2n = 2 \times 23 = 46$ chromosomes

Each pair of chromosomes is called a pair of **homologous chromosomes** and they carry genes for the same characteristics, arranged in the same order. Genes which occupy similar positions on homologous chromosomes and control the same characteristic are called **alleles**.

As each chromosome is represented twice in the normal diploid cell, each gene must be represented twice. During mitosis, exact duplication and distribution of the chromosomes in the cell nucleus takes place prior to nuclear division. Therefore identical nuclei are produced containing identical chromosomes and genes.

During meiosis, each one of a pair of homologous chromosomes passes into a separate gamete. Gamete cells are described as **haploid** (n). They contain 23 chromosomes, i.e. $n = 23$. Each gamete therefore contains one gene for each characteristic. Random fusion of gametes occurs during fertilization and the diploid number of chromosomes is restored. The zygote now formed has two genes controlling each characteristic.

MONOHYBRID INHERITANCE

Where the members of the gene pair are alike (**AA**) the individual is described as **homozygous** or **pure-breeding** for that character. Where the genes are different (**a**) it is **heterozygous** (**A** and **a** are alleles). The total genetic content of an organism or a cell is its **genotype** and may carry thousands of gene pairs affecting all aspects of the organism's development and activity. The observed condition of the organism is its **phenotype**.

Where one of a pair of alleles shows its effect in the phenotype, whatever other allele is present, this allele is said to be **dominant**. The member of a pair of alleles that does not show its effect in the presence of another allele is said to be **recessive**.

The following are examples of a dominant allele producing a dominant trait in humans.

1 **Tongue rolling** Many people possess the dominant gene for controlling the tongue muscle. When this muscle contracts it enables the tongue to be rolled into a tube.
2 **Shape of bottom of ear** Your ear lobe may be 'free' or 'attached'. Free lobes are dominant (see Fig 10.3).

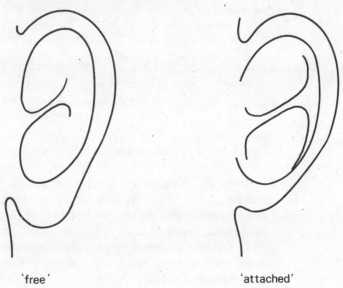

'free'   'attached'

Fig 10.3 Types of ear lobe

QUESTIONS INVOLVING MONOHYBRID INHERITANCE

The inheritance of specific characteristics can be written out diagrammatically as shown on p.252. This is the correct way to describe a genetic situation or problem and must always be used in questions which ask 'Describe or explain fully how . . .'

As a rule always begin by stating which allele is dominant and which is recessive. Use the initial letter of the dominant gene as the genotypic symbol and its capital form, e.g. **T**, for dominant and ordinary form, and e.g. **t**, for recessive. Always include all the stages such as parental phenotype, parental genotype, etc., in your explanation (see worked example on p.252). This may be shown diagrammatically as in Fig 10.4.

EXAMPLE OF MONOHYBRID INHERITANCE

A pure breeding tall plant is crossed with a pure breeding dwarf plant.

Let **T** = dominant gene for tallness.
Let **t** = recessive gene for dwarfness.
The F_1 generation will be as in Fig 10.4.

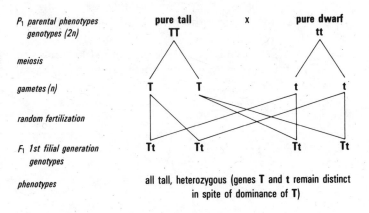

Fig 10.4 The F_1 generation in a monohybrid cross

The F_1 generation is then allowed to fertilize, giving the result shown in Fig 10.5. The ratio of 3:1 shown in Fig 10.5 is called the **monohybrid ratio** because only one pair of contrasting characters is being considered.

The above explanation may be used directly in answering questions such as the following, where the F_2 phenotypes show an approximate 3:1 ratio.

Specimen question The seeds resulting from a cross between a tall pea plant and a dwarf one produced plants all of which were tall. When these plants were allowed to self pollinate, the resulting seeds produced 908 tall plants and 293 dwarf plants. Using symbols and a

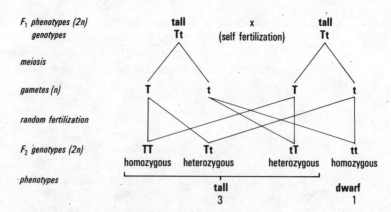

Fig 10.5 The F₂ generation in a monohybrid cross

written explanation, account fully for these results. What would be the results of interbreeding the dwarf plants?   (16 marks)

[ULSEB]

BACKCROSS

This is an experimental technique used to determine the genotype of an organism, e.g. the genotype of a long-winged *Drosophila* (fruit fly) may be homozygous (**LL**) or heterozygous (**Ll**). In order to establish which, the fly is backcrossed with a double recessive (**ll**) vestigial(short)-winged fly. If the offspring are all long-winged, the unknown parental genotype is homozygous dominant. A ratio of 1 long:1 vestigial wing indicates a heterozygote, as in Fig 10.6.

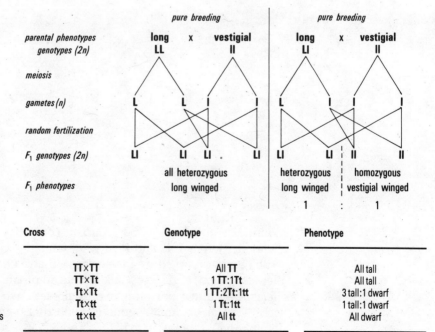

Fig 10.6 A backcross

Table 10.1 Summary of genetic crosses

T = dominant allele for tallness
t = recessive allele for dwarfness

Cross	Genotype	Phenotype
TT×TT	All TT	All tall
TT×Tt	1 TT:1Tt	All tall
Tt×Tt	1 TT:2Tt:1tt	3 tall:1 dwarf
Tt×tt	1 Tt:1tt	1 tall:1 dwarf
tt×tt	All tt	All dwarf

INCOMPLETE DOMINANCE

This condition occurs where two or more alleles do not show complete dominance and recessiveness. In most cases where this occurs the heterozygote has a phenotype which is intermediate between the homozygous dominant and recessive conditions. Two examples are given.

EXAMPLE 1

In some plant species a red-flowered plant crossed with a white-flowered plant produces an F_1 generation with all pink flowers. Neither the red nor the white allele is dominant. When self fertilized, the F_2 progeny are in the ratio of 1 red:2 pink:1 white – see Fig 10.7, where R = red allele, and W = white allele.

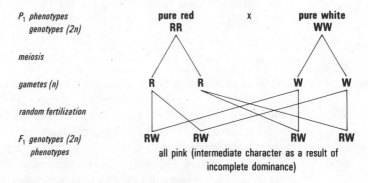

Fig 10.7 Incomplete dominance in flower colour

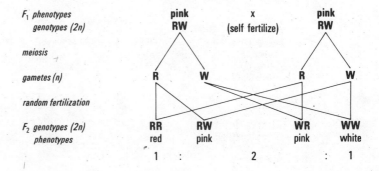

EXAMPLE 2

Inheritance of human blood groups is controlled by a group of three alleles written as $I^A I^B$ and I^O. I represents the region of the chromosome (gene) occupied by the alleles **A,B** and **O**. This is the multiple allele condition, and shows incomplete dominance with regard to two alleles **A** and **B**. A person may only possess two such alleles (one on each of a pair of homologous chromosomes). **A** and **B** are equally dominant; **O** is recessive to both **A** and **B**.

Table 10.2 Genetics of
human blood groups

	Possible genotype	Phenotype of blood group
$I^A I^A$	homozygous	} Group A
$I^A I^O$	heterozygous	
$I^B I^B$	homozygous	} Group B
$I^B I^O$	heterozygous	
$I^A I^B$	incomplete dominance	Group AB
$I^O I^O$	homozygous recessive	Group O

It is possible for two parents of blood group A and B respectively to produce children exhibiting all phenotypes (see Fig 10.8).

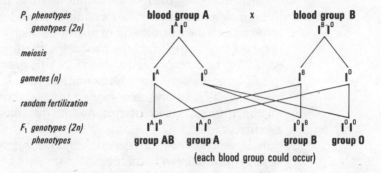

Fig 10.8 Incomplete dominance in human blood groups

Genetics problems involving the inheritance of blood groups are very common. Using information given above try to answer the following question.

Specimen question Explain fully how two people of blood group **A** may have three children all of whom are blood group **O**.   (13 marks)

[O&C]

SEX DETERMINATION IN MAMMALS

This is determined genetically as shown in Fig 10.9.
Female body cells have 23 pairs of chromosomes, of which one pair are both **X** chromosomes. Male body cells have 23 pairs of chromo-

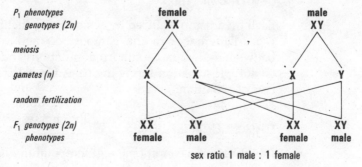

Fig 10.9 Sex
determination in mammals

somes, one pair of which contains an **X** and a **Y** chromosome. All eggs contain an **X** chromosome; 50% of sperms contain an **X** chromosome and 50% contain a **Y** chromosome. The sex of the offspring depends upon which type of sperm fertilizes the egg.

GENETIC ENGINEERING

This is the practice of moving sections of DNA from a donor cell to a recipient cell. This produces carefully controlled changes in the metabolism of the recipient cell, resulting in the manufacture of a prescribed substance.

This process is being increasingly used to manufacture proteins, hormones and vitamins. For example, some human DNA has been inserted into the nucleic acid of microorganisms. The microorganisms respond to this treatment by producing the human protein which is coded by the transplanted human DNA. If these microorganisms are then placed in very large fermentation vats, large quantities of the 'engineered' substance are made. In this way substances such as insulin, human growth hormone and hepatitis vaccine have been produced.

It is anticipated that genetic engineering will enable enzymes, detergents and even fossil fuel alternatives to be manufactured. Genetic engineering is a branch of the rapidly developing science of **biotechnology**.

VARIATION

This term is used to describe the infinite number of combinations of characteristics seen among individuals of the same species.

PHENOTYPIC VARIATION

This is variation in the physical characteristics of the organism. It is determined by genotype but may be modified by the environment, e.g. the basic human body shape and size is inherited but final size can be modified by environmental factors such as quantity of food eaten, exercise, disease, etc.

GENOTYPIC VARIATION

Each organism produced by sexual reproduction has a unique genotype. Differences in the composition and combinations of genes between individuals result from mutations and genetic reassortment. Genotypic variation forms the basis for natural selection in the process of evolution.

ENVIRONMENTAL INFLUENCES

Environmental conditions, e.g. temperature, light, water, food availability, disease, etc., may allow or prevent the full expression of the genotypes, e.g. a variety of pea plants that normally grow 2 metres tall will only do so under conditions of adequate light, water and soil nutrition. Any reduction in the supply of these conditions (limiting factors) will result in the gene for height not being able to exert its full effect.

Differences in physical characteristics (phenotypic variation) can be measured, e.g. index-finger length, height, blood group, ability to roll tongue, etc. When these results are examined they are seen to fall into two categories:

1 **continuous variation;**
2 **discontinuous variation**.

Continuous variation

The height of a large group of children of the same age and sex is taken and the results plotted as shown on the graph in Fig 10.10. This type of smooth curve is called a **normal distribution curve**. The highest point represents the average height and there are as many very tall people as very short people.

This is **continuous variation**. Characteristics showing this pattern of variation are controlled by several genes and influenced by environmental factors, e.g. weight in Man, seed number and fruit size in tomato.

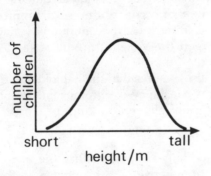

Fig 10.10 Distribution curve for height

Discontinuous variation

Here there is an abrupt jump from one characteristic to another. There are no intermediates. In **discontinuous variation** the characteristics are controlled by one or a few major genes. Environmental factors have no effect on them and they are passed on to the next generation, i.e. they are inheritable, e.g. blood groups, sex of individual.

Specimen question Variations between individuals are either continuous or discontinuous. From the list below, select one example of each type of variation.

(a)   presence of ear lobes
(b)   rate of heartbeat
(c)   length of handspan
(d)   ability of roll tongue
(e)   colour of iris
(2 marks)   [SCE]

SOURCES OF VARIATION

Genetic reassortment

This results from the rearrangement of genes during meiosis in gamete formation and from the random fusion of gametes at fertilization. The process occurs as follows.

1   An initial exact duplication of chromosomes occurs.
2   The chromosomes move together to form homologous pairs of chromosomes (see Fig 9.5).
3   One chromosome of each pair enters each daughter cell. This occurs at random and is termed independent assortment.
4   This produces a halving of the chromosome number – the haploid condition.
5   A second division occurs, producing four haploid gametes containing different sets of alleles.
6   The fusion of a male gamete with a female gamete to produce a diploid zygote is completely random and causes further variation.

This source of genetic variation accounts for the normal process of gene 'mixing' that occurs during sexual reproduction. It is the main factor contributing towards continuous variation. The environment then acts upon the varieties produced, and those best suited to it survive successfully.

Meiosis also ensures that the haploid and diploid stages alternate. This ensures constancy of chromosome number from generation to generation in sexually reproducing species.

Mutation

This is a sudden change in either the amount or structure of the chromosomal material (DNA). A change in the amount of DNA produces a chromosome mutation, e.g. in Down's syndrome each cell has 47 chromosomes instead of the normal 46. A change in the structure of DNA produces a gene mutation, e.g. sickle cell anaemia. Mutations are rare and usually occur during cell division (mitosis or meiosis).

A gene mutation may involve the addition, loss or rearrangement of the DNA code in the gene. Those which occur during gamete formation are transmitted to all the cells of the offspring. Mutations that are spread by mitosis are inherited only by those cells that are produced from the mutant cells, e.g. malignant tumour – cancer.

Sickle cell anaemia occurs when the chemical code in the DNA in one of the genes involved in haemoglobin production is changed.

This change causes the red blood cells to become sickle shaped and their oxygen-carrying capacity is reduced, leading to acute anaemia.

The rate of mutations can be increased by X-rays, ultra-violet rays, radioactivity (α, β, γ rays), and chemicals such as mustard gas, nicotine, tar and some drugs. Whilst most mutations are recessive (see p.249) and harmful, they do provide the main source of genetic variation within the population – the raw material of evolution.

Influenza, spread by droplet infection, is caused by three strains of virus designated as A, B and C, which vary in their degree of severity. Strain A is the most highly infectious. The genotype of the virus varies from time to time due to gene mutation. This makes it difficult to control, for immunity to one form is specific and cannot last indefinitely. Each year different vaccines must be produced to combat the modified viruses.

SELECTION

ARTIFICIAL SELECTION

Man selectively breeds from a natural population of organisms to obtain individuals possessing characteristics or traits that have economic importance or usefulness. New breeds, strains and varieties are produced in this way.

Hereford and Aberdeen Angus cattle have been selected for the quality and quantity of their meat. Jersey cows have been selectively bred for their high milk yield.

Outbreeding is the crossing of individuals from genetically distinct populations. The resulting offspring (**progeny**) are called **hybrids**. They possess characteristics which are better than those exhibited by either parent. Their condition is termed **hybrid vigour** or **heterosis**. They may show advantages such as increases in resistance to disease, food values and yields, e.g. with maize (sweet corn) outbreeding methods have increased yields by over 250% in some species.

NATURAL SELECTION

The occurrence of variation within a species means that some individuals will be better suited to living in the environment than others. Charles Darwin recognized this as the basis of the process by which new species arise from pre-existing forms. After receiving a letter from Alfred Russell Wallace, who had independently reached the same conclusions, Darwin and Wallace made their views known at the same meeting in London in 1858. In 1859 Darwin published a book called *On the Origin of Species by Means of Natural Selection*. In it he recognized the process of evolution, he presented data demonstrating it, and he developed a theory of how evolution took place. His theory is based on the following three observations.

1 **Organisms tend to produce as many offspring as possible.**
2 **The number of individuals in a species remains remarkably constant.**
3 **Variation exists among members of a species.**

From **1** and **2** he concluded that there exists, within nature, a **struggle for survival**. Some organisms survive and reproduce whilst others do not. Darwin's studies of variation (observation **3**) suggested that those organisms best adapted phenotypically to the environment survived, reproduced and passed on their advantageous characteristics to their offspring. By this means the ever-changing environment continuously selects those organisms best fitted for survival (survival of the fittest). This forms the basis of evolution by **natural selection**.

MALTHUS ON POPULATION GROWTH

In 1798 Thomas Malthus published an *Essay on the Principle of Population*. He concluded that whereas a population would increase in numbers by **geometric progression** unless checked somehow, food supply would increase only by **arithmetic progression** (Fig 10.11).

Charles Darwin took into account these ideas when formulating his theory of **natural selection**.

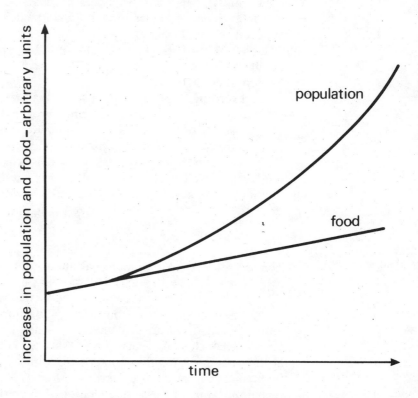

Fig 10.11 Malthus' theory concerning population increase and food supply

EXAMPLES OF NATURAL SELECTION

MUTATIONS

These occur in insects and bacteria, making them resistant to pesticides and antibiotics respectively. New pesticides and antibiotics have to be produced to kill these mutants.

Insects and bacteria breed very quickly and have a high mutation rate. Some of these new mutations give these organisms resistance to the newly-developed pesticides and antibiotics.

INDUSTRIAL MELANISM

The normal form of the peppered moth (*Biston betularia*) possesses pale mottled wings resembling a peppery pattern. Robins, thrushes and other birds prey on the moths by plucking them from the surfaces of trees. In 1848 a melanic (dark) mutant appeared in Manchester. In smoke-polluted areas, e.g. Manchester, the melanic form was well camouflaged when resting on the soot-covered trees, whereas the normal form was easily seen and more frequently preyed upon by birds. Therefore dark colour provided a selective advantage in this environment.

In non-polluted areas the reverse was true and the melanic forms were more easily seen and preyed upon (selective predation). Even today the normal form still predominates here.

Current figures: Manchester 99% melanic form; N. Scotland (unpolluted) 99% normal form.

These proportions have remained relatively stable from one year to the next for some time.

SICKLE CELL ANAEMIA AND MALARIA

Sickle cell anaemia causes acute anaemia and early death of individuals *homozygous* for the sickle cell allele.

Heterozygous individuals exhibit the **sickle cell trait** – red blood cells appear normal and only 40% of the haemoglobin is abnormal. This produces mild anaemia only.

In Africa and Asia, the sickle cell trait prevents carriers of it from contracting malaria. The protozoan *Plasmodium*, which causes malaria, cannot survive in the red blood cells containing abnormal haemoglobin. Therefore individuals possessing sickle cell trait may possess a selective advantage over those who do not in these continents.

FORMATION OF NEW SPECIES

Isolation is a factor in producing evolutionary change. It separates a population of a species into two or more groups. No exchange of genes occurs between the separated groups. Mutation and selection take place independently within each group and new species may develop (see Fig 10.12).

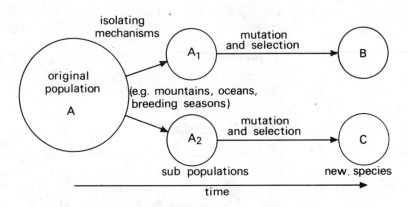

Fig 10.12 Summary of species formation

KEY WORDS ▶

Chromosomes	Monohybrid ratio	Selection
Deoxyribonucleic	Backcross	Artificial
acid	Incomplete	Outbreeding
Gene	dominance	Progeny
Homologous	Multiple alleles	Hybrids
chromosomes	Sex linked	Hybrid vigour
Alleles	Variation	Natural selection
Homozygous	Continuous	Population growth
Heterozygous	Discontinuous	Industrial melanism
Genotype	Genetic engineering	Sickle cell anaemia
Phenotype	Biotechnology	Malaria
Dominant	Genetic reassortment	Isolation
Recessive	Mutation	

SPECIMEN EXAMINATION QUESTIONS

1 DNA is a molecule containing a number of alleles arranged lengthwise.
   (a)   Where would you find DNA inside a cell?   (1 mark)
   (b)   Why is DNA such an important substance?   (2 marks)
   (c)   (i) What is an allele?   (1 mark)
         (ii) Give one example of an allele found in humans.   (1 mark)
                                                        [SEG]

2 Fig 10.13 shows the chromosomes of a cell from a woman. Fig 10.14 shows the chromosomes of a cell from a woman who is suffering from a genetic disorder.

diagram A

Fig 10.13

diagram B

Fig 10.14

(a)   (i) How many chromosomes has the cell from the woman in Fig 10.13? (1 mark)

(ii) What difference is there between the chromosomes of this woman and those of the woman with the genetic disorder? (1 mark)

(b)   (i) In which part of the cell are chromosomes found? (1 mark)

(ii) What could damage the chromosomes of a human egg so that a baby developed a genetic disorder? (1 mark)

(c)   Study of the chromosomes can be used to make sure whether a person is really male or female, for example in an athlete's sex test. How would the chromosomes of a man differ from those of a woman? (1 mark)   [NEA]

3   Examine Fig 10.15 and answer the following questions.

(a)   Given that the number of chromosomes in human body cells is 46, enter in the circles on Fig 10.15 the number of chromosomes for each of the structures shown.

(b)   A scientist carried out four crosses of true-breeding pea plants. Each cross showed contrasting characters. The F_1 plants which resulted were then allowed to self pollinate.

Table 10.3 summarizes the four crosses. It shows each of the original parental crosses and the resulting F_1 plants. It also shows the F_2 plants which resulted from the self pollination of the F_1 generation, and the F_2 ratios.

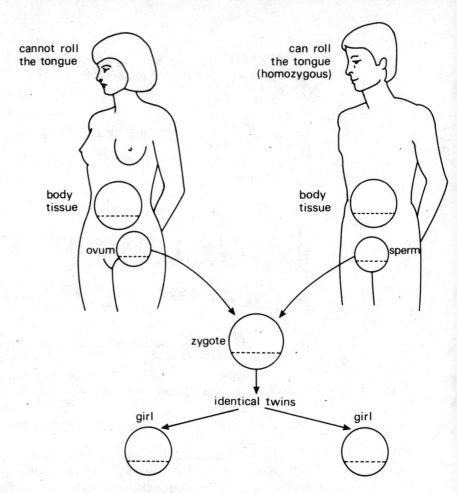

cannot roll
the tongue

can roll
the tongue
(homozygous)

body
tissue

body
tissue

ovum

sperm

zygote

Fig 10.15

identical twins

girl

girl

Table 10.3

Cross number	Original parental cross	F₁ plants from parental cross	F₂ plants from F₁ cross	F₂ ratio
1	Tall×short	All tall	787 tall:277 short	2.84:1
2	Round seeds×wrinkled seeds	All produce round seeds	5474 round:1850 wrinkled	2.96:1
3	Yellow cotyledons×green cotyledons	All produce yellow cotyledons	6022 yellow:2001 green	3.01:1
4	Grey seed coat×white seed coat	All produce seeds with grey coats	705 grey:244 white	2.89:1

(i) Complete Table 10.4 to show the dominant and the recessive characters in each of the crosses.   (2 marks)

Table 10.4

Cross number	Dominant character	Recessive character
1		
2		
3		
4		

(ii) Explain how you can tell from Table 10.3 which character is dominant and which is recessive. (2 marks)

(c)   (i) Calculate the F_2 ratio of plants producing grey-coloured seed to plants producing white-coloured seed in cross 4. (*Show your working*) (2 marks)

(ii) To the nearest whole number, what is the ratio of dominant to recessive characters in all four crosses? (1 mark)

(d)   (i) Using the letters, **T** and **t** to represent genes for tallness and shortness, enter in the circles in Fig 10.16 the genotypes of each parent in cross 1. (1 mark)

tall parent   short parent

Fig 10.16

(ii) All the offspring (F_1 plants) resulting from this cross are tall plants. State the genotype of the F_1 plants. (1 mark)

(iii) Complete Fig 10.17 to explain the F_2 results obtained in cross 1. (3 marks)   [*MEG*]

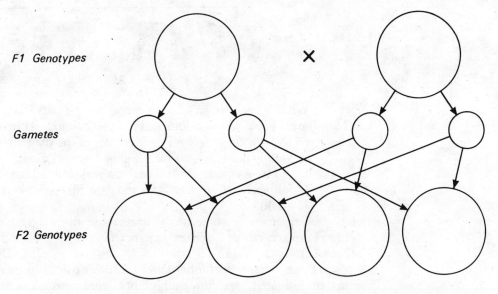

F1 Genotypes

Gametes

F2 Genotypes

Fig 10.17

4   In genetics symbols are used as a code so that a lot of information can be given simply. **D** is the symbol for the allele that controls the dark colour and **d** is the symbol for the allele that controls the light colour in these mice.

(i) If a mouse's genotype is $\frac{D}{d}$, what colour is it?

What are the possible colours of its father and mother?   (3 marks)

(ii) What would be the phenotype and the genotype of the offspring of a pair of light mice?   (2 marks)

(iii) A pair of dark mice produced both dark and light offspring. Give the genotypes of each of the dark parents.   (1 mark)

(iv) Another pair of dark mice had only two offspring which were both light. How do you explain this?   (2 marks)   [SEG]

5   Fig 10.18 shows the offspring of crosses between pure-bred Aberdeen Angus bulls, which are black, and pure-bred Redpoll cows, which are red. The ratio of the colours of the offspring of the first generation is also shown. Coat colour is controlled by a single gene which has two forms (alleles): one for black and one for red coat colour.

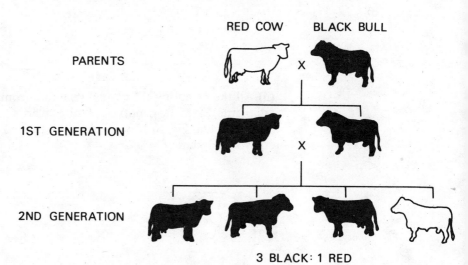

Fig 10.18

(a)   What letters are suitable to represent the two forms (alleles) of the gene, i.e. black coat colour and red coat colour?   (1 mark)

(b)   (i) Draw a circle around each animal in the diagram which is definitely homozygous for the gene for coat colour.   (1 mark)

(ii) Draw a square around each animal in the diagram which is definitely heterozygous for the gene for coat colour. (1 mark)

(c)   Explain why some of the animals in the diagram could be either homozygous or heterozygous for the gene for coat colour. (2 marks)   [LEAG]

6   When the mechanism of inheritance of flower colour in garden peas was investigated, red-flowered plants were crossed with white-flowered plants. The first generation of plants all had red flowers. However, when these red-flowered plants were allowed to self fertilize, about 25% of the offspring had white flowers, the remainder having red flowers.

In a similar investigation with snapdragon plants, when red-flowered plants were crossed with white-flowered plants, the result-ing first generation all had pink flowers. When these pink-flowered plants were self fertilized, 25% of the offspring had white flowers, 25% had red flowers and 50% had pink flowers.

(a)   Suggest why the results obtained with the garden pea are different from those obtained with the snapdragon plants.   (1 mark)

(b)   By means of a diagram, show how the results for the snap-dragon can be explained genetically.   (4 marks)

(c)   Some barley plants are susceptible to attack by mildew (a fungus) whilst others are resistant to mildew attack. In an investiga-tion by a plant breeder, it was found that susceptible plants produced only susceptible offspring when self fertilized, but that a resistant plant produced a mixture of resistant and susceptible plants when self fertilized.

(i) How would the plant breeder obtain a stock of barley plants which were all resistant to mildew?   (2 marks)

(ii) Assuming that resistance to mildew is controlled by a single gene, what must be the genotype of the resistant stock?   (1 mark)   [NEA]

7   The heights of the 30 pupils in a biology class were measured and the results are shown in Table 10.5.

Table 10.5

Pupil	Height (cm)	Pupil	Height (cm)	Pupil	Height (cm)
1	150	11	152	21	140
2	150	12	138	22	144
3	148	13	144	23	146
4	150	14	146	24	148
5	146	15	148	25	150
6	150	16	150	26	152
7	152	17	152	27	154
8	144	18	154	28	156
9	148	19	160	29	158
10	150	20	138	30	160

(a)   (i) Complete Table 10.6 to show how many pupils there are at the various heights.   (2 marks)

Table 10.6

Height in cm	138	140	142	144	146	148	150	152	154	156	158	160
Number of pupils												

(ii) Use graph paper to make a bar graph of the results. (3 marks)

(b)   Name the kind of variation shown by your bar graph. (1 mark)   [NEA]

8   The kiwifruit originally grew in China. In the 1960s a New Zealand

farmer planted a number of seeds intending to select plants with the best features.

(a)   What name is given to this form of selection?   (1 mark)

(b)   Why was it important for the farmer to use seeds from a large number of different plants?   (1 mark)

(c)   The best variety is called Hayward, after the farmer who discovered it. Most of the world's cultivated kiwifruit is now the Hayward variety.

(i) How must Hayward plants be reproduced to keep the variety the same?   (1 mark)

(ii) What could research workers do if they want to improve on the Hayward variety?   (2 marks)   [LEAG]

9   The graphs in Fig 10.19 show the patterns of survival in the brown trout and man.

(a)   Give two reasons why the pattern of survival for man is different from that for the brown trout.   (2 marks)

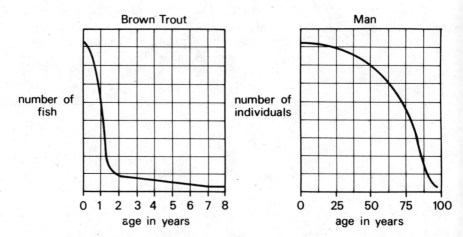

Fig 10.19

(b)   Explain how the pattern in the graph for the brown trout would support Darwin's theory of natural selection.   (3 marks)

[NEA]

10   (a)   The histograms in Fig 10.20 show the variation in length of minnows from samples caught in a river during 1960 and 1961.

(i) What type of variation is shown by these results?

(ii) Explain why the frequency of occurrence of any named variant can change within a population.

(b)   Mutations can bring about a change in a characteristic in an organism. Mutations can also be transmitted to the next generation through the gametes.

(i) Give one example of a mutation which is useful to man.

(ii) Give an example of an environmental factor which can increase the rate of mutation in populations of organisms.

[SCE]

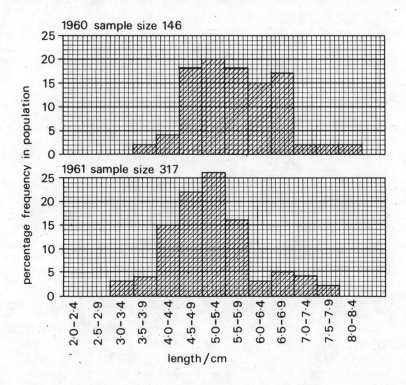

Fig 10.20

11 (a)   Briefly explain the theory of evolution by natural selection. Include in your explanation the following terms:
mutation; competition; inheritance; survival of the fittest; genotype; over-production.   (10 marks)

(b)   Man has domesticated a number of animals and cultivated many plants.

(i) How does this artificial selection differ from natural selection?   (2 marks)

(ii) Describe TWO examples of successful artificial selection in plants and animals.   (4 marks)

(c)   Sexual reproduction is considered to be essential if evolution is to take place, yet many higher plants reproduce asexually much of the time. Comment on this situation.   (4 marks)   [MEG]

ECOLOGY AND MICROBIOLOGY

CONTENTS

Environment The surroundings in which an organism lives.

Habitat The region in which an organism lives.

Ecosystem The living and non-living components of a region, which interact to produce a stable system.

Capillarity The rise of water in narrow spaces due to molecular attraction.

Photoperiodism The response of a plant to the relative lengths of light and dark periods.

Producer An organism which synthesizes complex organic compounds from simple inorganic materials.

Consumer An organism that takes in ready-synthesized organic material.

Food chain A food relationship where energy is transferred from one group of organisms to another.

Pollution Unusually high levels of natural or unnatural constituents in the environment, which cause undesirable effects.

Vector An animal which transmits a pathogenic organism from one organism to another.

Biotechnology The use of biological processes or organisms in manufacturing and service industries.

Genetic engineering The alteration of the structure of chromosomes by man.

Quadrat A structure of known area, usually 1m^2, useful for the study of density of populations.

Monoculture The repeated cultivation of the same plant species in the same area.

Colonization The appearance of a new species in a habitat and the growth in population size over a period of time.

Succession The various stages of colonization seen in a habitat. Relative numbers of different species vary throughout the succession.

Climax The final stable state of a community as it appears at the end of a succession.

ECOLOGY

Ecology is the study of the relationships between living organisms and their **environment**. There are three major environments – marine, freshwater and terrestrial – containing many **habitats**. The environment can be divided into two natural divisions – the **abiotic** or non-living environment and the **biotic** or living environment. These two interact in such a way as to produce a balanced system called the **ecosystem**. Populations of animals and plants that occur naturally together in a common environment form a **community**.

ABIOTIC ENVIRONMENT

The main features of the non-living environment concern the climate, nutrient cycles and the soil. These factors influence the number and distribution of organisms within a given area. While primarily affecting plant growth, they also affect animals which feed on them and the whole balance of nature.

LIGHT

The intensity and amount of light varies with the seasons of the year, latitude and weather conditions. Light is essential for green plants, and they possess numerous adaptations for obtaining optimum illumination for photosynthesis (see Chapter 3). Some plants, e.g. henbane, respond to long periods of daylight by flowering, whilst others flower only when day-length is short. This response to light is termed **photoperiodism**.

Light may also influence vegetative development of tubers, development of fruits and seeds, onset/break of **dormancy** in seeds and buds and **hibernation** and nesting in animals.

WATER

Water is required by plants for photosynthesis and by all organisms for metabolism. Plants living in deserts must possess efficient adaptations to cope with the dry conditions, e.g. reduced number of stomata, thick waxy cuticle, water storage tissues.

TEMPERATURE

The rate of enzyme reactions and metabolism varies with temperature. All organisms live within a narrow temperature range and possess many physiological and behavioural adaptations to remain within these limits, e.g. hibernation in animals – the animal sleeps deeply as its body temperature and metabolic rate fall. In plants the rates of photosynthesis and water uptake vary with temperature.

NUTRIENT CYCLES

All living organisms depend upon adequate supplies of nutrients. Plants are able to synthesize food from these nutrients using energy from the sun. Whilst the major nutrient elements (carbon, hydrogen, oxygen and nitrogen) are constantly cycled and recycled through ecosystems, energy is not.

CARBON CYCLE

Carbon exists:
1   as a component part of tissues of living organisms;
2   in natural and Man-made organic compounds; and

3   as carbon dioxide in the atmosphere (0.03–0.04%).

Carbon dioxide is the source of carbon for all plants and therefore, indirectly, for all animals. Photosynthetic activity of green plants extracts the carbon and incorporates it into carbohydrates. Some of these carbohydrates are later converted into proteins and fat. Carbon is returned to the environment by respiration of all organisms and by decay of dead organisms (see Fig 11.1).

Fig 11.1 The carbon cycle

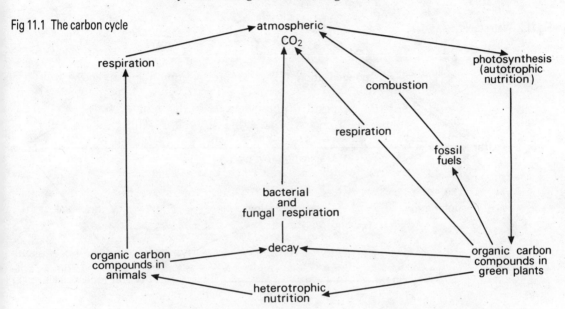

The burning of fossil fuels has increased the content of carbon dioxide in the atmosphere by 20% this century. Carbon dioxide traps infra-red radiation and prevents its escape from earth, yet interferes little with radiant energy coming from the sun. Some ecologists believe that this has caused the increase of 1.6°C in mean world temperature since 1900.

The level of atmospheric carbon dioxide can be reduced by rain, which dissolves the gas forming hydrogen carbonate (HCO_3^-) ions, and by plants photosynthesizing.

It is of vital importance that land is carefully managed to ensure that plant life is preserved and, where habitats have been destroyed, new ones created. If the number of producers were to be severely reduced, the delicate balance between photosynthesis and respiration would be upset because the amount of carbon dioxide that could be utilized by plants during their photosynthetic activity would be reduced.

Questions based on these nutrient cycles are common, so learn them well.

Specimen question Describe what is meant by the following: carbon cycle.   [UCLES]

WATER CYCLE

Water circulates between the atmosphere, land and sea, but a significant amount passes through living organisms. Water is a raw material of photosynthesis and a source of hydrogen and oxygen for all living organisms. Plants and animals return water to the atmosphere in many ways, including respiration.

Fig 11.2 Water cycle

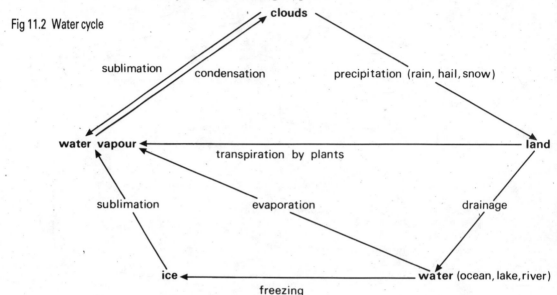

If trees on steep slopes are cut down (**deforestation**) the soil is no longer protected from the atmospheric elements. Rain will wash the soil away into rivers, which consequently become silted up. This can lead to flooding when the rivers burst their banks.

NITROGEN CYCLE

Nitrogen is necessary for the formation of protein. Air contains about 79% nitrogen but as a gas it is biologically inert and unavailable to most living organisms. It is absorbed by plant roots as nitrates from the soil and used for protein synthesis. Animals obtain their protein by eating plants.

Certain bacteria and fungi are capable of continually cycling nitrogen through the ecosystems, as shown in Fig 11.3. The nature of each process involved is as follows.

1 **Production of ammonia** Aerobic bacteria and fungi decompose organic matter with the release of ammonia (**putrefaction**).

2 **Nitrification** Aerobic bacteria oxidize ammonia, initially to nitrite and then to nitrate. This is a source of nitrogen readily available to plants.

3 **Denitrification** Under anaerobic conditions bacteria reduce nitrate to ammonia and nitrogen gas which is lost to the atmosphere.

4 **Nitrogen fixation** The biochemical reduction of gaseous nitrogen to

Fig 11.3 The nitrogen cycle

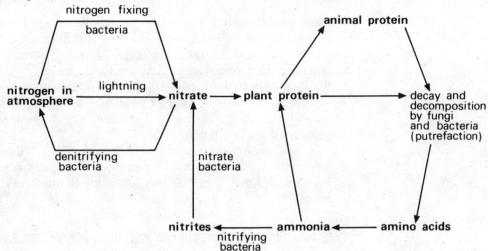

form ammonia may be carried out by saprophytic bacteria present in the roots of leguminous plants, e.g. beans, peas, clover, or by free-living soil bacteria.

The information given in Fig 11.3 may be useful in answering questions such as the following.

Specimen question Explain how the nitrogen of plant protein is changed, after the death of the plant, into a form which other plants can use.
(5 marks)   [JMB]

SOILS

Typically, soils are composed of the following constituents.
1 **Mineral particles** of different sizes.
2 **Water**.
3 **Air**.
4 Dissolved **mineral salts**.
5 **Humus**.
6 **Microorganisms**.
6 Other soil-dwelling **organisms**, e.g. earthworms.

The above are all points which should be learned and related to the part they play in soil fertility.

Specimen question
(a)   List the living and non-living components of a well-balanced soil. (10 marks)
(b)   Explain the contribution of each component to soil fertility.
(15 marks)   [ULSEB]

MINERAL PARTICLES

Mineral particles are formed from weathered rocks. Their size and nature determine the character of the soil. This in turn dictates which plant and animal species may live there. The crumb structure of a soil depends on the proportions of clay, sand and humus.

Sandy soils with predominantly large particles are light, warm and easy to cultivate. They have a loose texture, afford poor support for roots and are susceptible to wind erosion. Rapid drainage in these soils leaves them deficient in salts.

Clay soils are heavy, cold and hard to work. The small particles are closely packed, hindering drainage and decreasing air spaces.

Fertile soils are generally **loams** consisting of mixtures of different types of particle.

EXPERIMENT TO INVESTIGATE THE COMPOSITION OF SOIL BY SEDIMENTATION

Method

Shake a sample of soil with water in a measuring cylinder and then allow the soil to settle out (**sedimentation**) as shown in Fig 11.4. Calculate the percentage of each component.

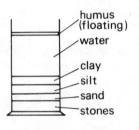

Fig 11.4 The composition of soil

Conclusion

Roughly equal proportions of all major components are present. This is called loam – a rich type of soil.

WATER

Water adheres to soil particles as a thin film and is held there by **capillary attraction** and chemical forces. The water content of a soil varies according to external conditions and the nature of the soil. Soil water may be (Fig. 11.5):

Fig 11.5 Soil water

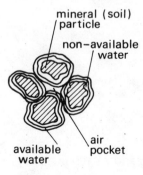

1   available water – capillary water which can be absorbed by plant roots, and drainage water remaining in the soil after rain;
2   non-available water – roots cannot exert sufficient force to remove and absorb this water by osmosis.

EXPERIMENT TO INVESTIGATE DRAINAGE IN SOILS COMPARED WITH SAND

Method

Three filter funnels are placed in three $250\,cm^3$ measuring cylinders, as shown in Fig 11.6. A separate dried sample of the following is placed on each filter paper:

1. $50\,g$ sand;
2. $50\,g$ clay;
3. $50\,g$ garden loam.

$100\,cm^3$ of water is poured into each soil sample and any water that drains through is collected. The volume of water held by each type of soil is calculated.

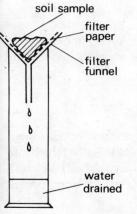

soil sample
filter paper
filter funnel
water drained

Fig 11.6

Results

Water poured into each funnel $= x\;cm^3$
Water drained through sand $\quad = y\;cm^3$
Water drained through clay $\quad =$ etc.
Water drained through loam $\quad =$ etc.

Quantity of water retained by $50\,g$ sand $= x-y\;cm^3$
Quantity of water retained by $50\,g$ clay $\;=$ etc.
Quantity of water retained by $50\,g$ loam $=$ etc.

Conclusion

Clay retains most water, followed by loam, then sand.

AIR

Air fills the spaces between mineral and organic particles in soil which is not waterlogged. The size of the air spaces depends on the size of the particles. This affects drainage. Larger air spaces allow more rapid drainage, but reduce capillarity.

The soil atmosphere is very similar to atmospheric air but usually there is less oxygen and more carbon dioxide. This is because the oxygen of the air is used for aerobic respiration by plant root tissues and other soil-dwelling organisms.

EXPERIMENT TO DETERMINE SOIL pH

Method and results

Allow $1\,g$ of soil to soak in universal indicator solution and distilled water in an evaporating dish for 3 minutes. Drain off the solution, compare its colour with the universal indicator colour chart and read off the pH.

MINERAL SALTS

These comprise 0.2% by mass of the soil content. They originate from the decomposition of plant and animal remains and from their waste products. They exist as a dilute solution in soil water and are essential for healthy plant growth. They affect the pH of the soil and therefore determine which plants can survive there.

HUMUS

Humus is composed of the remains of dead organisms and their waste products. It is formed at the soil surface and mixed into the soil by earthworm activity and ploughing. Bacterial decay of humus releases the soluble nitrates and other mineral salts required for plant growth.

   Humus can improve the texture of soils, e.g. if added to heavy soils it improves aeration and if added to light soils it prevents loss of salts (**leaching**) by too rapid drainage.

MICROORGANISMS

These include bacteria and fungi. Microorganisms break down organic compounds and humus to release soluble salts which are absorbed in solution by plant roots. (NB Denitrifying bacteria break down humus to release substances virtually useless to living organisms.

EARTHWORMS

Earthworms contribute to the maintenance of soil fertility in several ways. Their burrowing activity allows air into the soil and easy penetration of root systems. During feeding they ingest fine particles of soil from underground which is broken up in their gizzard. Much of it is eventually redeposited at the soil surface, providing a good **tilth** for seed germination. Earthworms drag dead leaves and other organic remains below ground, where they are decomposed more quickly by microbes.

AN IDEAL SOIL

All the above factors contribute to the fertility of soil. The 'ideal' soil is light in texture, warm, rich in dissolved salts and plentifully supplied with water, but not waterlogged. A loam meets most of these conditions.

AGRICULTURAL PRACTICES

MANURING

The continual harvesting of crops removes large amounts of mineral salts from the soil. These must be replaced to maintain soil fertility. This can be done by a system of manuring.

1   **Organic** manures (animal faeces, green manures and compost) are

derived from dead plant and waste animal materials. They contain many, if not all, of the necessary elements for plant growth. They decay slowly, add humus and minerals to the soil and are best ploughed in in the autumn.

2   **Inorganic** manures are now widely used. They are relatively simple chemical substances which contain the necessary elements for plant growth. **Advantages** of inorganic manures are:

(*a*)   quick acting when dissolved;
(*b*)   can supply one particular mineral which is deficient; and
(*c*)   easy to apply.

Disadvantages include:

(*a*)   high cost;
(*b*)   precipitate colloidal particles of soil and decrease water retention capacity;
(*c*)   contain no humus; and
(*d*)   if not used carefully, may upset mineral balance of soil and its **crumb structure**.

PLOUGHING

In **spring** this:

1   increases surface area for water evaporation;
2   crumbles soil, good for seed germination; and
3   aerates soil, stimulating microbial activity.

In **autumn** this:

1   mixes manure into soil where it decomposes rapidly;
2   furrows prevent water run-off; and
3   frost penetrates easily, kills pests, weathers clods of earth, provides better soil texture.

LIMING

The addition of lime:

1   flocculates (clumps) the small particles of clay soils, so aiding drainage and improving aeration;
2   neutralizes acid soils; and
3   kills unwanted pests.

CROP ROTATION

Different crops follow one another on a given piece of ground in successive years in a definite pre-arranged order. For example the Norfolk rotation is a four-year rotation:

1   clover (leguminous crop);
2   wheat;
3   root crop, e.g. turnips, swede;
4   barley.

Clover finishes growth in autumn. It is ploughed in and wheat is sown later that autumn. The wheat crop is harvested in the following late summer. The land is then ploughed deeply and left during winter. In the following spring it is cultivated and a root crop is sown in May. The root crop receives most manures for the rotation. It is harvested in the following winter. Barley is then sown the following spring.

Advantages

1　Clover brings about an increase in nitrate content of soil because of activity of nitrogen-fixing bacteria in root nodules.
2　Disease/damage less likely since most pests are specific for one particular crop.
3　Weeds more easily kept down when rotation occurs.
4　Economical on manure. Also some crops are deeper rooted and draw mineral ions from the subsoil whilst others are shallow rooted. In this way ions at different soil levels are utilized.
5　Labour requirements spread throughout the year, since different crops have different seasons for sowing and harvesting.

BIOTIC ENVIRONMENT

The biotic environment supports living organisms (biotic factors) and determines their number and distribution. Energy is needed for the constant recycling of materials within an ecosystem. It is lost as it flows through the ecosystem and must constantly be replaced by energy from the sun, which is the principal source of energy input into biological systems.

Fig 11.7 Interactions within an ecosystem

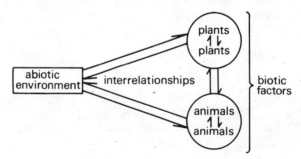

Only green plants can utilize solar energy, which is incorporated into sugars by photosynthesis. Plants are able to build up proteins, fats, and vitamins from sugars. They are thus called the **producers** of the ecosystem. All animals (**consumers**) derive their energy for growth and metabolism from producers. These feeding relationships can be summarized as a **food chain** (see Fig 11.8), where each stage of the chain is known as a **trophic level**. Microbial consumers which aid decay of dead organic matter and recycling of nutrients at all levels are called **decomposers**.

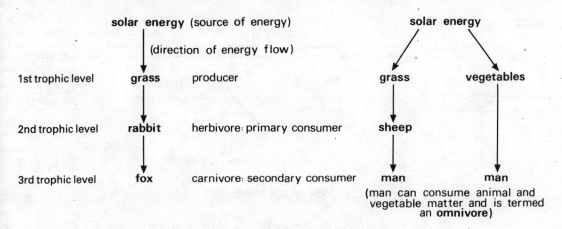

Fig 11.8 Some examples of food chains

It is rare to find a simple food chain in an ecosystem. Usually there are several organisms at each level which may obtain food from any one of the lower levels. These complex feeding interrelationships are called **food webs**, e.g. freshwater crustacea are eaten by a variety of fish and amphibia (Fig 11.9).

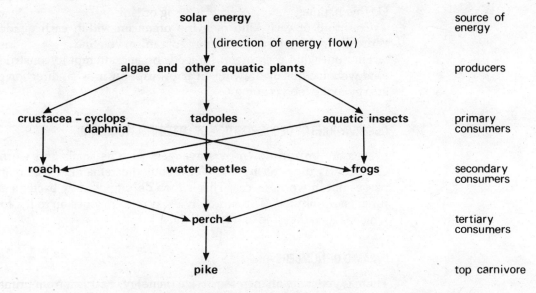

Fig 11.9 Food web in a freshwater pond

Only 1% of the total energy that reaches the plant as light is incorporated into plant tissues. As energy is passed along the food chain there is about a 90% loss between each level. These energy losses are accounted for in Fig 11.10 and explain why there are rarely more than five trophic levels.

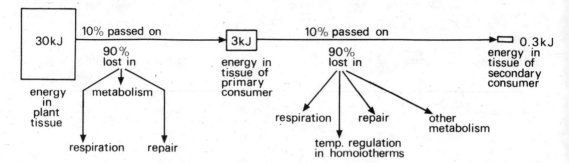

Fig 11.10 Energy flow through a food chain

The food chains in which Man is involved usually comprise no more than two or three trophic levels. Hence more energy is available than would be at the end of a longer chain.

EXPERIMENT TO STUDY THE POPULATIONS OF A LAWN ECOSYSTEM

Method
Having chosen a suitable location, throw a marker at random on to the grass. Place a quadrat over the spot where the marker has landed. Do this 10 times.

Count all of each kind of living organism within each quadrat. Write down the total of each type of organism you find.

Find out what each organism feeds on and attempt to construct a food web. Do this by drawing an arrow to show in what direction the energy in the food is going.

OBSERVATIONS OF DECOMPOSITION OF LITTER IN A WOODLAND

Leaves are broken down by **scavengers** such as snails and worms. Cellulose is digested by the worms but the remaining leaf matter passes out in worm faeces. This is then decomposed by bacteria and fungi (saprophytes). The saprophytes secrete enzymes on to the food which is then digested extracellularly.

PYRAMID OF NUMBERS

There is generally an increase in size (mass) of organism from primary consumer to the final carnivores in the food chain, but a decrease in number (Fig 11.11). As there is a decrease in available energy at each successive link in the food chain, there must be a corresponding decrease in the overall amount of living material that it can sustain.

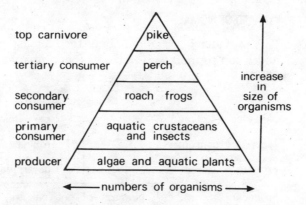

Fig 11.11 Pyramid of numbers

INVERTED PYRAMID OF NUMBERS

Many food chains, when presented in the form of a pyramid, do not show the broad-based pyramid shape as in Fig 11.11. Instead an inverted pyramid is produced, as shown in Fig 11.12.

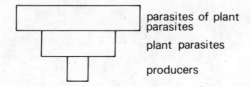

parasites of plant parasites

plant parasites

producers

Fig 11.12 Inverted pyramid of numbers

Presenting food chains as pyramids of numbers often gives a distorted view of interrelationships because they equate an individually very small organism with a very large one, e.g. flea with oak tree (see Fig 11.13). This can be overcome by comparing the **biomass** of organisms instead of their numbers.

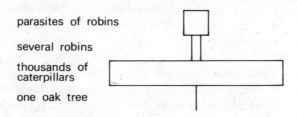

parasites of robins

several robins

thousands of caterpillars

one oak tree

Fig 11.13 Distorted pyramid of numbers

PYRAMID OF BIOMASS

This provides information about the biomass of a primary producer which can support a given biomass of primary consumer, etc. (see Fig 11.14).

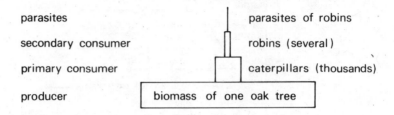

parasites	parasites of robins
secondary consumer	robins (several)
primary consumer	caterpillars (thousands)
producer	biomass of one oak tree

Fig 11.14 Pyramid of biomass (amount of living material)

POPULATION SIZE

The size of a population is controlled by its birth rate and death rate, immigration and emigration. In the absence of any limiting factors the growth rate continues unchecked, as shown in Fig 11.15.

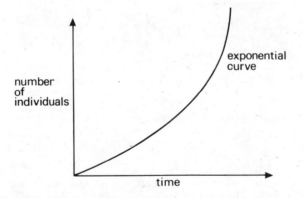

Fig 11.15 Growth curve of a single bacterium placed in a culture medium of large volume and constant nutrient supply

In nature such explosive growth does not occur. This is because of **limiting factors** (checks) such as space and food supply. Where these checks occur, populations show an initial geometric increase which is soon limited, with the population size ultimately becoming stable (see Fig 11.16).

Variation in numbers within a population

Populations of organisms fluctuate in response to changing conditions within an ecosystem, but over a long period of time the average size of each population remains the same.

If the predators become too numerous they will deplete the

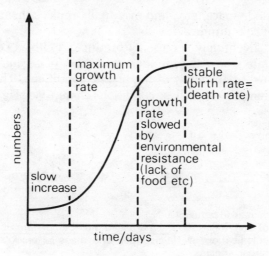

Fig 11.16 Population growth curve – water fleas in a pond

numbers of herbivores. Then the predator number will decline because of food shortage. Subsequently, with fewer predators, the herbivore numbers will again begin to rise (Fig 11.17). (What will happen to the vegetation in this ecosystem?) Thus over a period of time there is a general balance in numbers of predator and prey. It is not an absolutely steady state and is often referred to as a state of dynamic equilibrium in the ecosystem.

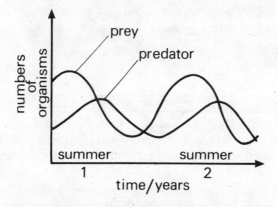

Fig 11.17 Predator/prey interactions

COLONIZATION AND SUCCESSION

Primary succession begins when a **pioneer population** begins to colonize an uninhabited area. This population of organisms affects existing conditions and thus provides new conditions for other organisms to exploit. They may compete with the pioneer population for food, space, etc., and eventually replace them, causing a succession of communities.

Eventually succession produces a **climax community**. This is the state where the numbers and types of organism exist in equilibrium (are balanced) with the abiotic conditions. The community will not change unless these conditions change (see Fig 11.18).

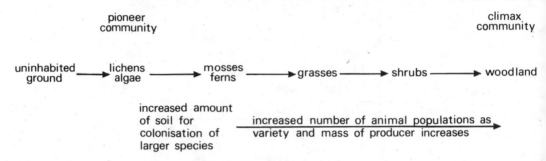

Fig 11.18 Primary succession

Some features of succession ·

1   Rate depends upon climate and availability of suitable plants which can move in to colonize the area.
2   Succession is associated with increased biomass of living and dead material.
3   Diversity of species increases.
4   Ecological niches become more specialized as succession continues.

If vegetation is destroyed or removed in any way, the newly bared land may undergo **secondary succession**. The early stages are different from primary succession and the whole process is much shorter.

MAN AND HIS ENVIRONMENT

As Man's industrial and technological ability has advanced, so has his ability to manipulate the environment. His remarkable success in combating disease and exploiting natural resources has led to a vast

Fig 11.19 Growth of world human population.

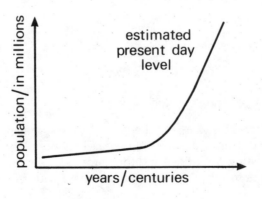

increase in the size of his population. The growth curve of the population takes the form of an **exponential curve** (see Fig 11.19).

Inevitably the curve must flatten out at some stage in the future or the population will outstrip food resources. Improved methods of food production will help this problem, but the only solution must be a reduction in birth rate. The increase in human population has meant that Man has affected his environment in two major ways – exploitation of natural resources and industrialization.

A number of developed nations have reached the stage where there is now virtually no growth in their population size. However in many developing nations the **population size** is still increasing rapidly. Now consult the population pyramids in Fig 11.20. Note particularly the age distribution of each pyramid.

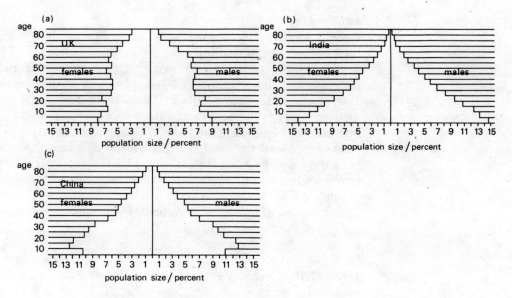

Fig 11.20 Population pyramids. (a) Fairly stable UK population; low birth rate, low death rate. (b) In India the population doubled in 40 years, while 100,000 children die of malnutrition each month; high birth rate, high mortality. (c) In China birth control has resulted in a drop in the birth rate but the population is 980 million and still growing.

Population size is an important world issue. It affects the quality of the environment in which we live. Pollution, food production and family planning are issues currently very much in the news.

BIRTH CONTROL

There must be an actual limit to the number of people who can inhabit the earth. Therefore it is important that the size of families is limited. If this does not happen, the only alternative is natural control by famine or some other form of disaster. Common methods of preventing pregnancy are given in Table 9.7 on p.228.

BIOTECHNOLOGY

Biological processes and organisms are used in manufacturing and service industries to mass-produce desirable products. Familiar materials may be made via new natural processes from unusual sources and by improved routes.

TRADITIONAL APPLICATIONS

1 Brewing of beer and wine-making using yeast.
2 Bread-making using yeast.
3 Manufacture of the antibiotic penicillin from the fungus *Penicillium*.
4 Production of cheese, yoghurt, sauerkraut and soy sauce.

NEW APPLICATIONS

Agriculture

1 **Genetic engineering** of plant cells leading to plants which can fix their own atmospheric nitrogen.
2 **Tissue culture**, enabling a chosen species to be reproduced many thousands of times. Single cells are placed in a nutrient medium. They multiply to form a **callus.** The callus is transferred to a fresh medium and develops into a plantlet which is then reared by normal nursery techniques, e.g. oil palm – the highest yielding palms have been cloned and the yield per acre on the oil palm plantations has been increased by a factor of the order 1.5. This process may be used to restock forests and plantations with faster-growing higher-yielding plants.
3 **Development of microbial insecticides** which are not dangerous for the rest of the environment.

Food

1 **Fermentation technology** has enabled the large-scale production of protein by microorganisms. Essentially single-celled bacteria make protein by digesting methanol. Called **single-cell protein** (SCP), it was originally developed as an animal feed. However there is no reason why it cannot be developed as a human food.
2 Production of fungal protein (**mycoprotein**) which is incorporated into food. Other 'dishes' can be made entirely of mycoprotein and disguised by flavours also produced by biotechnological methods.

Medicine

1 Supplies of highly specific antibodies are produced by using animal cells (called hybridomas) as cellular 'factories'.
2 Production of **interferons**. These make cells resistant to virus attack and may be used to fight cancer.

Energy

The biologically-based conversion of plant material into important energy compounds such as methane and methanol, which may be used as a substitute for petrol.

Waste/pollution
Biotechnology plays a major role in improving sewage treatment (p.295) and the treatment of other effluents. Microorganisms feed on all types of waste and may be used to convert it into useful products thereby recycling materials. This would aid the conservation of present resources.

PREVENTION OF DISEASE

CHEMOTHERAPY

The use of chemicals to treat and cure disease. These may be manufactured drugs, e.g. mepacrine to cure malaria, or natural or synthetic antibiotics, e.g. penicillin extracted from the mould *Penicillium* and used to control many kinds of bacteria.

FOOD PRESERVATION

1 **Sterilization** – food is cooked at very high temperatures, canned or bottled and finally sealed whilst still very hot. Bacteria and fungi are killed by heat in excess of 100°C, as are the more resistant spores. The seal prevents entry of any further microbes.
2 **Pasteurization** – milk is heated to 72°C for 15 seconds and quickly cooled to below 12°C. This kills pathogenic bacteria, but other bacteria which survive can cause milk to turn sour and clot under appropriate conditions.
3 **Refrigeration** – at low temperatures microbial activity is slow and they can neither cause appreciable decay nor multiply.
4 **Dehydration** – food is dried. Microbes cannot survive without water, but their resistant spores can. They will begin to germinate immediately the food is moistened.
5 **Osmotic preservation** – food is immersed in concentrated solutions (brine or syrup). Microbes die in this situation because of loss of water.
6 **Cooking** – prolonged heating of foods kills microbes and their resistant spores.
7 **Blanching** – food is plunged into boiling water to destroy the enzymes within it. Therefore no further ripening of the food can occur.
8 **Freezing** – activity of microorganisms is stopped at temperatures between −5°C and −20°C.

EFFECTS OF MAN ON THE ECOSYSTEM

AGRICULTURE

MONOCULTURE

This is the concentrated growing of a single species of plant in one area. It is the major method of crop production today. However, high densities of crops provide optimum conditions for pests and spread of disease.

USE OF PESTICIDES AND HERBICIDES

Herbicides
These remove weeds from amongst crops, but can upset the ecosystem by removing a food source or habitat of other organisms.

Pesticides, especially insecticides
Though these are effective, they are expensive. For example, DDT is effective in controlling a wide range of insect pests. However, like many other pesticides, DDT also kills many harmless as well as harmful organisms, so upsetting the balance of the ecosystem; it may even kill the pest's natural enemies, thus removing a form of biological control of the pest.

Non-degradable pesticides, e.g. DDT again, can accumulate within the tissues of organisms and be passed along food chains so that they become increasingly concentrated. Animals at the end of the food chain may receive a dose of the pesticide large enough to be fatal.

Tolerance of such pesticides varies from one pest to another. Those showing tolerance possess a selective advantage and their numbers increase dramatically. Tolerance can build up in a few years. Hence new insecticides have to be developed. A similar situation exists for herbicides.

Avoiding the use of pesticides and herbicides
Man is becoming increasingly aware of the harm he has caused to the environment. The general public is now being encouraged by education and law to be much more careful in the exploitation of the land. By studying the life cycle, behaviour and predators of a pest, Man is attempting to avoid the use of pesticides.

1 Eradicating mosquitoes in tropical countries by draining swamps and spraying stagnant water with oil. Think out what effect these measures will have on the mosquito.

2 **Biological control** Introducing a natural enemy of the pest into the habitat, e.g. in Australia the prickly pear cactus thrived and invaded many pasturelands. Larvae of a moth which feed on the prickly pear were introduced, and the spread of the prickly pear was controlled within 10 years.

OVERUSE OF CHEMICAL FERTILIZERS

When crops are harvested, nutrients which have been absorbed by the plants are removed at the same time. If nutrients are not returned to the soil the yield of future crops will be reduced. If chemical fertilizers are used to replenish the soil instead of organic substances, soil humus is reduced and a poorer crumb structure develops. Soil porosity is decreased, leading to a reduction in oxygen availability. Plants are unable to absorb salts efficiently and the salts are leached out of the soil into rivers and lakes.

Increased nutrient content of freshwater stimulates increased algal growth. More algae subsequently die and are decomposed by aerobic bacteria which use up vast quantities of oxygen. There is insufficient oxygen left in the water for other aquatic animals, which then die. This process is called **eutrophication**.

Poorer crumb structure means that **erosion** is more likely to occur, with top soil becoming dry and powdery and being blown away.

DEFORESTATION

When forests on mountain slopes are felled, weather elements such as rain and wind erode the soil, which is washed into rivers. Hence topsoil is removed and river beds become silted up. This causes flooding.

This can be countered by **afforestation**. Mountain slopes are replanted with trees, thus reducing erosion by run off and decreasing the risk of flooding.

POLLUTION

The following notes cover the main points concerned with the effects of industrialization, but you should consult your own notes and textbooks for further details.

1 Depletion of areas of natural vegetation to make room for housing, factories, roads, etc.
2 Depletion of non-replaceable resource for energy and by industry.
3 Over-exploitation of replaceable materials, e.g. timber, wood.

The major anxiety caused by industrialization is, however, **pollution** of the atmosphere, soil and water. The main factors in this are:

1 the release of chemical wastes from industrial processes;
2 use of pesticides and herbicides;
3 accumulation of unwanted materials (rubbish); and, increasingly
4 disposal of radioactive waste.

AIR POLLUTION

Caused by dust, smoke, soot, sulphur dioxide from burning fossil fuels. Reduced by Clean Air Act (1956 and 1968). Combustion engines produce carbon monoxide, lead and nitrogen oxides – all serious health hazards.

The lead that is inhaled accumulates over a number of years. Since it cannot be excreted it may build up to harmful levels. Some countries are taking steps to reduce the lead content of petrol.

Oxides of sulphur and nitrogen dissolve in rainwater, producing acid rain. This is a major environment problem, harming wildlife, forests, crops and buildings. It is of international concern as winds carrying the gases blow across continents. It is estimated that 20% of air pollution in Great Britain is blown in from abroad.

Radioactive materials may enter the ground via rain and be concentrated by food chains. When strontium 90 gets into an animal it replaces calcium and releases radiations that harm or kill living tissues.

SOIL POLLUTION

Caused by dumping of rubbish and chemicals. It produces both an aesthetic problem and a health hazard.

WATER POLLUTION

Industrial and domestic wastes enter inland waterways and the sea. Oil spillage at sea kills wildlife and damages seashores. Detergents, sewage and fertilizers encourage algal, bacterial and fungal growth. They use up oxygen which animals need (eutrophication). Pesticides that reach rivers and lakes either poison aquatic organisms or accumulate in their tissues. Legislation is now being introduced to limit these problems.

INDUSTRIAL WASTE

This contains long-lasting pollutants such as lead, mercury and cyanide compounds. They enter aquatic organisms and become concentrated in body tissues.

CONSERVATION

This means preventing the over-exploitation of plants and animals, and preserving the stability of ecosystems. This can be achieved in several ways.

LEGISLATION

1 Many species threatened with extinction may be protected by the law, e.g. Protection of Birds Act 1954.
2 Since the Clean Air Act many species have returned to industrialized areas.

3 Local authorities can pass byelaws to prevent removal of wild flowers from the environment.
4 Nature reserves protect endangered species which live there, e.g. Brownsea Island Bird Sanctuary.
5 National parks have been created which preserve areas of outstanding beauty and protect them from over-exploitation.
6 National Trust preserves places of historic interest or natural beauty.
7 Forestry Commission controls the management of forest plantations. Forest reserves, national forest parks and nature trails have been established.
8 Fishery management. This involves habitat conservation and fish culture, e.g. trout fishery – the success of trout in a river depends on the following factors:
   (a)   good quality water;
   (b)   sites for breeding;
   (c)   areas of shelter for the young;
   (d)   areas of shelter for the adults;
   (e)   adequate food;
   (f)   freedom from predators, parasites and competitors.
   Each factor is examined carefully and appropriate action taken where necessary. Beyond all else, trout conservation depends on fishing intensity.

RECYCLING OF MATERIALS

Many waste manufactured components are now being efficiently recycled, e.g. old cars can be packaged and sent to factories which recover some of the metal for re-use. Paper can be recycled, as can glass. The principle of recycling can be shown by the treatment of sewage.

Treatment of sewage
Solid matter in sewage settles out as sludge whilst the sewage stands in sewage tanks. Either of the following treatments then takes place.

Biological filtering The liquid sewage is sprayed over a bed of stones which provides a large surface area on which protozoa and bacteria can live. Organic matter and solid particles are removed from the sewage before it reaches the bottom of the bed. In this condition the liquid is safe for discharge into a river. Sludge from the sewage tank is transferred to other tanks for digestion into simpler compounds. These are dried and eventually recycled as fertilizer.

Activated sludge process Alternatively, liquid sewage plus some sediment (containing protozoa) is mixed together by bubbling air through it. Good aeration increases the rate of digestion. The liquid is discharged into the river. The sludge is digested by anaerobic bacteria. During this process methane gas is formed and utilized as fuel. The sludge is dried and used as fertilizer.

NEW SYSTEMS OF POWER

Systems are being developed which utilize the inexhaustible supplies of solar and wave energy.

RECLAMATION

Many schemes are in existence which are reclaiming derelict land.

1   British Coal has an efficient organization for the restoration of land used for open cast coal mining.
2   Local authorities with government finance have landscaped derelict land in an effort to raise the quality of the environment under their control, e.g. Lower Swansea Valley Project.

Specimen question Having read of the effects of Man's activities on the environment, draw up an essay plan for the following question.

Describe some of (a) the beneficial, and (b) the detrimental effects of Man's activities on the environment. (25 marks)   [UCLES]

PEST CONTROL

The control of the malarial pathogen shows how the relationship between host and parasite can be broken.

Plasmodium (an **endoparasite**) is a protozoan which causes malaria and is a useful example of a parasite involving an insect vector. The female mosquito fly 'bites' an infected person and sucks up blood. It takes in the *Plasmodium* parasites with its meal of blood. Within the insect the parasite rapidly increases its numbers. When the mosquito bites another uninfected person, it injects the parasites into his blood. Here they live in the red blood cells and liver cells, multiplying and absorbing nutrients, and causing their host cells to collapse.

infected→*Plasmodium* parasites in mosquito→infects
person   uninfected
                                                                              person

The following measures are taken in order to control the spread of the disease (**prophylaxis**).

1   Prevent breeding by destroying breeding grounds, e.g. draining stagnant water where eggs are laid, spray oil on to water to prevent larvae breathing.
2   Spray insecticides on to water and inside houses.
3   Prevent mosquitoes reaching people, e.g. mosquito nets.
4   Biological control – capturing large numbers of male mosquitoes which are then sterilized by radioactivity. These sterile males are then released into the population where they compete with fertile males during selection of females for mating.
5   Use of drugs to kill parasites in the bloodstream, e.g. Paludrine, Chloroquin.

Reliable collecting and sampling methods and accurate identification are essential to any ecological survey. Some methods are listed below.

TRANSECTS

Used when studying changes in plant populations that occur during succession, e.g. from water to land.

BELT TRANSECT

A line is marked out on the ground with string. Then a series of quadrats placed end to end are used, with the side of the quadrat lying adjacent to the string. Vegetation within the quadrat is recorded. From this information the frequency of species and their percentage cover are deduced.

POINT QUADRAT

Percentage cover is a useful parameter for measuring success achieved by different plant species. To do this a point quadrat is used which has a series of points equally spaced which are let down onto the vegetation at random. The number of 'hits' and 'misses' that the points make are recorded for a particular species.

Fig 11.21 Presence/absence histogram of species on a seashore.

$$\% \text{ cover} = \frac{\text{Hits} \times 100}{\text{Hits} + \text{Misses}}$$

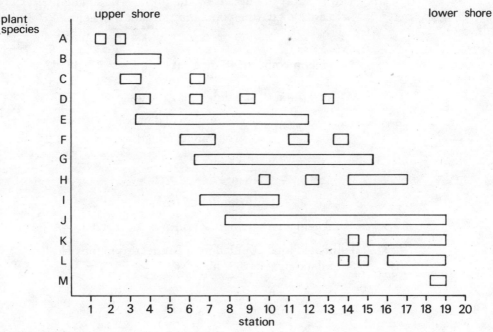

The presence or absence of a species should be examined in conjunction with habitat factors, e.g. tide, salinity. Results can be presented in the form of a histogram (see Fig 11.21).

LINE TRANSECT

A line is marked out on the ground with string. Plants which touch or cover the line are recorded at regular intervals along its length. Information from this is less informative than that of a belt transect. Height variations recorded along transects provide a profile transect which is used when analysing data.

RANDOM SAMPLING

In some habitats transects will be less informative. In this case a quadrat is thrown at random within the habitat on a prescribed number of occasions. All vegetation within the quadrat is recorded. This is a useful method when determining the population density of a single species.

EXPERIMENT TO DETERMINE THE SIZE OF A DANDELION POPULATION

Method
1   A quadrat is thrown 10 times at random in the area to be sampled.
2   All dandelions present in each quadrat are counted. A plant is only counted if more than half of it is within the quadrat.
3   All figures are recorded.
4   The mean population per square metre is calculated.
5   The mean is multiplied by the number of square metres in the total field area to give the population size for that field.

Calculations
Dandelion count in 10 quadrat samples = 14, 16, 13, 17, 16, 15, 14, 15, 12, 18

Total number of dandelions in 10 quadrats = 150

$$\text{Mean} = \frac{\text{Total number of dandelions}}{\text{Total area of quadrats}}$$

$$= \frac{150}{10 \text{ m}^2}$$

$$= 15 \text{ dandelions m}^2$$

Total field area = Length × Width = 100 m × 20 m = 2000 m^2

Estimated total population of dandelions in the field
= 15 dandelions × 2000 m^2
= 30 000 dandelions

COLLECTING METHODS 1 **Sweep net** – a large fine-mesh net is swept through vegetation as the collector walks forward. This disturbs invertebrates, which are trapped in the net.

2 **Plankton net** – a net of bolting silk attached to a metal frame and rope harness is towed slowly through water. Specimens are collected in a small glass specimen tube at the end of the net.

3 **Kick sampling** – a net of prescribed mesh is set up in a stream. Organisms are deliberately dislodged from a position upstream and are swept into the net. Size of mesh will determine the size of organisms trapped.

4 **Pooter** – insects can be collected directly from vegetation or off beating trays.

5 **Beating tray** – shake a tree branch whilst holding a large white tray of known area underneath. Invertebrates fall on to the tray and are collected by pooter.

PRESENTATION OF DATA Tables are a very efficient way of presenting data collected for analysis. Graphs, bar charts and histograms reveal patterns and relationships between organisms and their environment.

GRAPHS

These provide a pictorial illustration of the relationships between two or more variables. The variable quantity to be measured is plotted on the vertical (y) axis. The known variable, e.g. time, is plotted on the horizontal (x) axis. Points may be joined with straight lines, or a single straight line representing as nearly as possible an ideal line between a scatter of points can be used (see p.317, Chapter 12).

BAR CHARTS

This is a means of recording discontinuous data (see Fig 11.22), e.g. measuring the frequency of plant species at different points along a belt transect, or the density of an animal population over a period of time.

Line graphs can be superimposed on the chart to add further information.

HISTOGRAM

This records continuous data, e.g. analysis of a sample of height or mass. Data are grouped into classes for recording purposes, 0–20 mm, 20–40 mm, etc. This method enables a specific characteristic of a population to be analysed (see Fig 11.23).

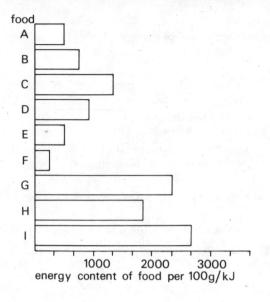

energy content of food per 100g/kJ

Fig 11.22 A bar chart

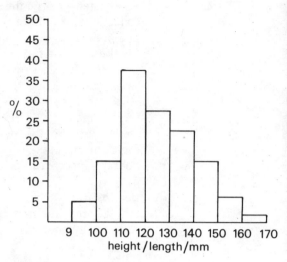

height/length/mm

Fig 11.23 A histogram

KEY WORDS ▶

Environment	Food chain	Insecticides
Habitat	Trophic level	Herbicides
Abiotic	Herbivore	Eutrophication
Biotic	Carnivore	Biological control
Ecosystem	Decomposers	Conservation
Light	Omnivore	Recycling
Photoperiodism	Food web	Reclamation
Dormancy	Pyramid of numbers	Industrialization
Hibernation	Pyramid of biomass	Air Pollution
Nutrient cycle	Population size	Acid rain
Carbon cycle	Exponential curve	Water pollution
Water cycle	Limiting factors	Industrial waste
Deforestation	Colonization	Sewage
Nitrogen cycle	Primary succession	Biological filtering
Putrefaction	Pioneer population	Activated sludge
Decay bacteria	Climax community	process
Nitrifying bacteria	Secondary	Chemotherapy
Nitrogen fixing	succession	Food preservation
bacteria	Birth control	Sterilization
Denitrifying bacteria	Biotechnology	Pasteurization
Soils	Genetic engineering	Refrigeration
Mineral particles	Callus	Dehydration
Loams	Tissue culture	Vector
Sedimentation	Fermentation	Prophylaxis
Capillary attraction	technology	Belt transect

Humus	Single cell protein (SCP)	Line transect
Decay	Mycoprotein	Random sampling
Leaching	Hybridoma	Sweep net
Microorganisms	Interferon	Plankton net
Tilth	Predators	Kick sampling
Manures	Prey	Pooter
Crumb structure	Dynamic equilibrium	Beating tray
Liming	Monoculture	Graphs
Crop rotation	Pesticides	Bar charts
Producers		Histogram
Consumers		

SPECIMEN EXAMINATION QUESTIONS

1 Equal amounts of a dry sandy soil and a dry clay soil were placed separately in each of two boiling tubes. The two boiling tubes were placed in a beaker of cold water which was heated for a period of 8 minutes and then allowed to cool. A thermometer was placed in each soil sample so that the temperature of both the sandy soil and the clay soil could be taken at 2-minute intervals during the heating and cooling period.

Table 11.1 Results

	Time (min)	Temperature of sandy soil (°C)	Temperature of clay soil (°C)
Heating	0	11	11
	2	16	13
	4	22	17
	6	29	21
	8	36	26
Cooling	10	35	25
	12	30	23
	14	24	21
	16	20	19

(a) Using temperature as the vertical (y) axis and time as the horizontal (x) axis, construct TWO curves, one to show how sandy soil heats up and cools and ONE to show how clay soil heats up and cools. Label your curves. (4 marks)

(b) Describe why the heating and cooling curves of the two soils are different. (3 marks)

(c) (i) Explain how the addition of lime to a heavy clay soil would improve its fertility. (2 marks)

(ii) State ONE environmental danger of adding too much artificial fertilizer to sandy soil. (2 marks)

(iii) State ONE way in which the productivity of a field can be increased without destroying its soil structure. (2 marks)

[MEG]

2   Fig 11.24 shows some of the pathways by which carbon is cycled in the ecosystem.

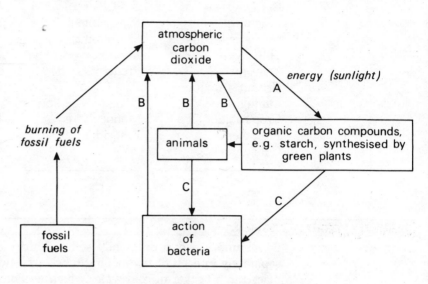

Fig 11.24

(i) What process does the letter A represent?
(ii) What energy conversion occurs during the stage represented by the letter A?
(iii) Give ONE example of the large-scale effects caused by plants or their use.
(iv) Explain the effects of excessive use of fossil fuels.

[SCE]

3   Fig 11.25 shows part of the nitrogen cycle in a woodland. The labelled arrows represent processes.

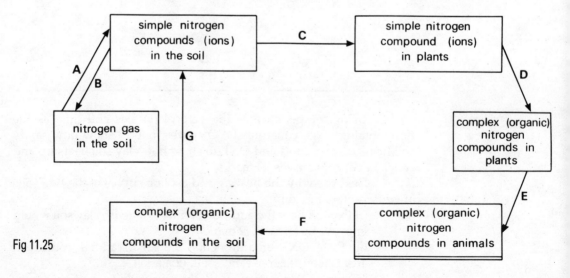

Fig 11.25

In Table 11.2 write the name of a process occurring at each labelled arrow. Two lines have been completed for you. (5 marks)

Table 11.2

Arrow label	Process
A	
B	Denitrification
C	
D	Protein synthesis
E	
F	
G	

[LEAG]

4   Fig 11.26 shows the processes involved in the water cycle.

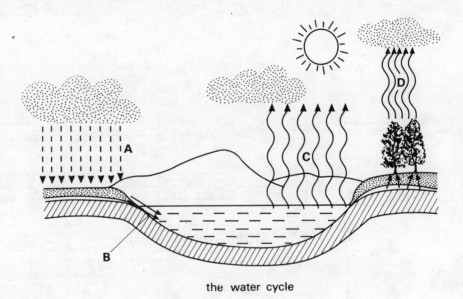

Fig 11.26

the water cycle

    (a)   Name the processes labelled **A, B, C** and **D**.   (4 marks)
    (b)   Name TWO substances which pollute water.   (2 marks)
    (c)   Name TWO substances which pollute air.   (2 marks)
[MEG]

5   Fig 11.27 shows part of a food web.
    (a)   Suppose all the field voles were suddenly killed by disease.
      (i) Why would the number of dandelions be likely to increase?   (1 mark)
      (ii) Why would the number of foxes be likely to decrease? (1 mark)
    (b)   You cannot be sure what would happen to the number of wood mice. Explain why their numbers might either decrease or increase.   (2 marks)   [SEG]

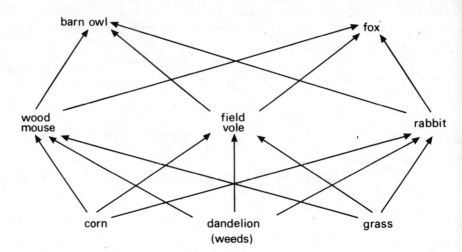

Fig 11.27

6   The food web in Fig 11.28 was constructed following a study of a grassland area.

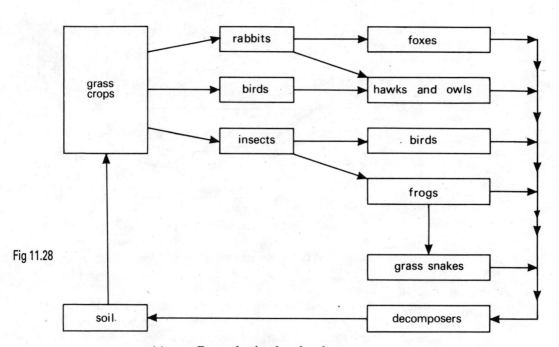

Fig 11.28

(a)   From the food web select:
       (i) a herbivore;
       (ii) a carnivore;
       (iii) a secondary consumer.   (3 marks)
(b)   What role is played by the decomposers in maintaining the food web?   (2 marks)
(c)   After the area had been sprayed with a pesticide to control insect larvae several small birds were found to have died from chemical poisoning. Suggest how this may have occurred.   (2 marks)

(d)   Some farmers have removed hedgerows and small wooded areas to increase the amount of land used to produce crops. The crops in these larger fields can then be harvested with large modern machinery. How would this action affect the hawks and owls in the area being studied.   (3 marks)   [NISEC]

7   Fig 11.29 represents a sealed aquarium placed in natural light and containing plant and animal pond life. All the living organisms in the aquarium must obtain energy to survive.

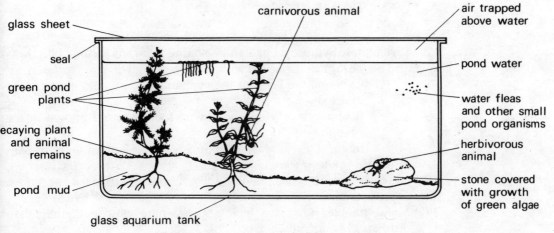

Fig 11.29

(a)   What is the source of energy for the green plants?   (1 mark)

(b)   What is the immediate source of energy for the herbivorous animals?   (1 mark)

(c)   What is the immediate source of energy for the carnivorous animals?   (1 mark)

(d)   In what ways would the aquarium be changed if all the animal life were removed and then the aquarium resealed? (2 marks)

(e)   In what ways would the aquarium be changed if all the plants were removed and the animals were sealed in on their own? (3 marks)

(f)   Would it be possible for the plants and animals to live indefinitely in the sealed aquarium as it was originally set up? Explain fully the reasons for your answer.   (3 marks)   [MEG]

8   Each year in Britain, 250 tonnes of lead from fishermen's weights reach the environment. It is feared that some types of birds suffer from this form of pollution because they swallow the lead weights during feeding. Study the data in Table 11.3 obtained between 1973–80 for mute swans and answer the questions which follow.

(a)   Using only the data given, suggest ONE reason why there is more lead in the blood of swans from near towns than from swans in the countryside.

(b)   Explain how the lead reached the swans' blood.

(c)   Lead affects the nervous tissues and the muscle tissues of

Table 11.3

Average concentration of lead in blood of swans (g/100 cm³)	Area inhabited
106.8	Trent (near a town centre)
28.8	Dorset (countryside)
104.6	Thames (near town centre)
107.4	Avon (near town centre)
18.6	Mid Wales (countryside)
16.4	Tweed (countryside)

Note: 40 g/100 cm³ is considered relatively harmless in swans.

vertebrates. Symptoms of lead poisoning in swans include blindness and the oesophagus packed with food.

(i) Name the layer of the eye which you would expect to be affected.

(ii) Suggest TWO reasons why food is found packed in the oesophagus.

(d) Suggest TWO ways of reducing this pollution without banning fishing *altogether*. (7 marks) [WJEC]

9 Describe how Man has polluted the environment. (Do *not* use smoke as an example.) (8 marks) [NEA]

10 Many people now use biological washing powder rather than ordinary washing powder.

(a) Name the substance obtained from living creatures which is contained in biological washing powder but not in ordinary washing powder. (1 mark)

(b) Name one kind of stain which is removed by using biological washing powder. (1 mark)

(c) Describe the best way of using biological washing powders to remove stains. (2 marks) [NEA]

11 Give a biological explanation for each of the following.

(a) Green plants are energy converters and food producers in food chains. (2 marks)

(b) Yeast is used in both the baking and the brewing industries. (2 marks)

(c) Conservationists are concerned with keeping hedgerows. (2 marks) [MEG]

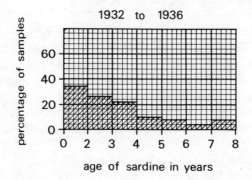

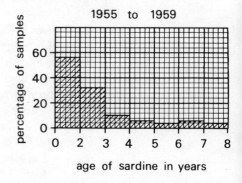

Fig 11.30

12   The histograms in Fig 11.30 show the age composition of a population
of Pacific sardines sampled during the two periods 1932 to 1936 and
1955 to 1959.

(*a*)   What is the main difference between the two samples?
(1 mark)

(*b*)   (i) What probably happened bewtween 1936 and 1955 to
bring about the difference between the two samples?
(1 mark)

(ii) Explain your answer to (i).   (1 mark)

(*c*)   State TWO conservation procedures which could be applied
to bring the population back to the composition of 1932 to 1936.
(2 marks)   [NEA]

13   The map in Fig 11.31 shows a river flowing through farms Y and Z.
Farmer Y changed from beef to dairy cattle. His herd no longer stayed
all day in the fields but came twice a day to the farm buildings to be
milked. Farmer Z had a fish farm and kept his fish in tanks filled with
water from the river. His fish began to die. Scientists analysed the
river water at A, B, C, D and E along the river. Their results are
shown in Table 11.4

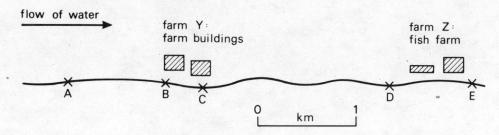

Fig 11.31

Table 11.4 River-water analysis

	Total nitrogen in chemical compounds (parts per million)	pH	Dissolved oxygen (parts per million)
A	0.40	8.5	10.0
B	2.60	6.8	3.6
C	2300.00	4.0	10.0
D	0.76	7.8	1.2
E	0.66	7.8	4.0

(*a*)   (i) What THREE factors shown by the table could have caused
the death of Farmer Z's fish?   (1 mark)

(ii) Which factor do you think the most likely to have caused
the death of Farmer Z's fish? Why would this factor have
caused the death of his fish?   (2 marks)

(*b*)   Suggest ONE explanation each for:
(i) the rise in nitrogen compounds between A and C;
(2 marks)

(ii) the fall in nitrogen compounds between C and D;
(2 marks)

(iii) the low pH at C;   (2 marks)

(iv) the low oxygen content at D.   (2 marks)

(c)   Farmer Y's cows had polluted the river.

(i) What is pollution?   (1 mark)

(ii) Suggest ONE way in which pollution by the cows could be reduced.   (2 marks)

(iii) Instead of fish, Farmer Z wanted to grow water cress in his tanks, but the local health authority would not let him sell it. Why not?   (1 mark)   [SEG]

14   What type of habitat did you study?

(a)   Name an organism you studied in this habitat.

(i) What apparatus did you use to study where this organism lives.   (1 mark)

(ii) How should you use this apparatus?   (3 marks)

(iii) What should you record?   (1 mark)

(b)   Name an environmental factor that you measured in this habitat.

(i) What apparatus did you use to measure this environmental factor?   (1 mark)

(ii) How should you use this apparatus?   (3 marks)

(iii) What should you record?   (1 mark)

GUIDE TO EXAMINATIONS

CONTENTS

Just as there is no foolproof way of revising, there is no foolproof way of passing an examination. A conscientious effort throughout the course and adequate revision will certainly help on the examination day. There are so many factors which may impair your performance in examinations and a few simple points may help produce a better frame of mind for tackling the paper.

1 Do not tire yourself out with last minute cramming the day (or night) before the examination.

2 Get a good night's sleep and get up in good time for the exam.

3 Be sure you know which subject you are taking, what type of examination it will be, the time it begins and the room in which it will be held.

4 Arrive at the examination room with all materials you will require, e.g. pens, pencils, ruler, eraser, etc., and your candidate number.

5 Allow yourself extra time to travel to school or college in case your bicycle has a puncture, etc.

These are all obvious points but every year many candidates enter the examination room either tired, late or in a panic because they had not considered them. Don't be one of these candidates.

When the examination begins there are several points which should be observed.

1 Read the instructions given at the beginning of the examination paper very carefully.

2 Answer all compulsory questions.

3 If the paper is divided into sections and a choice of questions is given within them, ensure you answer the correct number from each section. Follow any advice given on how long to spend on each section.

4 Fill in your name, candidate number and centre number on all sheets as instructed.

5 Always answer the correct number of questions. Never decide to give three detailed answers in the time allocated if the instructions ask for four. The maximum number of marks to be obtained by this can only be 75%, and few people ever achieve full marks in an answer.

6 Most exam papers now give the distribution of marks for each question. Use this as a guide to how long you should spend on answering each part question or question.

7 Read through the questions and decide which you are going to answer. It is worth spending a few minutes over this and being certain you possess enough information to give complete answers. As

a general rule begin by answering what is the easiest question for you or any compulsory questions. **Remember to stick to your time allocation**.

(*a*)   Answer the question which is set – do not rewrite to suit yourself.

(*b*)   Only give information which is relevant to the question. Do not write down all you know about that topic.

(*c*)   Examiners prefer answers which are concise and written in good English. Credit is sometimes given for orderly presentation.

8   Remember that the examiner is looking for the correct use of biological facts in your answer. Marks can only be awarded for what you write on the paper – not for what remains in your head.

9   Detail given on diagrams should not be repeated in words unless the diagram is making an answer more easily understood.

10   If you are running out of time in a question put down the important points in note form and do not worry about sentences. You may not gain full marks but you will gain some.

11   If time is available at the end of the examination read through your answers and correct any mistakes.

TYPES OF QUESTION

There are a variety of types of questions set at GCSE and SCE level and you should know how to tackle those which will be used in your examinations.

OBJECTIVE QUESTIONS   Answers usually have to be written in pencil on a special answer sheet and are then marked by machine. Between 30 and 60 questions are set – all are compulsory and vary in difficulty. This is a good way of testing your knowledge on all parts of the syllabus, so revise all topics.

Special question Which of the following shows correctly the exchange of gases and water vapour that occurs in flowering plants between the internal leaf spaces and the outside atmosphere during darkness?

	Gases and water vapour passing into leaf	Gases and water vapour passing out of leaf
A	Carbon dioxide	Oxygen and water vapour
B	Carbon dioxide and water vapour	Oxygen
C	Oxygen	Carbon dioxide and water vapour
D	Oxygen and carbon dioxide	Water vapour
E	Oxygen and water vapour	Carbon dioxide

Only one of these choices (**A–E**) is correct. The question deals with the exchanges of carbon dioxide, oxygen and water vapour between leaf cells of a flowering plant and the atmosphere during darkness. The two chemical reactions involving these materials are photosynthesis and respiration. Photosynthesis requires carbon dioxide to pass *into* the leaf and oxygen passes *out* of the leaf. Respiration requires oxygen to pass *into* the leaf and carbon dioxide and water vapour pass *out* of the leaf. Photosynthesis does not occur in darkness so the correct answer is concerned with respiration and the inward movement of oxygen and the outward movement of carbon dioxide and water vapour. Hence **C** is the correct answer.

If you cannot immediately tell which answer is correct try to eliminate the four which are incorrect. Usually three are easy to eliminate, e.g. **A**, **B** and **D** because they all contain carbon dioxide as the gas passing into the leaf. **C** and **E** could possibly be correct but as water vapour is a waste product of respiration it must pass out of the leaf; hence **C** is correct.

SHORT ANSWER QUESTIONS

Answers are written on the question paper in the spaces provided. This gives some indication of the length of answer required. In some cases a photograph, diagram, table, graph or passage is given, and candidates are asked to answer several short questions, e.g. Fig 12.1.

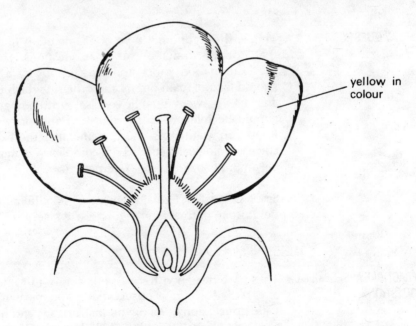

yellow in colour

Fig 12.1

(a)   How many stamens are there in this half flower?   (1 mark)
(b)   What is meant by the term *pollination*?   (2 marks)
(c)   (i) Name TWO features of this flower which suggest that it might be pollinated by insects.   (2 marks)

(ii) How does each of these features help in pollination? (2 marks)

(d)   How would the stigma be different in structure in a wind pollinated flower?   (1 mark)

(e)   Suggest ONE other feature of the flower, not shown by the diagram, that might be important for attracting night-flying moths. (1 mark)   [*MEG*]

STRUCTURED QUESTIONS

These are intermediate between a short answer question and an essay and are mainly used in question papers designed for candidates in the grades A and B target range. The questions are usually in several parts. No guidance on length of answer is given and you should be guided by the mark allocation.

Specimen question

(a)   The liver and the pancreas have important roles to play. Describe these roles in detail.   (10 marks)

(b)   The liver and the pancreas also have roles beyond that of digestion. Describe any ways in which these organs are involved in:

(i) the storage of carbohydrates;   (4 marks)

(ii) the excretion of wastes.   (6 marks)   [*MEG*]

ESSAY QUESTIONS

This is the traditional type of examination question. It is important that a plan is drawn up for these questions. This should be made on the examination paper and crossed out by a single line. The plan should list the main points and order in which they will appear in the answer. Answers must be concise, written in good English, and facts should be relevant to the question and presented in logical order. Keep your sentences short. Remember the examiner is looking for correct biological facts and not complex sentence construction. This is *not* an English language examination.

Specimen question Explain how the skin helps to return body temperature to normal after vigorous exercise?   [*LEAG*]

PRACTICAL ASSESSMENT QUESTIONS

These are designed to test your ability to follow instructions, make and record accurate observations and measurements and produce valid conclusions. Follow all instructions carefully and, when asked to record your observation, include all detail, e.g. size, shape, colour, smell, etc. Drawings should be accurate representations of the specimens, and you should follow all the advice given on how to draw on p.316. Marks can only be given for information you provide on the answer sheet. Answers must therefore be precise and detailed. Conclusions should be made on the basis of your observations and practical and theoretical knowledge acquired during the course. The following practical work is often set: drawing and labelling half flowers, fruits, seeds, bulbs, corms, rhizomes, twigs, bones, teeth, insects, and other small invertebrates; food tests; simple experiments, including osmosis and observation of behaviour in small invertebrates.

TERMS USED IN EXAMINATIONS

The following is a list of terms commonly used in examination questions. In each case a brief explanation is given of how you answer this type of question.

1   **Name** – write down the names of the structures, processes or organisms required by the question. Usually, these relate to a diagram or photograph.

   Specimen questions
   1   Name the structure which attaches muscle to bone.   [WJEC]
   2   Name the nitrogenous compound present in human urine.
                                                            [SCE]

2   **List** – write down the facts as briefly as possible. Each fact should be numbered **1,2,3**, etc.

   Specimen question List three mistakes the student is making. [NEA]

3   **State** – write down as briefly as possible the answer to the question.

   Specimen question State TWO features that suggest that the flower is insect pollinated.   [NISEC]

4   **Describe** – state in words (using diagrams when appropriate) the main points of the topic you are asked to describe. The instruction requires you to provide the examiner with knowledge and understanding.

   Specimen questions
   1   Describe the main methods used in the control of malaria.
                                                            [WJEC]
   2   Describe one method you could use to collect animals from the shrub layer in a wood.   [LEAG]

5   **Explain** – state all the details which affect the subject and enable it to be clearly understood. Clear answers are required.

   Specimen questions
   1   Explain how the body loses weight when it is at rest.   [SEG]

2   Explain the effects of the excessive use of fossil fuels.   [*SCE*]

6   **Discuss** – give a critical account of all the points involved in the topic being written about and their relative importance. You should make a list of all these in your plan and present them in an orderly way in your answer.

Specimen question

'Man has brought more and more biological knowledge to bear upon the problem of producing more food, and food of the right quality to keep him healthy.'

Discuss the role of the following, in this context:
(i) protein production by microorganisms;
(ii) butter and margarine;
(iii) legumes;
(iv) artificial fertilizers.   [*MEG*]

7   **Compare** – state the similarities and differences between the two or more topics given in the questions.

Specimen question Compare the two sets of results. [Given a table of experimental results.]

8   **Calculate** – show all the stages involved in deriving the answer to a numerical problem.

Specimen question Calculate the F_2 ratio of plants producing grey-coloured seed to plants producing white-coloured seed in cross 4. (Show your working.)   [*MEG*]

9   **Suggest** – state your answer on the basis of theoretical knowledge. It is not anticipated that you will 'know' the answer.

Specimen question (A graph is provided showing the relationship between respiratory tract disease and air pollution along a straight line from a rural area into a city centre.) Suggest a cause for the difference in the death rates from bronchitis between men and women.   [*NEA*]

10   **Diagrams** – may form the basis of a question or be used to illustrate a point in another type of question. In all cases diagrams must be large, fully labelled and have a title. They should be drawn as simple pencil lines and labelled with pencil or pen. Never sketch and avoid colouring and shading. Labelling lines and arrows must touch the structure and should be neatly arranged around the diagram. They must not cross. A diagram represents a simplified or idealized representation, whereas drawings are (usually) made directly from the object and appear in practical questions. Drawings must show correct proportions.

Specimen question Make a large labelled diagram of a vertical section through the mammalian skin.

11 **Graph** – these questions may involve the construction of a graph or interpretation of presented data.

(a)   Graphs should always be drawn in pencil on graph paper.

(b)   The graph should fit the middle of the paper.

(c)   The horizontal x-axis should represent the variable which is under the control of the experimenter, e.g. time, temperature.

(d)   The vertical y-axis should represent the variable being investigated, e.g. length changes, weight changes.

(e)   Axes must be labelled, equal intervals marked and the units stated, e.g. 0,2,4,6,8, . . . Time (minutes).

(f)   Points should be clearly marked either with a ⊙ or X.

(g)   Points should be joined either with a smooth curve or straight lines drawn with a ruler.

(h)   The graph should have a title, 'Graph of . . .'.

    If asked to determine a value on the x-axis corresponding to a value on the y-axis, draw a line from that point parallel to the x-axis. Where it cuts the line on the graph draw a line down to the x-axis and parallel to the y-axis. Where this line cuts the x-axis read off the value. If asked to interpret the graph, relate the changes shown by it to the biological situation illustrated. Remember that the steeper the slope, the faster the change.

INDEX